MURDER CAPITAL

MURDER CAPITAL

LIFE AND DEATH ON THE STREETS OF GLASGOW

REG McKAY

BLACK & WHITE PUBLISHING

First Published 2006
by Black & White Publishing Ltd
99 Giles Street, Edinburgh EH6 6BZ

ISBN 13 978 1 84502 093 4
ISBN 10 1 84502 093 6

Typeset by RefineCatch Limited, Bungay, Suffolk
Printed and bound by Creative Print and Design Group Ltd

ACKNOWLEDGEMENTS

Thanks to . . .

Victims' families who bared their pain.

Killers' families who bared their grief.

Grace and John for making sure I never forget about those for whom there is no answer – yet.

Paul for making sure my feet stay firmly on the ground, especially when my head floats off into the clouds.

Big Bob C for being the second biggest blether in Glasgow and great company over a swally.

The Rogano for the frequent asylum and strong liquor.

All the taxi drivers who got me there and back with an interesting tale or two.

Gerry for still putting up with the nightmare that is me.

All the booksellers who flog my books and don't look down on true crime as those luvvies do.

The team at Black & White for taking another risk on the scribblings of this dirty stop-out. A small crew, punching way above their weight. Watch their space.

Thanks mainly to The Boss – the punters who have bought, borrowed and half-inched my books. Power to you.

Reg McKay
Glasgow
April 2006

CONTENTS

I BELONG   1

PART 1
ORGANISED CRIME   5
THE BLOODY BLUES   7
AS COLD AS DEATH   14
NO BODY, NO PROBLEM   25
THE BIRDMAN OF POSSILPARK   32
SAINT OR SINNER?   39
SAFER IN JAIL?   46

PART 2
FEMMES FATALES   51
HONEY TRAPS AND HIT MEN   53
KILLING COUSINS   62
LAMB TO THE SLAUGHTER   66
LOW LIFE IN HIGH PLACES   70
HOUSE OF BLOOD   74

PART 3
CHILD KILLERS   81
A GOOD LITTLE BOY   83
RON AND REG   91
SUFFER THE LITTLE CHILDREN   98

RECLESS AND WICKED   107
THE GHOST OF THE FATHER?   115

PART 4
SEX KILLERS   **123**
A GOOD DAY TO KILL   125
GREEN-EYED MONSTERS AND RED MISTS   133
DEAD LONELY   136
DYING ON DEAF EARS   144
THE BLOODY BLUEBELLS   154

PART 5
KIDS WHO KILL   **159**
WASTED WARNINGS AND IDLE THREATS?   161
THE REVOLVING DOOR TO HELL   167
THE CARING KIND   173
CHILD'S PLAY   179
MASTER HYDE?   182

PART 6
THRILL KILLERS   **185**
DOGGING DAYS AND DEADLY NIGHTS   187
LIFE IMITATES ART   194

PART 7
WHODUNNIT?   **205**
NO ANGEL BUT . . .   207
NOSE IN THE AIR   220
LOST AND FOUND   227

INDEX   239

To *R* the loyal lover and *M* the wild child.
You keep my bogeyman at bay.
Precious souls.

I BELONG

See me? See Glasgow? See love?

Maybe it helps that I'm an adopted son of the city. When I was a teenage boy, my old man was set free from his wage slavery as a train driver. They call it redundancy. The Tories had shut down most of the backwater train stations so he went on walkabout, working wherever they'd have him – London, Alloa, Lincoln and then Glasgow. No offence to the other places, but thank God it was Glasgow who offered him the permanent job and where he decided we would live.

He put an advert in the *Evening Times* and now-departed *Citizen* asking if anyone wanted a council-house swap – Glasgow for Keith, a wee town up in Banffshire – a big vibrant city for a white-trash village. Like, right.

One offer came in. Because of the old man's shifts he could only go to see the place at night. It seemed a nice wee house in a quiet cul-de-sac and it was. He signed the deal that night. We were moving from the hills and glens to Govan. He didn't know it was Govan. Well, it was dark.

Glasgow folk would call my new neighbourhood Drumoyne and quite right too. On my first day at school, there were two guys in the playground chopping lumps out of each other with meat cleavers. Now, I was a bit wild then but a cleaver fight at 8.55 a.m.? I thought I'd arrived in Hell. And I had, of course. Heaven and Hell – that's Glasgow.

It took a while. Within a year, folk could understand what I was saying. After another year, I was settled. A year later, I'd bore anyone I could corner about how Glasgow was the centre of the universe. It's a habit I haven't lost – a feeling that's as strong as ever.

The people are the warmest on earth with a sense of humour so deadpan and black that, on first hearing it, you don't know if they're picking a fight or cracking a joke. Usually, they're taking the piss and they expect you to reciprocate.

The people are the hardest working, the most stylish and the most willing to help a stranger. If you're a tourist and you get lost, pray that it's in Glasgow.

Where else can you shop at Armani and come out to a Big Issue seller calling you by name? Or have a drink at Fat Boab's bar where all the punters eye you up suspiciously and silently for a full ten minutes? But all strangers and outsiders *can* drink at Fat Boab's bar – that's the point. That's Glasgow folk.

It's a beautiful city beyond measure. Stand in the old city centre with its buildings in blocks like some original New York scene and it looks uniform, organised, solid, plain. Ah, but just look up. Up high, the architects have built in their joy like a homage to some god – if only He or She looks over our place. And they do.

It's the city with the best clubs, the best music, the best artists and, of course, the best writers. It's a city of poets as the sing-ring-sing tones of the voices turn words into folk songs, ditties, rhyming slang and, aye, even proper poems.

Comedians are us. Not just the Billy Connollys and the *Chewing the Fat* guys or *Naked Video* or Rab C Nesbitt or Rikki Fulton or that adopted son from doon the water, Chic Murray. Want a laugh? Hang around a Glasgow pub or bus stop or queue at the cash machine among ordinary Glasgow people. Comedians are us.

But what the hell do we have to laugh at?

Listen to the white coats and the grey suits for a while and you could get depressed. Glasgow to them is all about heart disease, lung cancer, heroin addiction, crime, abused kids, alcoholism, unemployment, early deaths and what not – all of it the highest anywhere. Oh, aye, and murder.

It's true. We can't just wish it away. It's the everlasting contradiction of this big, beautiful city. The place where I feel safest, where outsiders feel relaxed, where a stranger will give you a helping hand without you needing to ask for it also witnesses more murders than any other western European city. The city is the witness – the people do the killing.

At a time when guns are so cheap and so easy to get hold of, we have a lasting love affair with the knife. Maybe it goes back to the days when men carried daggers – skean-dhus they're called – in their socks, handy for settling a bit of a dispute. We're still doing it.

It's something about the Glasgow way. Even top gangsters, with teams of armed men at their disposal, will often choose to settle a grievance by a knife fight. Or the same type of men, ordering a hit, will instruct that it's done with a blade. Ask them why and some of them will say that with a knife you can't accidentally shoot a passer-by. But is that all it is?

It's also up-close and personal. That's the Glasgow way.

Yet it isn't just knives or hit jobs that kill our people. We have crimes of passion, mental murderers, mysteries, poisonings, thrill killers, sex slayers. It isn't just men who murder but women, kids and groups. In Glasgow, you can get anything you want and everything is possible and it's no different with killing – we have it all here.

Anywhere you go, someone you know well is the most likely person to be your killer. Glasgow's no different. Don't waste your energy being wary of the city. Choose your friends and lovers carefully – very carefully.

London, Belfast, Dublin, Paris, Berlin, Amsterdam – all have high murder rates. By comparison, Glasgow is blood red. In Glasgow, you are twice as likely to be murdered as in London or Amsterdam, three times more likely than in Madrid, Dublin or Paris, more likely even than in Belfast with all its post-Troubles violent ways.

Yet it's the place people love, where folk feel safest, the best place for anything you can think of – apart from sunny weather. That's the contradiction that's Glasgow.

See me? See Glasgow? See murder?

PART 1
ORGANISED CRIME

Career criminals is a nice way to describe them. Mobsters, gangsters and street players are more common terms. This section deals with those people, the men and women who kill mainly for business though sometimes it is personal – as personal as it gets.

No apologies are given for omitting many of the well-known cases. In every section of this book, the idea is not to tell *all* the tales – that would take several books just to cover the last twenty years, which is the period the book focuses on. The aim is to relate accounts that give a fuller sense of what really happens in this part of our world. If a case has been well written about before, then you are unlikely to find it here. Some important cases are excluded – like the unsolved hit on Bobby Glover and Joe Hanlon. Paul Ferris and I have covered that in *Vendetta*. So there's no Fatboy Thompson or Billy McPhee or Justin McAlroy. But there are many new names and famous names whose murders are exposed fully for the first time.

You will, however, find passing reference to the Doyle Family slaughter. Not to go over ground already well covered but to tell the tale of another murder that people seem to have ignored – I don't ignore it.

Now and then in this book, I solve some murders for the first time but some of the stories in this section have no happy ending – or maybe I should say they aren't finished yet. So many of the murders of those involved in organised crime in Glasgow seem to

5

remain unsolved. No apologies are offered for this. I'm a writer writing about how it is and that is how it is.

Want an answer to unsolved killings among Glasgow's mobsters? Ask the cops.

THE BLOODY BLUES

Violence. One word summed up his life. That was his way, always had been. Now he walked out into the weak Glasgow sun and smelled their fear. Only the stupid weren't scared of The Equaliser.

From an early age John Simpson had done it all. Sometimes that was hard and lonely but that was the price men like him paid. But now, at twenty-three, he could at least walk about his neighbourhood knowing that he was safe. Safe through fear, everyone else's fear. That's how he had made it.

His area was what they now call the Greater Pollok area, a strip of urban jungle stretching south from Pollok through Priesthill, Nitshill, Darnley, Arden and beyond. It was a wild area full of hard men where too often life was too cheap. Of them all, he was the one they feared most.

Cast into care when a child, Simpson had run away and lived on the streets. They say that can't happen in modern Scotland but all too often it does. No begging or scrounging for him. He robbed houses and mugged adults. He was only eight years old.

Then he spotted older guys with a lot of money. It was the mid 1980s and heroin had hit the streets and nowhere harder than Pollok. He got himself a couple of knives and went after the young dealers, stabbing and slashing them, stealing their cash and their stash.

By 1985, Simpson was ten years old and dealing smack on a street corner. In 2006 there would be outrage when an eleven-year-old girl fell asleep in class and was found to be hooked on heroin. Apparently she was buying tenner bags at the Pollok Centre. That was the middle of his patch back then in 1985 when he was dealing as a ten-year-old.

Other dealers tried to muscle in on the scrawny kid that Simpson then was. He chibbed them too.

They paid for a heavy team to get him. He took to his heels and they'd thought they'd won. No chance. John Simpson picked them off one by one and, in a week, he was back at his stance, selling smack.

Pollok was peppered with abandoned houses – boarded up by the council because everyone refused to live there. Simpson broke into several and set up homes. If the cops and social workers sussed where he was and came for him, he'd flee out the back or through the ceiling or some other escape route he had prepared. By night, he'd be well settled in one of his other bases.

When the cops and social workers caught him, he'd go back to the children's home, kick his heels for a week and then hit the road again. He preferred living in a derelict house with no heating or lighting and walking those bloody streets with a chib in his hand. Most kids go to school. John Simpson's education was on the street.

By the age of thirteen, he had a fearsome reputation and had expanded his repertoire to guns. If people feared him before, now there was no holding him back. Some of the older men – still teenagers themselves – recruited him for a bit of armed robbery. At thirteen years old, he was carrying a loaded shotgun into warehouses and banks.

By the time he was fifteen, he was getting fussy about who he worked with but one older guy convinced him that they should work together on a heist. A month after the successful job, Simpson still didn't have his share of the cash. He reckoned his partner in crime was taking the piss and decided he had to teach him a lesson.

The young Simpson took the much older bloke hostage, kept him locked up for days in one of his abandoned houses, periodically beating him and raping him. He got the man to tell him where the money was stashed and took him out to get it. Simpson took all of it, the other guy's cut as well, and then marched him back to the house where the torture continued. A couple of days later, he walked out and went down the street to where the guy's brothers and gang were hanging around.

'John, you seen Jaimie?' one of them asked, as he knew they would.

'Aye, I've just left him,' replied Simpson, not breaking his stride. ''Fact, he was asking if youse lot would go see him.' Simpson gave them the address and kept walking. He knew what they'd find. It wasn't a pretty sight and it was obvious who had done in their mate. So now they'd come for him or accept that he was worth leaving alone. They left him alone.

Within a couple of years of that, Simpson agreed to work with the top man in the south side. Stewart 'Speccy' Boyd looked a bit like a mild-mannered bank manager. His nickname wasn't subtle and with his trendy spectacles, colouring of hair and round smiley face there were those who said he looked a bit like Elton John – but never within his hearing.

A graduate of the Priesthill Young Team, Speccy was as intelligent as he was vicious. When he and Simpson got together, Boyd was about twenty years older than Simpson. When Speccy was a young man, the south side of Glasgow was split up into small patches ruled by small but very dangerous gangs who spent a lot of time battling with each other. Speccy decided to unite the south side and there was only one way to do that – by conquering it. It had taken time and lot of brutality and even more street cunning. Speccy learned that being a diplomat was often the best way to win hearts and minds but it helped if the diplomat had a loaded gun in his paw.

By the time John Simpson hit eighteen years, Speccy ruled the south side. It was a huge territory with a highly lucrative drug market and many other scams as well. Speccy had a lot of hard men around him. There was his lieutenant John 'The Joker'

McCartney often known as 'The Richest Dustbin Man in the World' because he was officially registered as a dustman. He now bribed someone to clock him in every day, giving him a visible source of income that kept the cops and taxman at bay. One of the other benefits was that he had the keys to massive council incinerators. Handy for disposing of bodies, the team used them frequently.

There were others – like Benjie Bennett, Scudder Scanlon and Chas Melvin. As a team, they ruled the roost in their patch and thought they were the bee's knees. Speccy reckoned that young John Simpson was harder than that lot put together so he signed him up.

Simpson became Speccy's equaliser, the guy he'd put into some crazy violent situation to settle a dispute or pay someone back – thus his nickname, The Equaliser. He was good at his job and Speccy would say to confidants, 'When I put John in, it isn't a question of him winning – he always does. It's a question of making sure he doesn't kill too many people.'

There is no doubt that John Simpson had killed a few people in the line of business. By the mid 1990s, street players from the south side who were in dispute with Speccy or independent from him were disappearing off the face of the earth. Officially they remain listed as missing by the cops – cremated in the incinerators more like.

Life could have been good for John Simpson. Wealth, power and respect were his for the taking but, by 1998 and at the age of twenty-three, it had all gone sour – it was just that he didn't know it.

Valium was his big habit. On the street they call them Blues. John Simpson took fifty or sixty at a time, several times a day. Taking that many Blues does things to your head – changes how you see the world. He started to believe that he ruled it.

Not a big drinker, he started regularly visiting pubs – not for the booze but for the sport. He'd spit on the floor of some packed bar and the first person to step on the spittle got done in – big time.

Then there was sex. When Speccy was on the run down south for a murder, John got off with one off his boss's several girl-friends. Once the way was clear for Speccy to return to Glasgow, he acted like it didn't matter. It did.

'That hurt Stewart a lot,' said one of his lifelong friends. 'No' that he'd ever admit it but I could tell. He was hurt and that meant only one thing with him – payback.'

A short while later, Simpson was sleeping in an aunt and uncle's house when two masked gunmen burst in and shot him in the head three times at close range. At the time, everyone assumed they had been some members of Speccy's paranoid team who had decided that Simpson was getting too big for their own good. It wasn't. Later in this book, we'll reveal the how and wherefore of that shooting. Right now, the important thing was that Simpson survived.

The gunmen had made a fundamental error but, again, more on that later. The shock, the wounds and the damage would have killed most strong men but John Simpson was exceptional. A few weeks later, he discharged himself from hospital early – he had a business to run.

He walked out into the weak Glasgow sun and smelled their fear. Only the stupid weren't scared of The Equaliser – or so he thought.

Standing in the street waiting for a taxi, the feel of his gun heavy and comforting in his waistband, he looked around his territory. Kids had just come out of school and were playing their madcap games, their shrill voices blowing frosty clouds. Two old women stood on a street corner, both arms weighted down with heavy carrier bags their mouths rattling off words non-stop. A dog ran past at speed. Going where? Does anyone ever know?

Simpson spotted the familiar car and lifted his arm in greeting and, at the same time, the driver braked and pulled in. Not the taxi he'd been waiting for but a pal – an associate from Speccy's mob, more like, but not a bad guy, one you could trust.

With a big smile on his gob, Simpson leaned over to the driver's open window, putting his hand on the car roof, leaning his weight. Pals, they even made him relax. He should've noticed the rear window was open – would've noticed nine times out of ten. Not that day.

The masked man sat up from where he had been lying across the back seat.

BOOM.

The first shot rang out echoing against the concrete tenements and turning all heads.

BOOM.

BOOM.

The car sped off, leaving John Simpson bleeding on the ground. He died where he lay, on the street in his own neighbourhood.

No one spotted the car. No one saw the driver. No one saw anything. It was that type of area – they were that type of people.

Three street players were accused by the cops, of course, but, even before the trial, everyone knew it hadn't been those guys. Speccy would make sure they walked free. They did.

Rumours ran wild about who had killed John Simpson. It was only then that the public sussed a family connection – Simpson was Speccy Boyd's cousin. Speccy was a hard man but sanctioning a hit on his own flesh and blood?

It had been a busy time on the south side. Three years earlier, Boyd had been cleared at trial of killing Mark Rennie from the hard scheme of Ferguslie Park in nearby Paisley. And, two years before, a bloke called Billy Weatherall had been shot on Speccy's orders to stop him giving evidence against some of his pals. One of Speccy's crew, Paul Bennett, had rowed with his boss over a drugs deal and hadn't been seen since. Now The Equaliser was dead. The south-side schemes ran red with rumours.

One whisper was that a bloke called Charles or Chas Melvin had been the driver of the hit car. Melvin was a loyal member of the crew and somebody most people got on with. In 1995, he had carried out a hit for them, shooting and killing a player called Bryan 'Dopey' Cochrane. Chas Melvin went to trial but played the game they expected, keeping his mouth shut and risking big-time jail. He walked free.

Most people liked Chas and that included Simpson who didn't get on with many people and trusted even fewer. Simpson wouldn't have hesitated to stroll across and blether to Chas in his motor.

In July 2000, thirty-four-year-old Melvin got a call while he was at home with his wife and their three young kids.

'I've got to go to a meeting,' he told her. She was used to that.

Minutes later, Chas climbed into the back of the red taxi that had called to pick him up. 'I won't be long,' he promised as he climbed into the minicab. As the cab drove away, Chas waved to his wife and kids. He has never been seen again.

For years, Chas Melvin's wife searched the bleak marshlands of nearby Fenwick Moor. That's where they told her they dumped her man's body.

Chas Melvin is officially listed as missing, not murdered. He is one of more than a dozen from that one stretch of Glasgow who, over a period of just a few years, are in the same category. They are all street players, of course, and not worth the cops' time. Or so it seems. Try telling that to Chas Melvin's wife and kids.

John Simpson's murder remains unsolved like so many hit contracts in this city. He was twenty-three years old, just starting his life as a man, when he lay cold on the mortuary slab. That's the way it is for some folk who walk the killing streets of Glasgow.

AS COLD AS DEATH

In a city of cold-hearted men only he earned the nickname, The Iceman. He earned it well.

Frank McPhie was born and raised in the hardest schemes of Glasgow in that post-war period when the Gorbals was still the stuff of *No Mean City* and the new urban deserts of Castlemilk, Drumchapel and Easterhouse were about to be born. The traditional heavy industry of the shipyards was already teetering and the old order was on the way out.

With no privileges or middle-class comforts, his generation would either fight with boot and blade to get on or perish in the drudgery of the dole, a haze of booze or bloodily on the streets. Frank McPhie was a fighter and good at it.

By his teenage years of the 1960s, Glasgow was in the grip of the razor gangs. As many as 300 teams of furious young men fought and killed each other for nothing more significant than street cred. Wielding axes, long swords, butchers' cleavers and heavy-headed hammers, they chopped, slaughtered and maimed each other in what was arguably the bloodiest time of street battles Glasgow has ever witnessed – and that was saying something. McPhie ran with the teams and did his share.

Yet, back then, he was just another mental team boy – someone you wouldn't want to cross, someone you'd want to avoid, but two-a-penny, all the same. It was later, in adulthood, that he'd make his real mark.

Like so many of the gang guys before him who decided they'd served an apprenticeship for a life of crime, McPhie started off as a bouncer on pub doors and was soon involved in the protection rackets. His reputation for fearless violence was well known and it gave him perfect credentials as a threat to landlords as well as a guarantee to them that he could stop some other player putting the squeeze on.

He soon had his regulars around his Maryhill patch in the west of the city, collecting weekly 'rents' from pubs, bookies, brothels and gambling dens. But that wasn't enough for Frank McPhie. When offered money to teach someone a lesson, he accepted straight away. After all, hadn't he spent years as a young man fighting for no reward? Now he was doing what he was good at, what he enjoyed, and getting paid top dollar.

McPhie soon established that he had the knack of hurting people bad. Better, he didn't much care who the target was. He'd had enough of running with gangs with their leaders and politics. From that time on, it was strictly number one.

A pub landlord had asked him to teach a guy a lesson. He'd been coming into the pub drunk and looking for a fight once too often. The landlord didn't know that McPhie and the aggressive drunk had been best pals since they were kids. Most men would have given the pub owner a slap for suggesting such a thing and warned their mate. Frank McPhie took the money and knifed his old pal so viciously he ended up in hospital on the critical list.

That's when the name The Iceman was first given to Frank McPhie.

By the 1970s, McPhie was an armed robber. There were several teams around Glasgow at the time – the Barlanark Team from the east end and Walter Norval's feared XYY gang – making a lucrative earning at the game. Frank McPhie was never slow to chase a quick buck.

McPhie would work with other established gangs as a freelancer. Not skilled in safecracking or alarms, he was used for what he was good at – terrifying people. Most often his role would be to hit the premises carrying the biggest, meanest shotgun he could find threatening to kill the first person who breathed too heavily. None did.

Eventually his luck ran out and, in 1978, he was sent down for five years for a robbery. In jail, he quickly adapted, cracked a few skulls and took over what was then the money-spinning business of tobacco baron.

With his furious temper and respect for no one, prison was almost a home for home for McPhie. As a result, he went straight back to his old ways once free – only to be nabbed again for armed robbery and jailed for another five years in 1986.

By the end of the 1980s and at the age of forty, Frank McPhie was infamous in the hard jails and bloody streets – at the top of his game, in other words – and ready to take on new work.

A regular source of wages for McPhie was Arthur Thompson, the reputed Godfather of crime in Glasgow. Thompson had broken the mould and created good working relations with the big London teams like the Krays and the Richardsons. It was a relationship of mutual convenience with London players coming to Glasgow for the occasional hit job. From time to time, Frank McPhie would travel in the other direction. The Iceman Cometh.

Along with this lucrative work, McPhie was still carrying on his protection rackets but had extended them to big, rich farms on the outskirts of the city. This was a new game and the bemused farmers at first told him where to go. Then their outbuildings started burning down in the middle of the night, their cattle died of poisoning and their horses had chunks cut out of their flesh as they grazed in the fields. Most soon paid up.

McPhie was still busy on the armed-robbery front but he was getting smarter and staying one step ahead of the cops. When eventually in 1990, they did arrest him and charged him with robbing a bank in Dundee he walked away, having been found innocent. But he wasn't always that smart.

The dogs' howling and whimpering in agony could be heard

hundreds of yards away. Slowly, carefully, the ring of cops moved closer and closer to the scene. The signal went up and they rushed the bloodthirsty mob at the illegal dogfight and right into a scene of carnage.

Experienced cops who have dealt with the most distressing human situations will confess that dog fights turn their stomachs, make them want to weep or lash out at the cruel men who organise them, bet on them, go along for some sick thrill.

This fight was out in the wild countryside of Fife. The police were happy enough to save some animals, put the badly wounded out of their misery and lift some of the men behind the trade but there was a bonus – miles away from his home in Glasgow, there was Frank McPhie.

The man who had dished out so much pain, robbed banks and factories and escaped capture more times than not was caught there at a dogfight. It wasn't like McPhie to be so sloppy. But the fact that he saw a trip to the blood-splattered pits of the fights as a day out tells us a lot about the nature of the man. He loved the pain of others – plain and simple.

The Iceman wasn't much to look at but anyone who allowed that to fool them would be making a big mistake. He had a foul temper and looked for violence. Would it be his downfall?

Like most other street players at that time, McPhie had moved into the trade in drugs. It was an arena he knew to be profitable but, like so many of his kind who were more used to the heavy act, he knew little about it.

The cops must have thought it was Christmas and their birthdays all rolled into one. There they were, trailing a big-time drug trafficking crew, and who should the crew make a delivery to but The Iceman himself?

McPhie was acting for a bloke called James King, then one of the top drug dealers in Glasgow. All he had to do was buy £29,000 of cannabis from a London firm – not a huge deal, even by 1992 standards – but the £200,000 of dope the Londoners were carrying was a different matter. The Iceman showed all his naivety of drugs by taking delivery of his consignment right outside his Maryhill home.

Caught red-handed, he was sent off to prison for eight years in 1992. It was a hefty sentence for cannabis dealing at that time and probably reflected the authorities' view that Frank McPhie had escaped prosecution too often on other matters. Bad enough as jail time was, it was to lead to another, more serious, matter – murder.

Perth Prison was a dank dungeon of Victorian hell where cockroaches and rats crawled over the prisoners as they slept in their cells. The regime was as harsh as the jail was decrepit and it was there they would dump some of the men the system couldn't handle like TC Campbell, Toe 'Little General' Elliot and one William 'Worm' Toye.

Toye was a hard man and drug dealer from Clydebank, an industrial desert of a town on the banks of the River Clyde to the west of Glasgow. Once world famous for shipbuilding, the industry had all but died for Clydebank, leaving it with unemployment, crime and drugs. William Toye was one of the top boys there.

When Toye's brother, Gavin, faced charges of killing a gangland rival, the family didn't fret. That had happened before but the cases collapsed due to terrified witnesses suddenly changing their minds about testifying. Not this time.

A guy called Edward Maxwell was going to give evidence against Gavin. Whether twenty-eight-year-old Maxwell was ever offered police protection isn't known. But he should have been.

As Edward Maxwell played football in the street with friends, William Toye appeared out of nowhere. Pulling an axe from under his coat, Toye cornered the terrified Maxwell and hacked him to death in broad daylight in front of screaming kids nearby.

The murder of poor Edward Maxwell might have prevented him giving evidence but it didn't stop a jury from finding Gavin Toye guilty and sending him to jail for life. There was one other problem – William 'Worm' Toye was sent down for life too for Maxwell's murder.

That's how Toye found himself in Perth Prison in 1996. Well settled and ruling the roost in the jail's D Hall, he was worrying prison staff. The jail was awash with home-made blades and too many people were getting hurt. In jail, no one sees any such attack, of course, but the screws were still convinced that Toye was the cause. No problem, they'd move him.

Prison halls are like small countries with their own leading powers and order of rank. When Toye was transferred from D Hall into A Hall, it was like an invasion by some enemy. And in charge of A Hall was Frank McPhie.

Toye made no secret that he would take over A Hall's thriving drug trade from McPhie. Within hours of his transfer, the two men had a blazing row in front of a stack of prisoners. But these weren't men who settled a dispute with mere words.

Not even, 'I'll fucking kill you, ye bastarding Worm.'

And, 'Any fucking time, you cunt, McPhie.'

That's what they roared at each other. Men like McPhie and Toye made no idle threats.

The next day, the two went at each other raining kicks and punches into bone and flesh. Pulled apart and cooled down, they went back to their cells but still the prison staff left them both in A Hall.

The following day, Toye was having a cup of tea in his cell with another prisoner. Three men, led by McPhie, ran in. One grabbed Toye round the arms, another threw a sack over his head and McPhie shoved a long knife into his chest.

It had taken seconds. The blade had gone straight into William Toye's heart and on arrival at hospital he was declared dead.

In every prisoner's file, there is a 'Friends and Foes List', warning staff about special association between the cons so that they'd know which ones to keep apart. There had been bad blood between McPhie and Toye before, both inside and outside prison. Yet the prison service insisted that there had been no warning of the trouble to come. Well, they would have no more trouble to come from William Toye.

McPhie was charged with murdering William 'Worm' Toye. Although the trial produced witnesses who had seen the hit, no one could identify the hit man. No surprise there. The case against McPhie was found not proven – that peculiar Scottish verdict which is neither guilty nor not guilty. The cops hate that verdict. To them, it means that the jury believe that the accused was guilty but there just hadn't been enough proof for them to return a guilty verdict. Either way, it results in freedom. Well, it would for McPhie once he served his existing sentence.

The Iceman didn't waste his time in jail. He kept in touch with street players from Maryhill and the nearby patches of Possil and Springburn. One guy in particular, Colin McKay, visited him regularly and, through him, McPhie got to know a young bloke by the name of Christopher McGrory.

McGrory, then twenty-five years old, was an ex-milkman. He had owned the round before selling it for a good price but still people were beginning to notice that, having bought three horses and the like, he was living way above his means. McGrory was a frequent traveller to Ireland. That alone interested Frank McPhie very much for one reason – drugs.

Freed from jail in 1996, McPhie spent an increasing amount of time with McKay and McGrory. McGrory had used some of his money from the sale of his milk delivery business to start trading in drugs, mainly cocaine and heroin. Though not an established player, he had cracked a commercial problem that McPhie had been thinking about for some time.

In the mid 1990s, most of the drugs reaching Glasgow came up from Liverpool. But the Scousers were often buying their supplies from teams in Ireland, helped by the deadly skill and contacts of ex-paramilitaries of the IRA and UDA. In supplying Glasgow, the Scousers upped the price so they made a handsome profit. How much cheaper it would be to cut out the middlemen. McPhie thought he'd found the man with the right contacts in Christopher McGrory.

A year later, in 1997, the three men had grown so close that

Colin McKay was the best man and Frank McPhie an usher at McGrory's wedding in Dublin. They had become close in other ways – a hefty drug deal had been set up that would make them all very comfortable.

After the big day, McGrory and his new bride, Anne-Marie, jetted off on holiday to Paris – actually to Disneyland where, by all accounts, McGrory let the child in him rule and had a great time. It didn't sound like the type of place a gangster would go. Whatever else he was, Christopher McGrory wasn't that.

Back from honeymoon, McGrory flew off again to Dublin, this time on his own. His new wife had noticed how, for weeks before their wedding, he had been avoiding contact with his close pal Colin McKay. She asked if there was a problem but got no satisfactory reply.

Three days after his return from Paris and back in Scotland from his trip to Dublin, McGrory went to the stables where he kept his horses. The next time he was seen, he was lying dead in the back of his own van at Douglaston Golf Course, some distance away. He had been strangled.

The cops had been watching McGrory as well as McKay and McPhie. They always watched Frank McPhie. Immediately McKay and McPhie were arrested and charged with murder.

At the trial at Glasgow High Court, the cops suggested that McGrory had returned from his trip to Dublin following his honeymoon with a large consignment of drugs – not for the first time. But he had decided to go it alone this time and his two erstwhile partners had been far from pleased.

The cops suggested that the two accused had trailed McGrory to the stables, forced him into his van, driven to the isolated golf course and tried to strangle the hiding place of the drugs stash out of him. They had just gone too far.

The jury weren't convinced. McKay and, once again, Frank McPhie walked away from the murder trial with a not proven verdict.

Outside the High Court, a large group of well-wishers were

waiting for the men. Twice accused of murder and walking free both times, Frank McPhie let it all go to his head.

The Iceman returned to his normal routine, even demanding protection money from the farmers again. Also, he'd learned a lot from his time with McGrory and McKay and he started his own supply route of drugs from Ireland. If he had just worked steadily at that, then all might have been well and Frank McPhie would have been a very rich man. But The Iceman had weaknesses.

Anyone who crossed him got slashed and beaten. One kid who fought with McPhie's teenage son was attacked and deeply wounded with a screwdriver. In a pub, he knocked over a table spilling a pint of beer into the lap of a young man. When the young guy objected, McPhie gave him a hell of a hiding, oblivious to the fact that he was a nephew of the Daniel Family, one of the strongest teams in Glasgow. Another time, he slashed an old man, not giving a hoot that he was a friend of the McGoverns from Springburn, another of the city's top firms. Frank McPhie didn't care. He thought he was invincible. But was he?

The folk near the allotment in Maryhill noticed the car pull up and four men get out. The witnesses were just ordinary folk who didn't recognise any of the newcomers. But they knew the man whose allotment the four were now approaching. It was Frank McPhie's.

In spite of all the money he earned, McPhie kept the wise counsel of showing little sign of his riches. He lived in a council house in a graffiti-strewn, rundown part of the city. His clothes were ordinary – no extravagant jewellery – and he even drove an old Transit van with a Q registration plate, indicating that it had once been written off after an accident. Then there was the allotment and growing his own vegetables – not exactly what a wealthy gangster would do.

Angry voices were raised in the air. The four newcomers were shouting at McPhie who was giving back as good as it he got. Then he took to his feet and ran for his Transit. The Iceman scared?

Whoever those guys were, they must have been known to him as real killers.

McPhie took off, the Transit's engine screaming. It might have once been declared a write-off but he could make it shift. The four men in the souped-up car were right behind him.

He knew the roads around Maryhill like the back of his hand but McPhie wanted to draw the men away, especially away from his own home and family, so he headed for the motorway – first the M8 and then the M74, heading south. A few miles out he cut off, drove at frantic speed through the village of Bothwell – all the time with the other car in pursuit.

By the time he cut back on to the motorway heading back to Glasgow, McPhie had already been on his mobile phone calling several associates for help. By the time he reached the cut-off for Maryhill he was still on the phone and the other car still behind him. Screeching through the built-up area of Maryhill, he knew he had no choice now but to get back home to Guthrie Street and hole up there till help arrived. Not even the blokes following him would want to hurt his wife and kids – he hoped. Besides, his place was only 400 yards from a cop shop. Who would risk dishing out the grief with the police so close?

What McPhie didn't see was that, as he reached Guthrie Street, the pursuing car slowed and turned away. Chase over. Or was it task accomplished?

Screeching his van to a halt, McPhie threw open the door and headed fast for his house, passing his young son. Just then one single shot rang out, blasting a dumdum bullet straight into his skull.

The Iceman was dead before he hit the pavement.

The cops were on the scene in a flash. Scouring the area, carrying out door-to-door checks, all they discovered was that a man with red hair was seen walking away from the street seconds after the shot was fired. Then there was a breakthrough. In an outside drying area on the eighth floor of flats across from McPhie's house they found a rifle.

They had the murder weapon all right and usually that's a

major step in solving any murder. Two weeks later, forensic tests found DNA on the weapon. That was another major step – surely they were closing in on the killer. Not when it was revealed that the DNA was from one of their own mob.

A full-blown murder investigation squad was based near the site for months. Eventually the cops took what was an unusual step at that time – they issued an e-fit picture of the suspect. It revealed nothing and few folk came forward with any information at all. Not even the men at the allotment who gave chase were identified although it was clear that they had set McPhie up for the sniper waiting at his home.

Five months after the killing, John McCabe, a close associate of the Daniel Clan, was arrested and charged – only to have the case against him dropped through lack of evidence.

Soon the cops were admitting that it was the most professional hit job ever in Scotland. It was as if the killer had never been there yet had calmly left them the murder weapon. Had it been a hired hit man from one of the Irish paramilitary groups? If so, who had hired him? One of the big Glasgow teams McPhie had upset or some Irish crew he had crossed in some drugs business? Some lonely soul he had dished a doing to some night? Lonely but, as with so many Glaswegians, connected to dangerous folks across the water in Ireland?

The trouble was, Frank McPhie had upset hundreds, maybe thousands, of people in his fifty-one years. In this case, there was just too large a number of suspects for there to be any usual suspects.

Frank 'The Iceman' McPhie was killed by a sniper in the year 2000. At the time of writing, his murder remains unsolved. Then so do the murders of William 'Worm' Toye and Christopher McGrory. Unusual? Maybe, but, as we'll find out, not so unusual when it comes to known street players being killed in Glasgow.

Frank McPhie caused a great deal of grief to many people during his lifetime. Maybe the cops weren't too bothered the day The Iceman truly became as cold as death?

NO BODY, NO PROBLEM

'It's Paul. He's been missing for days.' Usually such a phone call to the cops would elicit at best some sympathy and form-filling but not for this guy. The cops immediately decided this was more sinister – murder, in fact.

The missing man was twenty-six-year-old Paul Thorne who was well known to the police in Bristol. For years, Thorne had run with a big mob of dreadlocked Yardies down there. In many of the big cities, the Yardies had taken over the streets. Across the country, they controlled urban areas and threatened terrible violence towards anyone who tried to get in their way but UK police forces agreed the single, most bloody and most lawless street in the country was slap bang in the middle of Bristol.

Yardies have often been said to be involved in disorganised rather than organised crime but that's misleading. That impression is created by their stance of always working as individuals as well as within the team and of constantly demanding respect from everyone – and that goes for those they are in crime cahoots with as much as anyone else. Show disrespect and you're a dead man – no questions asked, no warning given, no matter who you are. One minute you're best friends, the next he's riddling your body with bullets.

It's easy to show a Yardie disrespect. Look too long at one of their baby-mothers (the name they use for the number of women each is expected to have for sex and breeding) or fail to look at her at all, implying that she isn't drop-dead gorgeous . . . it all depends on the Yardie in question. Once he's decided you need to be taught a lesson, there's no turning back for one obvious reason. In Glasgow, the knife fight remains the predominant way to resolve such disputes but, for the Yardies, it's guns – the bigger and deadlier the better.

It was the Yardies who first took up MAC-10 sub-machine guns. Nicknamed Big Macs, the term doesn't do the weapon justice. One touch of the hair-fine trigger and hundreds of bullets a minute go spewing out the barrel on their lethal way.

Perfectionists will slag off automatic and semi-automatic guns as lacking accuracy. But what does that matter when so many bullets are flying and you are only feet away from your target? That's the Yardie way.

Macho isn't a strong enough word for the Yardie world. They are modern-day gladiators fighting in an arena with no walls, no rules, no leaders, no obvious enemy. Unpredictable? You might say that. The type of group you'd want to avoid? Be extremely wary of? Sure, apart from one thing – their drugs. Yardie groups had specialised in bringing in large consignments of drugs and delivering on time. Drugs meant large profits. Yet, even taking that into consideration, most other big gangs in Britain preferred not to work with them – apart, that is, from some Scots.

For some time in 1988, cops in Glasgow and Bristol had been tracking the movements of Yardie couriers to Glasgow. No doubt they had planned to nab the teams when a particularly large delivery was being made. Then Paul Thorne went missing and it was a dramatic change of plan.

In the dock were Ricardo Blanco, Thomas Collins and John Paul McFadyen. Paul Thorne hadn't been found and already the cops had formed the view that he would never be. Few folk in Scotland had ever been convicted of murder in those circumstances before but that didn't deter them from charging this threesome with his murder for a very good reason – they had an informant. He was Stephen Mitchell and he was charged along with the others. He was trading charges that, if proven, could lead to him spending most of his adult life behind bars for his testimony against the others – turning Queen's evidence, in other words.

A great many of the convictions we now accept to be unjust have relied on just this type of witness. But this was 1988 and no one – aside from the accused men – thought anything was amiss. It was game on in Glasgow High Court.

Almost from the start of the trial it was Ricardo Blanco who attracted most attention. Despite all the murder trials that Glasgow has seen over the years, having a foreign national in the dock was a bit unusual. Though born in France, Blanco was from a Spanish family. He had been in both the French and Spanish Foreign Legions and was described as the group's enforcer. It was already an exotic cocktail for the followers of true crime but it got even more interesting when Blanco sacked his lawyer, Bill Turnbull QC, and conducted his own defence.

The prosecution established that Paul Thorne was a drugs courier for a large team of Yardies based in Bristol; that he'd been regularly travelling to Glasgow to meet up with John Paul McFadyen and Ricardo Blanco to deliver hefty consignments; and that, on this occasion, unbeknown to Thorne, something had gone wrong – lethally wrong.

Maybe the Scots reckoned that he had been cheating them. Maybe he'd been taking a slice of the goods for himself – a regular and weighty temptation to couriers. Maybe they were concerned that the outsider might be a weak spot – someone likely to trade information to the cops. Or maybe they had sussed that Thorne was being tailed by the police and decided to sever all links with him irrevocably. Whatever the reason, the cops and their witness then said that Thorne had been led out to the lonely, misty Fenwick Moor between Glasgow and Ayr. There, the three accused and one other – presumably the man who was turning Queen's evidence – each shot Thorne in the head. It's an old Mafia approach so that no one man to take the blame – no man is free to grass to the cops. This works fine and well except when the cops are prepared to drop charges against one of the shooters. How can the jury be sure they're being told the naked truth?

The prosecution then said that the accused buried Thorne's body in an unmarked grave. In spite of extensive search parties, Thorne's body had not been found and was unlikely ever to be in that barren, desolate place, booby-trapped with boggy marches.

The jury bought it and all three were found guilty of murder. John Paul McFadyen was seen as the leader of the group and was hit with a minimum of twenty years. Word on the street was that McFadyen played no part in the hit – no part at all – but he was too honourable to speak out and the others were too concerned with self-preservation to tell the truth. In spite of all the public attention falling on him, Blanco got the lesser sentence of fifteen years, as did Collins. That would normally be the end of the story but not as far as Ricardo Blanco was concerned.

During the trial, the media have limited privilege to report on the people involved. What this roughly means is that they can report on the trial but nothing else that might prejudice a jury for or against any of the accused. But, as soon as a trial is finished, particularly with guilty verdicts, it's happy hunting time and this time their target was Ricardo Blanco.

Soon stories started to appear claiming that in the French Foreign Legion he was trained to be extremely disciplined and hard and he had been taught different ways to kill – so far, so accurate. But the stories went on that he had deserted after allegedly killing a man and then he had drifted through France and Spain, using the skills garnered in the Legion – the Spanish Assassin, in other words.

Whether these stories had any truth in them or not, there wasn't much that Blanco could do to defend himself. Convicted prisoners, especially murderers, are seen as having no reputation to defend – they're sitting ducks for any journalist. But Blanco fought back in other ways, against the prison system.

He was involved in scraps with other prisoners, knifed two guards up in the hellish regime of Peterhead Prison and was so difficult to manage that he spent long, lost months in solitary confinement. But he did make progress on one front, making a new close friend in one William 'Worm' Toye.

As is detailed in the story 'As Cold as Death', Toye was serving life for the axe murder of a young man who was going to stand witness against his brother, Gavin. William 'Worm' Toye was also a jail hard case and ran the drug smuggling rackets in whichever one he was in. Toye and Blanco made a formidable pair.

Then, of course, Toye was stabbed to death in his cell in Perth Prison by Frank 'The Iceman' McPhie. Blanco made no secret of swearing revenge for his mate's death. It wasn't just that he'd lost a friend but the word was that, with Toye's assistance, he was going to take over the Clydebank area on his release. Within days of Toye's death, Blanco made his move and two prisoners received severe beatings.

This time, the prison system knew when they had trouble on their hands and transferred Blanco to another jail. While the trouble in prison cooled to a low simmer for Ricardo Blanco, he was to be involved in other matters that would put him in the headlines again. This time it wasn't murder but sex.

Jacqueline Wylie was tiny but most people would say attractive, sexy even. She had also been Toye's live-in lover. When her man was murdered, Jacqui continued visiting his best pal, Ricardo Blanco. The two became close, very close, and in July 2001 they were married.

Blanco was nearing the end of his sentence. Usually, the prison system would show some heart and try to arrange as normal a wedding as possible. By that time, he'd been moved to Greenock Prison and the local registry office was set up for the big day. Then the prison staff thought again.

It might have been thirteen years before that Paul Thorne had been murdered but the Yardies have long memories. Consultations with the police in Glasgow and Bristol revealed what the prison dreaded – the Yardies were waiting for the first chance to take Ricardo Blanco out in revenge. Most gangs might let him have his day. Most players wouldn't risk attacking a room full of prison screws with police guarding the door. But this was the Yardies – they did things their way.

The wedding was quickly rearranged for inside Greenock Prison – not the most romantic of settings but the prison staff did their best. Their best wasn't enough for Blanco. Soon he was demanding the right to have sex with his new wife to consummate the marriage. In most other European countries this would have been a given right but not in Britain.

In prison weddings, sympathetic staff often turn a blind eye while the happy couple sneak off to a nearby room for half an hour. In allowing this, they're breaking the law of the land and putting their jobs in jeopardy.

Blanco was vociferous in his demands for conjugal visits. So much so that unofficial statements soon emerged from the prison service and cops that all he was trying to do was avoid deportation to Spain on his release. As a foreign national who had committed a serious crime, being sent back would be automatic unless he had a valid marriage to a UK passport holder.

The Home Office was understandably reluctant to concede that Blanco and Wylie's marriage was anything other than a ploy to allow him to stay on in Scotland. If, on the other hand, she was pregnant by him they would have to relent.

Blanco was big on fighting for his rights. He had taken legal action over the amount of time they had kept him in solitary. On another occasion, he accused prison staff of brutality and torture. He made progress on these points but none at all on the sex visits – until he was allowed a visit home as part of Training for Freedom. It was a day visit to Jacqui Wylie's for a couple of hours and he was escorted by only one prison officer. There are contradictory tales about what happened next but what we do know is Blanco and Jacqui ended upstairs alone in a room – he says with the prison officer's permission, the prison officer says not.

An altercation then happened between the screw and the con that resulted in damage to the screw's nose and eye. Then Blanco and Jacqui drove off and the Spanish Assassin was on the loose, only to be arrested twelve hours later at a house in Glasgow's Pollok scheme.

When Ricardo Blanco appeared in court later, on related charges, he claimed the prisoner officer's face 'accidentally' smashed into his head. The prison officer said there was nothing accidental about it. Amazingly, the jury believed Blanco and he was acquitted, only to be returned to jail to serve his sentence. He was never allowed near any prisoner from Clydebank, though, since the cops believed he planned to take over those streets when he was freed.

Just weeks before the publication of this book, Ricardo Blanco was released from jail and deported to France. From a secret bolt-hole near Bordeaux, he contacted the *Daily Record* newspaper to give them his account of what happened that night out on Fenwick Moor.

According to Blanco, he was just a visitor to Glasgow. At the time, he was living in Bristol and he was a friend of the drugs courier, Paul Thorne. He said the Glaswegians had decided to kill Thorne and his friend, Nicola Hughes, to steal their drugs. For some reason, they told Blanco this, giving him a stark choice – shoot or be shot. Blanco claims he pled for Thorne and Hughes's lives but only managed to save the woman. He admits firing the first shot at Thorne out on the moor but says he deliberately missed. However, with no body, this, of course, can never be proved.

The word on the street was that Blanco was expected to speak out – that he had information that would help the other convicted men. Instead, when he went public, it was to clear his own name and, in doing so, he damned the others.

Meanwhile, the other convicted men have remained silent – just as the code of the street would expect them to. What really happened on the moor that night? We'll never know till that silence is broken or Paul Thorne's body is discovered . . .

Stranger things have happened on the bloody streets of Glasgow.

THE BIRDMAN OF POSSILPARK

Hit contracts, protected witnesses, armed cops in armoured cars, a bloodthirsty team of killers in the dock ... the court at Dunfermline was hardly used to such scenes. That's because the crew concerned were one of the most lethal in Glasgow.

It was 2005 and there was a war for control of the lucrative drugs trade in Possilpark. The top man was Robert O'Hara who was known as The Birdman – a nickname handed down in his family over generations. Still only twenty-seven years old, The Birdman lived in luxury and drove fast cars but life hadn't been easy for him.

O'Hara had been brought up in Possilpark, one of the roughest areas of Glasgow. It was back in the 1970s, when drugs started to seep into the city, that the main dealers first emerged in that no-man's-land, bandit territory. With the cops struggling and failing to control Possil, where better to start off such an illegal trade?

The area already reeked with violence and gangs but, by the early 1980s, drugs had created organised firms. Men were getting rich on dealing and there was so much profit at stake that shootings were commonplace. That was the Possilpark where Robert O'Hara grew up. By all accounts, the young kid learned well.

At the age of nineteen, he was already well on the way to carving out his own patch. But, in his world, there was always someone ready to take his place and every bit of progress had to be protected – whatever it takes.

In 1997, he blasted a rival with a handgun in the streets of Possil. The guy was hit in the arm and survived but it could have gone either way – or so the court thought. At O'Hara's trial the judge, Lord Abernethy, said, 'You were convicted of a very serious charge and the sentence for a charge of this kind has to be a substantial period of custody.'

He was given six years for attempted murder.

Unless they've seen the light and decided to convert to honest citizens, street players like The Birdman don't give up their business while in prison – especially not when they will only be out of circulation for a few years, as he would with a six-year sentence. During such a short spell inside, he would have kept in contact with his team and his allies, trying to make sure that his business, his patch, wasn't taken over by outsiders while he was away.

Before his imprisonment, it was believed that he was working closely with the McGovern Family, a powerful crew from nearby Springburn who were reckoned to be one of the top teams in Glasgow. Allegiances on the street are always more complex than Hollywood portrays. Sometimes teams work together. At other times, they have a simple agreement not to interfere with each other's business. Now and then, there's a war pact that one lot will help out another if either is challenged by a third mob. And they frequently change sides – often it's simply a matter of friendship.

Always alert to major threats, many other street players see only friends and foes. You are with someone or against them.

Trouble was brewing for The Birdman. One evening in September 2000, Tony McGovern went for a sociable drink in one of his regular haunts, The New Morvern Bar. Tony was part of the McGovern team that ran Springburn and a close associate of O'Hara. The rough and ready New Morvern Bar was well known as a street players' pub and had a long association with Glasgow faces. At one time it was run by the brother of Arthur 'The Godfather' Thompson and later by Ian 'Blink' McDonald, who'd go on to be an armed bank robber in Torquay and put on the

Most Wanted list of every cop force in Britain as he fled from prosecution. For Tony McGovern it was a local and regular haunt slap bang in the middle of his home patch. It was a safe place for him to go – or it should have been.

Tony McGovern and his brothers Joe, Tommy, Jamie and Paul, had worked hard from poor beginnings to establish themselves as major players with all the trappings. Such was their power that some journalists took to calling them The McGovernment. But their success brought strife as well as wealth.

Ten years earlier, Tony's home had been blasted by a firebomb. Three years earlier he and other members of the clan were the targets of a shooting at the Vulcan Bar. In turn, the McGoverns were also accused of dishing out the heavy stuff. Just five years before, Tommy McGovern had stood trial for gunning down a competitor but walked out of court a free man.

In 2000 the McGoverns were having problems though. A former associate, Jamie 'The Bull' Stevenson, had broken away from them and turf wars were in the air. In June of that year, Tony had survived a hit attempt on him at his home in the middle-class suburb of Bishopbriggs. Message received – he was taking no chances. From then on, a top-of-the-range bulletproof vest was worn by Tony all the time – even on the night he popped into one of his locals, The New Morvern Bar.

Tony had only had one or two drinks as he chatted to a couple of pals. They'd later report that he seemed tense, worried, but then that would be expected, given his family's troubles.

Leaving the pub on his own, Tony McGovern headed for his Audi car parked nearby. That's when the gunman struck.

Up close and personal, the hit man pumped several bullets into Tony McGovern. The shooter would have expected him to be wearing a bulletproof vest – most men in his business did. But, as many street players wryly say, with the black humour that's typical of Glasgow, 'Vests don't have hoods.' – or trousers, come to that. So shooters and blade merchants get up close, aiming for the neck, head and the soft, vulnerable organs below the waist.

Rushed to Glasgow Royal Infirmary, Tony McGovern was declared dead soon after.

For months, newspaper headlines screamed about blood on the street and with some justification. Anyone brave enough to take out a McGovern wasn't going to stop there or care who else tried to get in the way.

Most street players reckoned the feud between Jamie 'The Bull' Stevenson and the McGoverns was the source of the grief. So did the cops.

Bull Stevenson was arrested only to be released again and, at the time of writing in 2006, Tony McGovern's murder remains unsolved. But, in 2001, barely a year after the killing, the situation on the streets remained very tense and Robert O'Hara was about to be released. The Birdman free was seen by most as yet another threat in the struggle for the north east of Glasgow so someone decided to neutralise that threat.

The first blast knocked O'Hara off his feet. Strong as he was, the force of a shotgun from close quarters is difficult to withstand. Then a second blast came from a nearby car as it crawled past. One in the leg, the next in the arm – the drive-by hit man was avoiding O'Hara's bulletproof vest – then another and another and another shot rang out before the car sped off.

The shooting had taken place in Possil, in an area where O'Hara felt reasonably safe. But, in a war with such serious players, there was no such thing as a safe place.

Bleeding heavily, O'Hara pulled himself to his feet and staggered into the nearest pub, the Brother's Bar. The young man was in bad shape and at the Glasgow Royal Infirmary he was placed on the critical list. But he was made of strong stuff and would pull through.

For the next three years, the turf wars appeared to calm but, as we all know, appearances can be deceptive. The streets of Possil and Springburn were like a swan – all serenity above the water, frantic paddling below.

The body lay on the pavement like a bloody rag doll, all bent and broken. It was broad daylight in Possil, a place used to routine violence, but at first sight this was worse. This was murder.

Twenty-five-year-old Paul McDowall had been beaten with heavy clubs and knifed repeatedly. Once the cops identified the man and began to investigate the background, notions about who his killer might be slowly emerged.

One of McDowall's friends was a bloke called Dougie Mills. Mills was a known drug dealer and the cops knew he was coming into conflict with another local team – one led by Robert O'Hara.

A lengthy search of footage from nearby CCTV cameras eventually came up trumps. There was O'Hara and one of his henchmen, Robert Murray, near the scene of the crime on the right day at the right time. But that wasn't good enough – after all, this was their home patch.

In an area like Possil, with its massive crime rates and drugs problems, the cops aren't slow to put pressure on those for whom they could make life difficult. Even so, most people were terrified of O'Hara and his mates and those who weren't wouldn't give the time of day to the police. However, maybe the cops found people with a great deal to lose or maybe it was because the victim, McDowall, wasn't seen as a bad guy or even a big player – whatever the reason, hundreds of interviews later the police got their witnesses.

Soon O'Hara's team of Colin McKay and Brian Kelly were arrested but the police had to wait for the leader and his deputy, Robert Murray. The Birdman and Murray had flown off for a luxury holiday in Mexico. Oblivious to what had been going on back home, the suntanned O'Hara and Murray were arrested as they walked through Glasgow Airport on their return.

The four weren't just facing murder charges but, thanks to the police witnesses, they were up on firearms and drugs charges as well. One of the witnesses, then in Barlinnie Jail, had made a phone call to O'Hara. According to the authorities, the call was 'intercepted' – a fancy term for taped – and, during this call, O'Hara talked openly about weapons and the like. This provided the cops with enough information to raid a house in Cumbernauld where they found a stash of drugs. They also did Kelly's house and there they seized the group's arsenal – and impressive it was too. The gang had a MAC-11 sub-machine gun, the first of its kind ever recovered in Scotland, that could rattle out 600 bullets a minute. A more run-of-the-mill revolver and a sawn-off shotgun were also recovered, along with a stack of ammunition. Murder was the most serious charge but the prosecution would use this evidence to argue that the men had prepared for and planned more violence.

The Crown's witnesses were understandably terrified. Not only were they placed under police protection but the trial was also moved from Glasgow to Dunfermline and intense armed security was put in place.

In spite of the authorities' fears that The Birdman's crew might arrange some violence at court, the trial went relatively smoothly – aside, that is, from a witness's sister claiming that O'Hara and his girlfriend had offered her a £10,000 bribe to get her brother to withdraw his testimony. These allegations would later be tried in court and found not proven.

The case against The Birdman's mob gradually unfolded, revealing brutality and cruelty of the lowest order. Colin McKay apparently owed O'Hara £2,000 for heroin. Instead of cash, O'Hara would take payment in kind in the form of killing Paul McDowall simply because he knew the team's rival, Dougie Mills. Without debate, McKay agreed.

On the day in question, he ambushed the unsuspecting McDowall, killed him in broad daylight in the most horrific manner and then calmly phoned O'Hara to tell him the act was done. The CCTV film of O'Hara and Murray near the scene caught them on their way to see the dead McDowall for themselves. If O'Hara was being callous, McKay didn't get the chance.

The audacious daytime murder meant that the world of Possil was up and about and local folk learned of the execution very quickly. Within minutes of murdering McDowall, McKay himself became the hunted prey as a group of furious men gave chase. They caught him, beat him and knifed him with the same blade he'd used on McDowall. McKay almost died as a result of the attack but he survived, only to face the murder charges.

The jury took little time to find all four men guilty. The judge decided that, such was the seriousness of the offences, they should be sent to the foremost court in Scotland, Edinburgh High Court, for sentencing. There it was revealed that Murray had also been found guilty of attempting to murder a man, James Elder, in Maryhill, just before the murder of McDowall.

Of O'Hara, the sentencing judge said, 'You literally terrorised a whole area of the city of Glasgow and reaped substantial rewards. There is little I can say to reflect the revulsion every decent citizen must feel about you.'

The judge saved his strongest words for Colin McKay, who he described as one of O'Hara's lackeys. 'You kept his drugs for him. You kept his guns for him. When he asked, you also killed for him, as casually as if he asked you to get him a pint of milk. You are no better than a hired assassin.'

Robert O'Hara was sentenced to a minimum of twenty years, Colin McKay to fourteen years, Robert Murray to twelve years and armourer Brian Kelly to ten years.

At the time of writing, Robert 'The Birdman' O'Hara is compiling an appeal against his sentence.

Out in the streets of Possil, the trade in drugs goes on. Guns are more common than ever and new faces rule the streets. There are always new, usually younger, people ready to step in and reap the rewards of crime – whatever it takes.

You can take The Birdman out of Possil but Possil . . . it stays the same.

SAINT OR SINNER?

It wasn't so much Friday night as very early Saturday morning when the call came in. A body lying in a bloody heap outside a pub – or at least another bloody body and another pub. As usual, it had been a busy night for the cops covering Glasgow's east end and they sent a patrol car to check it out. What they found was going to rock the city.

The uniforms didn't need to wait for the forensic and scene-of-crime folk to work out what had happened. The man had been shot several times up close – hit style – and had been dead for a few hours. Nor did they need their scientific colleagues to identify the body. It was local man John Linton, a man some east enders thought of as a saint.

Thirty-four-year-old Linton had a track record with the cops going back to his teenage years but he had turned his back on that to sort out another matter. He worked full time trying to prove the innocence of TC Campbell and Joe Steele – the two men who had been convicted of murdering six members of the Doyle family in so-called Ice-Cream Wars in 1984.

The Doyle murders had disgusted all decent people. As the family slept, someone had torched a large cupboard – called a cellar – next to the front door of their flat. The cellar was jam-packed full of old tyres and cans of oil. In seconds the place was blazing and the fire wiped out almost a whole family, including a young baby.

After a high-profile murder trial, most members of the public would have gladly seen Campbell and Steele hang, such was their horror at the crime. It was generally accepted that the two men were guilty – street players knew better.

On the day after the murder, the cops launched one of the biggest manhunts ever in Scotland. They were pulling in known criminals from every corner of Glasgow and farther afield – Paisley, Greenock, Kilmarnock – but there was only one name on the cops' lips – TC Campbell.

Even before the investigation proper began, known players were being threatened and bribed to produce some evidence that would tie Campbell in to the murders. Witnesses near Bankend Street, where the family lived, were being cajoled and pressured to say that TC Campbell had bought a can of petrol and asked two junkies to torch a door on the night of the murders. None of them had seen him do this but the message went out loud and clear. It was a set-up and TC Campbell was going down no matter who the real killer was.

Long before the trial, east-end folk thought they knew who was behind the killings even if he didn't actually torch the cellar himself. Thomas 'The Licensee' McGraw was identified as the man in Bankend Street that night buying petrol and asking the junkies to torch a door. He also had a dispute with one of the Doyles – Andrew who was also known as 'Fatboy'. Along with a dozen other people, The Licensee had initially been arrested, charged and even held on remand but suddenly he was released without explanation.

When TC Campbell and Joe Steele were eventually convicted, east-end folk just sighed and said it was 'more of the same old same old'.

McGraw was called The Licensee because people believed he was licensed by the police to commit crime in return for information. Sure enough, he had escaped conviction or even being charged for many years in spite of being an active armed robber, drug trafficker, protection racketeer and being behind a great deal of violence.

In prison, TC Campbell and Joe Steele didn't lie down but set up a campaign to prove their innocence. TC started riots – at one point, he took over Peterhead Prison – and later he went on long hunger strikes that came close to ending his life. Joe escaped from different jails. He would enjoy a couple of days of freedom before inviting the media to some event – like tying himself to the top of a massive tower or chaining himself to the gates of Buckingham Palace. Every time he went back to jail, he'd plan his next escape, only to hand himself in again.

Gradually people not in the know began to wonder if TC Campbell and Joe Steele were innocent. Early on, they were visited by a firebrand young socialist politician, Tommy Sheridan. They convinced him and he went on to organise demonstrations and protests on their behalf. But an even earlier supporter was brave John Linton. Linton was brave because he lived in the same part of the city as Thomas 'The Licensee' McGraw and his troops and frequently and openly accused them of being behind the Doyle murders. These were lethal people who didn't take kindly to being blamed for anything.

Linton was also brave because he turned his back on his livelihood – crime – to organise the campaign. He worked with Campbell's and Steele's families, along with supporters such as Sheridan. And he took other risks as well. One night in 1994, he broke into the House of Commons. Wandering through those hallowed halls and offices of state, he planted hundreds of campaign leaflets in drawers and filing cabinets. At least now there wouldn't be a politician or civil servant who could claim they hadn't heard of The Glasgow Two, as Campbell and Steele were now being called.

On another night, he broke into Buckingham Palace but, just one room away from the Queen's private quarters, he was intercepted by security. John Linton was in trouble again but this time for a good cause.

By the mid 1990s Linton was running a very efficient campaign office that distributed thousands of leaflets, letters and press releases in the names of TC Campbell and Joe Steele or The Free the Glasgow Two Campaign. Linton was an unknown to all the journalists and politicians who were encouraged to change their views about Campbell and Steele's convictions. He might have been the hidden face of the campaign to them but east-end people knew fine well who he was – and so did the east-end faces.

Most days and nights, Linton could be found beavering away in the campaign's office. This was based in the east of Glasgow in a small former factory that had been made into several small offices. It wasn't the most secure setting and, on a number of occasions, when he emerged late at night into the dark, he was jumped by several men intent on beating him up. John Linton was no pushover and he held his own. Nor was he going to be scared away by those tactics.

Then, one day, Linton received a formal letter advising him that the building that housed the office had been bought over by some company he had never heard of. A week later, he was given notice to quit on the grounds that the new owner intended to change the use of the building.

The campaign survived on supporters' donations and it was going to be really hard to find another affordable office base. Things weren't looking good for the campaign. TC Campbell was on his longest hunger strike and had grown frail and ill – so frail the screws at Shotts Prison had moved him out to Law Hospital, Carluke, on the orders of the Secretary of State for Scotland. The politicians didn't want to create a martyr by letting him die in jail.

That was bad – the worst. Yet the situation with the office – that was just bad luck, wasn't it?

Some months after the campaign had been evicted from its office space, Linton noticed the other tenants hadn't moved out. Some dirty digging later, he discovered that the man behind the new owner was one George 'Crater Face' McCormack, a local taxi driver who was well known for officially fronting businesses for Thomas 'The Licensee' McGraw. That meant only one thing to John Linton – McGraw had deliberately seen to it that the campaign no longer had its office.

A few weeks later, in April 1996, Linton bumped into McGraw at The Sheiling Bar. The Sheiling was then well known as the local of Gordon Ross, one of McGraw's top men, and a regular haunt of his followers. It wasn't the best place to choose to fall out with McGraw but that's exactly what John Linton did – and not for the first time.

'YOU'RE A FUCKING MURDERER, MCGRAW,' Linton roared in the packed pub. 'AND A FUCKING GRASS – AN INFORMANT THAT LETS INNOCENT MEN ROT IN FUCKING JAIL.'

In Glasgow, they call a showdown like this where somebody is embarrassed in public a 'sherricking'. A sherricking was something that men like The Licensee couldn't allow.

'WHAT YOU SCARED OF, EH? WHY YOU TRYING TO FUCK UP TOMMY AND JOE'S APPEAL? WE ALL KNOW THEY DIDNA DO IT. THEY SHOULD BE FREE. BUT YOU'RE FUCKING TERRIFIED. WHAT OF? WE ALL FUCKING KNOW WHAT OF, YOU MURDERING BASTARD.'

The night ended in fisticuffs and grief but nothing that John Linton couldn't handle. He had sherricked The Licensee before and would do so again, given half the chance. Linton was never going to get the chance.

Just over a week later, John Linton was invited to a meeting with some guys he'd known for many years. We know he wasn't worried about the meeting since he went alone and unarmed. Linton was brave, not stupid.

Another reason he would have felt relaxed was the venue. The Roadhouse pub was in the city's sprawling Easterhouse scheme, not unfamiliar territory to Linton. Better still, it was widely known to be the pub of Jim Steele, Joe Steele's older brother. What did the campaign manager trying to set Joe free have to fear from Joe's own brother?

A few hours later, at the back of The Roadhouse, a group of men surrounded John Linton and fired. It was that old Mafia trick. No one was going to take sole responsibility and no one was going to be free to grass.

The old Mafia trick worked this time in that the cops were met with stony silence in their search for his killers. Then some people started letting it be known that Linton had owed a large sum of money to some serious players for some drugs transaction. Had John Linton been up to his old tricks? Had he reverted to sinner?

The news was orchestrated and spread fast. But the storytellers weren't ordinary folk. They were east-end players, well-known faces – The Licensee's people.

A short while later, the cops leaked that a warrant was being issued for Jim Steele in connection with the murder. But the Steele Family was outraged by the suggestion and Campbell's brother-in-law, Thomas 'Shadda' Lafferty, went public, claiming it was all a police tactic to discredit the campaign. Why would the police do that?

On hearing the news of his friend's death, at death's door himself, TC Campbell ended his hunger strike declaring, 'Now that John's gone, I'll never prove my innocence from six feet under.'

In 2005, TC Campbell and Joe Steele had their convictions for the murder of the Doyle Family quashed at appeal. The presiding Law Lords allowed evidence from two independent forensic linguists. Both concluded that statements taken by more than a dozen police officers during the murder investigation – which proved highly incriminating for the accused men – had to have been made up. Every single police officer swore that they had exactly the same notes of a verbal confession by Campbell, word for word. The forensic linguists both concluded that the odds against this were so high that it was impossible.

In plain language, the cops lied to convict TC Campbell and Joe Steele.

At the time of writing, Strathclyde Police has carried out no inquiry into the cop lies. No police officer has been disciplined, sacked or jailed.

At the time of writing, two unjustly imprisoned men, TC Campbell and Joe Steele, have been deemed innocent and set free yet no further investigation into the Doyle murders has been launched.

The people who wiped out almost an entire family in 1984 are still walking the streets of Glasgow, free men – and so, since 1996, have the killers of John Linton, a sinner turned saint.

SAFER IN JAIL?

Life and death are daily parts of country life, even in pastures as lush and beautiful as Langbank in Renfrewshire. As farmer John Baxter trundled down the single-track road, he was on his way to collect nothing more sinister than bales of silage. Then he saw the body.

'When I saw it, I thought the worst,' he said, once he had time to calm down. God knows what panic had thumped in his chest as he'd hurried out of his vehicle and up to that odd-shaped bundle lying only yards from the isolated road. It was the badly decomposed corpse of a man.

From anywhere in Glasgow, a thirty-minute car ride will take you out into a rural landscape as barren and unpopulated as anywhere in the country. Most citizens see this as a benefit, enhancing their quality of life. There are others who see it as a way of disposing of death.

It was summer, 13 July 2004, and the cops had a problem. Alerted by John Baxter, the police were quickly at the scene. They soon sealed it off and had a helicopter sweeping the area – all to no avail. Whoever had left the body was long gone.

Modern police rightly make a great song and dance about how useful modern forensic science is. DNA, blood categorisation, dating procedures and many more techniques have all made tasks like the one that now confronted them possible. But sometimes easier, older systems can be of value – like checking lists.

Two weeks before, on 30 June 2004, one Michelle Toner had gone to the police near her home in Pollokshields, Glasgow, a worried woman. Her husband, Martin, had gone out the day before and not returned. Here was a frantic woman with two young children whose man had gone out to a meeting and not returned a full day later – decent people might expect the police to be sympathetic, understanding. Not this time.

After just twenty-four hours' absence, the cops, more often than not, play it all down. They know people go away for many reasons and are unwilling even to fill in a Missing Person Report till the absence is much longer. But there was another reason they were reluctant to listen too much to Michelle Toner.

Martin Toner was facing serious drug-trafficking charges. Along with Glasgow men James Cameron, Douglas Fleming and Finbar Brady, he stood accused of smuggling drugs between 2000 and 2002 in Belgium, Holland, Colombia, England and the Caribbean. The movement of drugs between those countries doesn't involved tenner wraps. Rest assured, large quantities featured in the allegations.

Shortly after the day he disappeared, Toner and the other accused men were due to appear at Edinburgh High Court on a pre-trial procedural matter. The cops knew all about Martin Toner's background and his forthcoming trial so they bluntly told his wife that they suspected he had fled to avoid court.

Michelle Toner kept insisting that her man would never just go away. Martin loved their two kids too much. In the event, she was right. It was Martin Toner's body that farmer John Baxter had found near that lonely country track.

On the day she had last seen her man, he had set off for Langbank, telling some friends that he was on his way to meet someone who owed him money. Officially, Toner ran a small cleaning business but he was well known to be involved in trading, dealing and more than a few shady scams. So going to a meeting to pick up a debt would have been normal routine for him. None of his friends or family worried about that. They should have.

The police set up a murder hunt team of thirty officers. The first stop was to interview his co-accused on the drugs charges. When charged, Fleming and Brady had been held on remand in Barlinnie Prison but Cameron and Toner were allowed to live at home.

The nature of the charges involved contact with a range of countries and inevitably well-proven underground routes to get there. It was the very set of circumstances that made an accused a risk of going abroad and avoiding court. Most men would have been held in jail pending the trial but Toner was not. He must have been delighted at that but should he have been?

The interviews of his co-accused didn't prove helpful to the murder team. Yet the cynically minded might say that they were useful to the men in the hot seats. Given the murder inquiry, their lawyers had no problem in obtaining a postponement of legal proceedings. In such trials, more time is always useful.

As is usual in street matters, Toner had not told his friends who the guy he was meeting was or anything about him, other than that he owed him money. Most street players worth their salt work on a strictly need-to-know basis. So none of his friends knew who the man was.

While Langbank itself is a small picturesque village, the surrounding area is a vast landscape of wooded countryside littered with overgrown lanes and clearings well hidden from the road. For that reason it's popular with courting couples as well as faces who want to do a bit of business without being spotted. Toner and the man he was meeting had chosen the venue well – no one had seen them.

The cops' extensive hunt abroad was particularly relevant, given the drug-trafficking charges Toner was to face. One of their first ports of call was someone not facing any charges. Kevin Lofthouse had been good pals with Toner and even lived in a house Toner owned. But after Toner was charged with drug trafficking, the pair had had a huge argument and hadn't spoken since. The trouble was that Lofthouse had left Scotland for France about the time of Toner's disappearance.

The cops caught up with Lofthouse in Marseille, where he was selling a boat. He knew nothing about his ex-pal's disappearance and death. Still no joy for the cops.

In September 2004, the original drug-trafficking trial eventually proceeded. They were one week into a trial heavily laden with evidence when the defence teams spotted something. A lot of prosecution staff and policemen were going into a room in the court, laden with cups of coffee. A staffroom? A rest room? No – a room set up with a direct camera link to the court.

A year earlier, the TV link had been set up at Glasgow High Court for a top-security case. They had left the equipment in place and some court administrator had been asked by one of the prosecution staff to switch on the link. Cops and court officials had been watching the show from the comfort of the room.

When this was brought to the attention of trial judge, the place went into uproar. Only with the judge's permission is such a link allowed. Besides, what if someone due to give evidence later had watched the proceedings? That was strictly a no-no.

Once again, the trial was postponed to allow an inquiry into the TV link. They convened again in June 2005, almost the anniversary of Martin Toner's body being discovered. By that time one of the accused had fled the country and another had to be searched down by warrant. Some of these guys just didn't want to go to court.

The judge, Lord McEwan, had considered matters very seriously and decided he had no option. The trial against the men had to be abandoned. It was set to be one of the biggest drug-trafficking trials Scotland had ever seen and yet it was abandoned due a technicality and the nosiness of some officials and cops.

Around that time, the police didn't appear to be much further forward in catching Martin Toner's killer – except for forensics. Toner's body had been so badly damaged that the first assumption was that he had been beaten to death in the most vicious manner but the forensic bods discovered differently – he'd been shot.

Up to that point, the scenario of two men meeting to settle a

49

debt, an argument ensuing and turning violent seemed eminently feasible. These scenes happen every day among Glasgow's street players and a few go the whole road – to murder. But most people – no matter how dodgy – don't shoot a business associate. Had Martin Toner been taken out by a hit? Had he messed with too many dangerous people in his business in Colombia and the Caribbean?

The cops knew that, if Toner had been killed as a hit, there was little chance of getting information from anyone associated with the crime or the killer. Their main hope was that some honest member of the public had spotted something of value even though it had been almost a year since Martin Toner's murder.

So they pled again for information from the public through the media, asking anyone with useful information to call Crime-stoppers. To add some incentive, they put a £3,000 reward on the case. Still no useful news. Rewards rarely work.

At the time of writing, the Crown has won the right to consider raising new charges against Martin Toner's co-accused on the drug offences. Martin Toner's murder case remains open but stagnant and collecting more dust every day.

Would he still be alive if held in jail on the drugs charges? Would he now be with his wife and kids? Only one person can answer that question – his murderer – and he's not saying.

PART 2
FEMMES
FATALES

The gentle sex? Whoever coined that phrase should be condemned to live forever with The Fighting McNeilly Women, a well-known east-end crew who have been sending strong men scurrying for safety for the past twenty-five years. Of course, women can be gentle but they can also be lethal. Those are the dames we pay attention to here.

There was a time when scribblers gave women murderers a particular slant. They were all arsenic and lace, slipping more and more poison gradually into some man's stew. Or theirs were crimes of passion. The poor dears were moved too much by love, lust and hormones to let someone else live. And that was it for women. Aye, right.

Sixty-one-year-old granny-of-twelve Angela Carroll had had enough. Her neighbour in the sheltered housing complex, seventy-six-year-old Christina Turner, had taken up with a neighbour, a man who drank a bit, and the two of them made too much noise. One day, it got too much. She was going to sort it.

She had told the woman straight that she thought her a slut and a whore and now she'd taken up with a man who'd been a pal of hers. One day in 1999, she spotted Christina Turner in the garden and something snapped.

'I'll kill you,' she screamed standing behind and above her. 'I'm going to kill you,' she shrieked again, as she brought the twelve-inch knife down to Christina Turner's neck.

Gentle sex? Sure. Thankfully Ms Turner had only a scratch and the High Court accepted that the accused didn't mean what she had said. They deferred sentence.

The point is that here were two elderly residents of a sheltered housing complex falling out so bitterly that their dispute could be settled by a blade and threats of murder. Want it real? That happens.

Henrietta Gibson went further. In 2005, in her Parkhead flat, she snapped. Her fifty-nine-year-old husband George had beaten and tormented her for almost their entire thirty-six years together. OK she was drunk but he'd hit her and burst her lip and she'd had enough. She chibbed him six times and killed him. The court was sympathetic and jailed the poor woman for only five years.

These are examples of everyday scenes from the hard side but they're not good enough tales for this section – domestic violence and neighbours in dispute are just too commonplace. Apart from changing the names and the dates, it would be more or less the same story again and again.

No, the women who populate this section are different – they're involved, complex, crazy ... What they aren't is gentle. Why should they be? Never heard of emancipation?

HONEY TRAPS AND HIT MEN

'Suicide,' said the cop, looking up at the body hanging from the noose, 'it's always a bloody waste.'

The cop was experienced and very little surprised him now – not even the fact that the man hanging before him was a respected Glasgow lawyer, nor that the man had chosen the entry hall at the office of his legal firm, Hughes, McVey and Quar, to carry out his final act, nor even that some of his colleagues knew the dead man, Jack Quar, as a respectable, cheery bloke who got on well with everyone.

'Such a bloody nice man,' said a detective attending the scene. 'Who would have thought he'd have killed himself?'

Who indeed? But, by the end of that day, Jack Quar's body was being processed and the conclusion of suicide was close to being reached. Maybe the cops should have hesitated and questioned the obvious hanging in front of them? Maybe they should have checked Jack Quar's business diary from just the day before? They might have spotted a name that would have interested them.

Everyone who was anyone in Glasgow knew Manny O'Donnell. Wealthy, outspoken, dripping in gold jewellery and fond of flash cars, Manny O'Donnell was hard to miss. O'Donnell had made his legitimate money from the building industry and his illegitimate cash from vice, theft and big-time fraud. His construction company was legitimate and he had blue-chip customers such as the Ministry of Defence and the nuclear submarine base at

Coulport on Loch Long. And that was in spite of his political affiliations.

As Irish as his name sounds, O'Donnell was an open and vociferous supporter of the IRA, making hefty personal donations and expecting all his workers to put £10 each week into an IRA collection box. If they didn't pay up, he sacked them. Most paid up.

One of his good friends was a pub owner, John 'The Irishman' Friel, another flamboyant figure on the Glasgow scene. But Manny kept other company both among IRA big names and top street players in Glasgow.

Manny O'Donnell was a man walking with one foot in the gutter and one on the pavement. It's a dangerous way to walk.

On 20 November 1998, one day after Jack Quar was found hanging by a noose, another gruesome discovery was made. In a lovers' lane in the town of East Kilbride near Glasgow, a man walking his dog lifted the edge of a large, filthy tarpaulin and immediately regretted it. Underneath the tarpaulin was the body of a man, so bloody he seemed to be cut to shreds. Manny O'Donnell, fifty-three, had finally favoured one leg and fallen into the gutter.

O'Donnell had been shot through the chest and then the head with a shotgun at close range. He had then been stabbed and slashed over twenty times. He had clearly angered someone very, very much.

In sussing who the killers might be, Glasgow cops were immediately faced with a big problem – not the lack of suspects but the excess of them.

In a city divided on political and religious grounds similar to Belfast, there were plenty of UDA and UVF supporters who would have gladly taken him out. In his legitimate business dealings, he was known to be a hard and callous negotiator, happy to leave his debts unpaid but very willing to send in the heavies when he was owed. More than one subcontractor had been forced out of business or out of town by O'Donnell. Plenty of folk blamed him for ruining their business, their families, their lives.

In his shady dealings, he was involved in controlling prostitutes – or at least paying people to manage them for him. There are big profits to be made in the sex industry but it is also a highly competitive business and it has attracted some very unsavoury characters – men like the Welsh brothers who fought a murderous feud with 'The Godfather', Arthur Thompson, for twenty-five years over the control of the city. The brutality that this feud provoked includes Thompson's mother-in-law being killed by a car bomb, at least three of the Welsh crew being taken out and a lot of other violence that has never reached the public domain. This was the calibre of some folk behind the sex business.

Then there was some of the company he kept. Not for nothing was O'Donnell's street name 'The Contractor'. The cops believed he was friendly with John Healy, one of the most feared faces in Glasgow. Earlier that year, Healy had been sent down for ten years for trafficking large amounts of cannabis from Spain to Scotland. Healy's co-accused were Thomas 'The Licensee' McGraw and his team. The Licensee's team had walked free while Healy had got time. He wasn't best pleased. Rumours were circulating that Healy had stashed a large quantity of drugs and wasn't telling where. Maybe Manny O'Donnell knew? Rumour or not, there were those who'd kill to find out.

That lot was just the start for the cops to ponder on. They were settling down for a long inquiry when they got a break – a drunken confession.

With its candyfloss, Kiss-Me-Quick hats and mobbed pubs, you either hate Blackpool or love it. Many Glaswegians love it and go there for September holiday weekends or to settle and work there or sometimes just to get away from Glasgow for a while.

The Glasgow cops had decided to do what they always do in any murder inquiry – look at those closest to the victim first. They very quickly cleared O'Donnell's wife and his many lady friends so then they looked at his work colleagues.

In particular they were interested in Francis O'Donnell – no relation to Manny – who worked as his driver. Another man they wanted to talk to was William McKinnon who helped run the prostitutes with Manny O'Donnell.

When they pulled Francis O'Donnell in, he insisted that he'd been in his native Ireland at the time of the murder. Although he couldn't remember which Dublin hotel he had stayed in, he stuck to his guns. He was going to be a tough nut to crack.

William McKinnon wasn't so stern. Interviewed by the cops, he was nervous, almost tearful, wringing his hands.

'Look, I know who did it,' he eventually blurted out. 'Let me tell you about this night in Blackpool.'

McKinnon claimed he and Francis O'Donnell had decided to get out of Glasgow for a while after the murder and headed to Blackpool. But it wasn't the tower, the trams or the leisure park they were interested in – just the pubs. One night, after ten or eleven pints of beer, Francis O'Donnell began talking about Manny's death and then he blurted out, 'I done it. I done it with they two bams . . .'

The cops quickly struck a deal that no charges would be brought against William McKinnon if he gave evidence against the others. By September 1999, the authorities were ready to go to trial with an interesting list of characters.

There was twenty-seven-year-old Francis O'Donnell, of course, who continued to deny any involvement but still couldn't remember what Dublin hotel he had allegedly stayed in.

Then there was beautiful, petite Mary Ryan. Ryan was known to have been involved with Manny O'Donnell in running his vice game. At twenty-seven years old, Mary was almost half Manny O'Donnell's age. They were frequently seen together around Glasgow and even went on a holiday to Spain together. The rich businessman and beautiful young woman – people assumed their relationship was sexual. Ryan always denied this but now she was going to have to prove it wasn't murder either.

The third accused was twenty-five-year-old Patrick Devine, Mary Ryan's lover. Mary had said that she was with Patrick at his house at the time of the killing and he had backed her up. The cops showed what they thought of that by charging him with murder too.

At the beginning of the trial at Glasgow High Court, the judge slapped a total ban on reporting the proceedings. While more common in England, this is a move Scottish judges are reluctant to pursue. It indicated that officials thought the witnesses would be at some level of risk if their evidence was revealed openly. But was their caution to do with gangsterism or O'Donnell's Irish links?

Early on, the Crown made a breakthrough when Patrick Devine withdrew his statement that Mary Ryan had been with him in his flat at the time of the murder. Now the heat was on Ryan and Francis O'Donnell. The prosecution case read like something out of a Hollywood film script.

Mary Ryan had been asked by persons unknown to lure O'Donnell to a quiet spot in East Kilbride, they claimed. For reasons unknown, Mary Ryan agreed. Ryan hired a Renault 19 for the night and went to meet Manny O'Donnell in his regular haunt of the Tinto Firs hotel in the city's south side. The staff knew O'Donnell well and remembered him and the pretty woman chatting over a drink and then leaving – not in his top-of-the-range Mercedes but in the Renault, with the woman driving.

Why had Manny gone with Mary Ryan? It's true they were work colleagues but they wouldn't have much business to conduct out in the new town of East Kilbride and he would have known that was the direction she was heading. On the promise of sex? Maybe – we know O'Donnell had a weakness for good-looking women.

With her alibi of having been with Patrick Devine that night now destroyed, Ryan was having to change her ground. She admitted being at the hotel with O'Donnell and leaving with him but, she clamed, it was to go to a meeting in the Pond Hotel in the west end of Glasgow. That made more sense in terms of the vice businesses the two ran together.

Ryan then claimed that, when she stopped at traffic lights in the Dumbreck area of the city, masked and armed men jumped into the car and took O'Donnell hostage. They drove him to a parkland area nearby and killed him. She claimed she didn't realise any of this was going to happen and, assuming she'd be next, she'd had to beg for her life. Eventually they let her leave to walk home to her south-side flat with warnings that, if she uttered a word to anyone, she would indeed be next. That's what Mary Ryan claimed.

The prosecution claimed that she had calmly driven Manny O'Donnell to his appointment with death in the lovers' lane in East Kilbride. Once the car was stopped, Francis O'Donnell and others unknown jumped into the car. Almost immediately, Manny O'Donnell was shot in the back, through his seat, with a shotgun. Fragments of the seat were found in his flesh. Then his head was pushed back against the headrest and he was blasted in the skull from close range. Then the assassins stabbed and slashed him repeatedly.

Frenzied is an overused word in describing this kind of attacks but it fits the assault on this occasion. The post-mortem would reveal that Manny O'Donnell was well dead before they drew their blades.

Later that night, Francis O'Donnell and persons unknown torched the Renault, the murder car, and had Mary Ryan report it as missing the next day. This procedure is common with hits and was the final damning nail in the coffin of the accused. Mary Ryan had hired the murder car so it had all been premeditated, the prosecution claimed.

The trial lasted five weeks but it didn't take the jury long to reach guilty verdicts on Francis O'Donnell and the honey-trap, bait Mary Ryan, both of whom were sentenced to a minimum of fifteen years in jail. As the verdicts were read out, Mary Ryan sobbed and teetered on her feet and had to be held up by a court official.

The murder charge against Patrick Devine, Ryan's erstwhile

lover, was found not proven. William McKinnon, who turned on his old friends and gave evidence against them, was, of course, not charged.

But even as Ryan and Francis O'Donnell were being led into the bowels of the court for the onward journey to jail, there were those who started puzzling over the unanswered questions. Assuming the prosecution description of the murder to be more or less accurate, it would have needed two, if not three, killers. There had been no suggestion that petite Mary Ryan had carried out any of the violence so where were the other killers?

In the years after Manny O'Donnell's murder, additional useful information has emerged. Not only had his building firm carried out work for the Ministry of Defence but it had also been involved in the Falkland Islands at a sensitive time after the hostilities with Argentina and in other nuclear submarine ports. He had met Prince Andrew and rubbed shoulders with most military leaders in Britain. This was a man with deep-rooted involvement in the IRA. Would MI5 and MI6 just allow that to continue?

Yet the IRA wasn't just a source of political fellow travellers for O'Donnell. He had fallen out with his former business partner, William Friery, and wanted him taken out. In the months before his death, O'Donnell had gone to Ireland with a suitcase full of money and asked the IRA to assassinate Friery.

Whatever your views on the IRA, they see themselves as soldiers, not gangsters. They refused to do the hit and were incensed that O'Donnell had dragged them into this personal business. Besides, Friery was also a supporter and fundraiser for them. It was no surprise that Friery went into hiding in Turkey shortly after O'Donnell's murder.

Then there was Jack Quar, the lawyer found hanging by the neck in his Glasgow office. In the hours before his apparent suicide, he had acted normally. He had bought a Christmas tree and stored it in the boot of his car. He'd dictated notes to his secretary for the next morning, asking that she leave out files for him. That same day, the always-dapper Quar had visited his tailor and arranged for some suits to be altered. Then a couple of hours later he calmly hanged himself?

It didn't ring true. Besides Quar was an ex-military intelligence captain with incredible self-confidence and discipline. No one but no one who knew him believed that he killed himself. Then there was that visit from O'Donnell.

Before his murder, rumours circulated that O'Donnell had agreed to store a load of cocaine for one of Glasgow's Mr Bigs. There is no doubt that, with his property and businesses, he had done this before. This time, the word was that he'd got greedy and helped himself to some – a cool £250,000 worth. People have killed for much less.

O'Donnell wasn't a drug dealer with outlets on the street. To complete this deal, he would have had to move the gear on to someone who could shift it and he'd probably get less than half the value for the cocaine – maybe £100,000 or £150,000 tops. It was still a tidy profit but he would have to clean this money, lodge it someplace the authorities wouldn't notice, and he wouldn't be able to touch it. Some place legal? Who better to consult than a lawyer like Jack Quar?

There is no suggestion that Quar knew anything about the source of this cash or that he was doing anything illegal. Wealthy people, entirely legally, seek this type of advice all the time.

It's likely that O'Donnell had sought Quar's advice on such matters before. After O'Donnell's death cops discovered £20,000 planted at his work, £22,000 under his floorboards in one of his houses, £200,000 in an Irish bank account and over £500,000 in a Jersey deposit. And that's just what they managed to find in the early days, without looking too hard.

If the word about O'Donnell stealing the cocaine is right, did someone go hunting for the money and pay a visit to Jack Quar as he finished up for the day at his office?

There were no physical signs on Quar's body of a struggle. So what? Men who deal in millions of pounds' worth of cocaine are professionals in business and as killers. A well-liked, successful lawyer is less likely to die a violent death than to commit suicide. So is that what they conjured up? And so successfully that, when Quar's body was cremated shortly after his death, all the evidence of wrong-doing was destroyed?

Did they then go after O'Donnell? With his links to the IRA and Glasgow gangsters, did they decide that his death had to look brutal? That it was the most likely way he'd meet a sudden end? Is that why he was stabbed so often after he was so obviously dead? To make it look like some random act of brutality? Exactly what it wasn't?

Was Mary Ryan used not just as a honey trap but as a patsy? Set up to take the fall for others? From her jail cell in Cornton Vale, the women's prison, she thinks so and still protests her innocence seven years on. Short protests by convicted people are two a penny – long protests are rare.

Maybe listening to Mary Ryan is the only way we'll learn the whole truth behind the honey trap and the hit men. Then again, maybe even she doesn't know the whole picture. That's often how it is in the messy world of organised crime and nowhere more so than in Glasgow.

KILLING COUSINS

One of the more polite names Glaswegians like to give to their city is the Dear Green Place. This comes from the huge tracks of lush parks laid down in Victorian days, often paid for by the well-to-do who had grown rich on tobacco, coffee and slavery. For such an urban, industrial landscape it's also rich in beautiful, council-run, golf courses. Around the world, this sport that's often only for the rich but, in Glasgow, it is available to any and every working-class citizen who fancies it. However, the parks and golf courses provide another facility – a dumping ground for corpses.

It isn't known if the stone was thrown deliberately or carelessly. What isn't in dispute is that it hit a car window and smashed it. There was going to be trouble.

The stone-throwing happened in the Royston area. In the old days, when heavy industry was at its peak, the area was called the Garngad – a long tunnel of tenements, cram-packed with folk, running from the city centre almost out to the Rhubarb Fields on the city's northern border.

Many of the families supported themselves by working in the big engineering plants making steam trains for every country in the world. Or the coal mines just a few miles away. Or the steel mills or the shipyards. The work was hard and dirty and the wages barely enough to support a family. Disease and early death were rampant and too many of the people knew that their lives were cheap.

Yet in the Garngad families also helped each other. Bailed each other out when money was short. Helped care for the sick and dying. Were the warmest, most trustworthy neighbours you could hope for. It was a place where you really did leave your door unlocked yet it was also a place where drunkenness and violence were a part of everyday life. The Garngad bore all the contradictions that are the city of Glasgow.

By 2004, the city fathers and mothers had tried to rid the area of old prejudices. One of their oft-tried devices was to rename the area. It didn't work, of course – just ask anyone who lives in Royston now.

The area is rife with heavy merchants, drug traffickers and gunmen. Shoot-outs in the street are common. Disputes are more often than not settled with blades. The place reeks of brutality and murders are not uncommon.

In 2001, local man John Keenan had been practically hacked in half during an attack by two adversaries, Brian 'Spud' Murphy and Richard Holmes. There was outrage locally when Murphy, who admitted stabbing Keenan twenty-five times, was jailed for only five years and Holmes, who admitted thumping Keenan with a baseball bat, was admonished and set free.

Three attempts were made on Holmes's life after that, including a drive-by shooting outside the Glasgow Royal Infirmary. Eventually, early in 2005, a lone gunman shot Holmes dead near his home in Royston Road and had a good go at doing the same to three of his mates.

The whole saga sums up Royston. So what had anyone to fear from something as minor as throwing a stone?

Eighteen-year-old Stephen McLeod chucked the stone. By bad luck or by design it hit the rear window of a car and smashed it. So what? Annoying as car vandalism is, the motors lining Royston's streets are all too frequently trashed. This was just a broken window. Then young Stephen McLeod disappeared.

Eleven days after he went missing, McLeod's badly decomposed body was found in some trees on Ruchill Golf Course, close to Royston. His body was so far gone that the exact cause of death proved impossible to determine but it was 2004 and the pathologists had the technology to confirm that he had been stabbed six times and slashed. Another murder hunt was on.

The cops dug into McLeod's background but they weren't coming up with any likely suspects. Then someone told them about the incident with the stone.

The car with the smashed window belonged to one Kara Heron, aged twenty-four. To say she had been angered by the smashed window was an understatement. She was incensed and admitted that she had decided to teach the vandal a lesson with the help of her cousin, seventeen-year-old William McElroy. By June 2005, the cousins were in court on a murder trial.

Kara Heron admitted seeking McElroy's help in exacting some revenge on McLeod. The pair went to Shuna Place in Royston on 2 August 2004 and forced McLeod into her car.

'Let me out, please,' cried the young captive as Heron drove. 'Please, I didna mean it.' As young McLeod struggled in panic and fear in the back seat, McElroy thumped him and threatened him. 'Please, my dad'll pay for the damage. If you just let me out.'

Kara Heron ignored the teenager's begging and continued driving, not stopping till they reached Ruchill Golf Course. Here the stories of the accused differ.

Kara Heron claimed that she let the two young men out of her car, then drove off. That all she expected was for McLeod to be given a beating. That she wasn't thinking of murder and knew nothing about the knife that was used on McLeod. Had never seen it.

William McElroy had a low IQ and had attempted but failed to have the murder charge dropped on grounds of diminished responsibility. His account was slightly but significantly different . McElroy claimed that at Ruchill Golf Course his older, female cousin had handed him the murder knife before driving off.

The jury at the High Court in Glasgow weren't convinced by McElroy's argument, which did nothing to take him out of the frame. Either version led to the conclusion that he and he alone had carried out the actual murder.

Finding McElroy guilty of murder, the judge, Hugh Matthews QC, ordered that he be imprisoned and not considered for release till he had served at least twelve years.

Kara Heron was also found guilty but of the lesser charges of abduction and culpable homicide and sentenced to six years in jail. In court, Judge Matthews said to Heron, 'You set up the circumstances that led to Mr McLeod's death. I cannot ignore the fact you were an accessory in bringing about his death.'

That is not in dispute. But did she bring the knife and hand it to her cousin? The murder knife? Her cousin the killer? All over nothing more than a broken car window? That's life in some Glasgow schemes for you.

LAMB TO THE SLAUGHTER

Any city at night can be a fearful place. It's worse when you've had a few drinks, you're in a strange neighbourhood and you can't find your way home. That can be terrifying.

Alan Lennox was only twenty-one years old but he was already showing much promise in life. Training to be an electrician, he was a hard and steady worker who had won the Apprentice of the Year award at Cardonald College. But that night, in August 2003, he was having a night off and enjoying a few drinks with friends in a strange part of town.

Calton is one of the oldest areas of Glasgow and can be confusing to outsiders. Just to the east of the city centre, it's home to the sprawling outdoor market, the Barras, and the Barras Ballroom, where serial killer Bible John picked up his victims in the 1960s. While developers have demolished and rebuilt slices of the area, the small winding streets with their ancient pubs remain much in evidence. It's an easy place to get lost in.

Edging on to Glasgow Green, Calton sees much human traffic. Working girls heading there to sell their bodies. The chickens, underage male prostitutes looking for the darkest corners. Drug dealers trailed by lonely junkies desperate for the next tenner bag of smack. Calton can be a dangerous place to get lost in.

Young Alan Lennox wasn't stupid. He would have avoided the rowdy drunks and groups of strutting young men in their baseball caps. But he needed to get home to his place in nearby Gorbals, just across the River Clyde, which runs along the southern edge of Glasgow Green. He was lost and had to ask someone. A young couple would do. They looked safe.

Amy Stewart and John Hopkinson were very helpful. Of course they'd show Alan the way to the Gorbals. It wasn't far. In fact they'd walk with him a bit of the way so he'd be sure to take the correct direction and not get lost again. That was the type of Glasgow folk Alan was used to. Always willing to go that wee bit further to help someone else.

The three walked through the streets of Calton chatting about this and that. They'd just take a short cut down this lane then Alan could practically see the Gorbals from the other end. The young electrician was grateful – so grateful he bought the pair chips and some cigarettes. What was a few quid to Alan Lennox who'd just been paid? He was that kind of young man – generous. Now he'd had a good night out but he wanted to get home to his own bed.

Except the lane near Bain Street wasn't a shortcut to the Gorbals. For those who knew Calton, it was an infamous place nicknamed Muggers' Alley.

Halfway down the lane at the darkest point, the mood changed. Amy Stewart and John Hopkinson both pulled knives and held them at Alan's throat. Wisely, the young man didn't struggle or protest much and soon they had robbed him of his hard-earned pay packet containing £140.

As the pair went to leave, Amy Stewart reached out and stabbed Alan in the thigh, once. Then she and her accomplice scurried out of Muggers' Alley, leaving their victim bleeding behind them.

Stewart and Hopkinson didn't need to debate what they'd do with the money. Heroin. The pair were smackheads with no cash – well, not until they robbed and stabbed Alan Lennox. Now they had enough money to keep their habit at bay for a couple of days. A couple of days free of that constant search for funds to feed the monkey. Two days she wouldn't have to go and sell her body and they wouldn't have to think of some scam to steal some dough.

Stewart and Hopkinson were so delighted by their change of fortune that they stopped for a cuddle and kiss. Unfortunately for them they were standing right under a CCTV camera that caught, timed and dated their celebratory embrace.

Back in Muggers' Alley, Alan Lennox was bleeding to death. That one stab wound by Amy Stewart had severed a main artery. The young man died there on his own, in the dark, in a strange place.

Thanks to the CCTV film, Amy Stewart and John Hopkinson were soon arrested and brought to trial at Glasgow High Court. Stewart's lawyer tried to have the murder charge dropped if she pled guilty to culpable homicide. However, the offered deal was rejected by the prosecuting QC Dorothy Bain.

After a protracted trial, during which Stewart and Hopkinson blamed each other for the stabbing, both were found guilty of murder. A date was then set for them to appear at Edinburgh High Court for sentencing.

Lord Abernethy, presiding in Edinburgh, was presented with a litany of human tragedy. Apparently, Hopkinson had come from a good, caring background and hadn't been in trouble till he got hooked on smack. His was a modern-day tragedy right enough and a waste but it was a tale Lord Abernethy must have heard so often before.

At the time of the assault on Alan Lennox, Amy Stewart had only been nineteen years old but they had been nineteen years of misery, according to her counsel, Ian Duguid QC.

Stewart had been physically abused through much of her childhood and had been taken into foster care. At the age of sixteen, she left care and formed a relationship with a man many years her senior. Even by then, she had been drinking heavily – a problem that worsened. Her older lover had a plan to deal with the booze – he put her on to heroin and on the streets selling sex.

The relationship staggered on for another couple of years through constant rows and several miscarriages for Stewart. All the time her smack addiction became worse and worse. Finally, just months before the attack on Alan Lennox, Amy Stewart had broken away from the older man and taken up with Hopkinson, still older at twenty-seven years but closer to her own age.

No doubt Lord Abernethy was sympathetic to the dreadful life that Amy Stewart had lived but he was a Law Lord not a social worker and the most serious of crimes had been committed. Before pronouncing sentence he said to Stewart and Hopkinson, 'You planned to rob the deceased and armed yourselves with knives. What you did can only be described as cruel and callous.'

Then, perhaps addressing the Glasgow love affair with knives as well as the two people in the dock, Lord Abernethy continued, 'Whatever your actual intentions – and I accept there was no intention to kill the deceased – it should be clear to everyone the use of knives in crimes can prove fatal. In this case, one stab wound was enough.'

Amy Stewart and John Hopkinson were jailed for life and will have to serve at least twelve years before they can apply for release.

At the time of Alan Lennox's murder, Amy Stewart had been bailed on three different occasions by different Glasgow courts. Only four weeks before the murder, she had appeared at Glasgow Sheriff Court charged with assaulting and partially blinding a seventeen-year-old Iraqi Kurd refugee, Rebaz Osman. Again the court had bailed Amy Stewart – bailed her to commit murder.

In March 2004, one month after being sentenced for the murder of Alan Lennox, Stewart pled guilty to the assault and to blinding Rebaz Osman in one eye. She was sentenced to four and half years in jail to be served concurrently with her life term.

Victims' organisations and Alan Lennox's family understand-ably spoke out angrily, saying that, if she hadn't been bailed, the young man would still be alive. There were demands for someone to overview bail orders and prevent this type of tragedy from hap-pening again. Prevent anyone else being released from custody only to lead another innocent, like Alan Lennox, like a lamb to the slaughter.

LOW LIFE IN HIGH PLACES

They tore down the dense rows of sandstone tenements of old Gorbals, replacing them with modern monstrosities built on stilts – flats as damp as dank dungeons – and high-rise flats. Killing a community, some called it. Then, one night in 2002, a passer-by looked up and saw a woman hanging by her fingertips from a twentieth-floor ledge. She didn't hold on for long, of course – no one could – but tumbled silently through the air and flopped lifeless on to the concrete below. Another sudden death in Glasgow.

By the next day, a shocked and upset woman called Rose Broadley was talking to the media. The dead woman was her friend, twenty-eight-year old Joanna Colbeck. Joanna was a heroin addict with no money for a fix. Rose and her common-law husband, Robert Butchart, had taken pity on her and given her a bed for the night in the twentieth-floor flat at Norfolk Court. Desperate for drugs, Joanna must have jumped out the window as they slept.

Poor woman, everyone thought. Imagine waking up to your friend's suicide. Then the cops checked their records.

Rose Broadley was known to them as a drug dealer and a pimp for at least two working girls, both of whom had heroin problems. One of those women was Joanna Colbeck. Worse, they had reports that Broadley would often hand out beatings with a baseball bat – especially to Joanna Colbeck.

That's when the cops decided to watch CCTV of the flats on the night in question. A camera covering the entry to Norfolk Court showed them clearly enough. Earlier on the night of her death, Joanna was being frogmarched into the flats by Rose Broadley. It was clear from the film that Joanna didn't want to go into the flats but was being forced there by Broadley. Once they reached the lifts, Broadley smacked Joanna hard across the face. That was enough for the cops – they started digging deeper.

In March 2004, almost two years after Joanna's death, Rose Broadley found herself in Glasgow High Court charged with murder and abduction. The evidence of abduction was in the CCTV film for all to see and Broadley pled guilty. But murder? The prosecution had no witnesses to any murder. That was going to be harder to prove and Rose Broadley pled not guilty.

Broadley, her man and her teenage son, who had been in the flat at that time, swore Joanna had been OK and alive when they went to bed and they were all fast asleep when she fell from the ledge. But, slowly, thoroughly, Geoffrey Mitchell for the Crown began to build a case for murder.

Joanna Colbeck had come from a highly respectable family and had been employed as a nursery nurse till she took to heroin. Quickly she lost everything and soon ended up on the streets selling her body for her next fix.

Her mother, an accountant, reported how they still stayed in touch and for months Joanna had been trying to break her habit and stay away from her old associates. She also told her mother that she was in trouble, owing several hundred pounds to someone who could turn nasty. She was scared that she'd be killed but she refused to say who that person was – though she did reveal that they lived in the high flats at Norfolk Court in the Gorbals.

The court heard how Broadley was well known to the cops. That she dealt heroin to Joanna and another woman then drove them to Edinburgh to sell their bodies to pay for that same heroin. Broadley was known to have a temper and be violent to both women at times, especially Joanna who had been taken to the flat at Norfolk Court and beaten with a baseball bat and a piece of wood on numerous occasions.

71

One person witnessed Joanna being abducted by Broadley and her man. As she was being forced away she had begged, 'No, Rose, don't. My mammy's got money to pay you.'

A teenage girl gave testimony that, on the night of Joanna's death, she saw Broadley force Joanna into the lift and heard her say, 'Wait till you get upstairs. Have I got a surprise for you. Your name's written on it.'

Another witness simply described Rose Broadley as a 'psycho'.

The most damning evidence of all came from a male friend of Joanna who, after her death, had approached Rose Broadley. The woman had apparently threatened him, saying, 'Don't you start on me or you'll be next to go out the window.'

Throughout it all, Rose Broadley maintained that she had been asleep and that Joanna, in a desperate state over drugs withdrawal, must have thrown herself from the window. But one witness who wouldn't be heard was Broadley herself, who used her right to refuse to take the stand. Of course that meant the prosecution couldn't cross-examine her but that wasn't going to stop them making the strongest possible case for murder.

In his closing speech, Geoffrey Mitchell, prosecuting, claimed that Rose Broadley had forced Joanna into the flat at Norfolk Court. He went on, 'She was treated worse than a dog and I suggest she was ordered to go out of the window as a punishment. Just to see how long she could dangle.'

In spite of there being no witnesses, no forensic evidence and no corroboration of Broadley's direct involvement in making Joanna fall from the window, the jury were persuaded by Mitchell and the prosecution witnesses. Rose Broadley was found guilty of murder and jailed for life with a minimum sentence of fifteen years for what the judge, Lord Bracadale called, 'A calculated and thoroughly wicked murder.'

That might well have been the end of a sad and pathetic tale, as tragic as the death of poor Joanna Colbeck was. But Rose Broadley and her legal team had other ideas. They appealed.

The grounds of appeal argued that there was insufficient

evidence of murder for a conviction. Further, there wasn't even any evidence that Joanna Colbeck had actually been murdered. An expert witness testified that the manner in which Joanna had been seen clinging to the ledge and the way her body had landed on the hard ground were more consistent with Joanna taking her own life.

An important feature was that she had landed a short distance from the building indicating that she'd dropped rather than been pushed. In fact, the original charges had included an accusation that Rose Broadley had pushed Joanna but that had been withdrawn by the Crown. Broadley had been found guilty of causing Joanna to fall but the conviction did not specify how.

But the Law Lords at the Court of Criminal Appeal found that the trial judge had been wrong to instruct the jury that there was enough evidence to convict of murder. Rose Broadley's murder conviction was quashed.

But Broadley wasn't set free. After the appeal, she was led away in handcuffs to return to Cornton Vale Prison where she was serving a three-year sentence. What for? The numerous beatings she'd handed out to Joanna over the years. Also for abducting her one night – the same night Joanna Colbeck died. The night she committed suicide. Or did she?

HOUSE OF BLOOD

The woman sat on the settee rocking and sobbing, her hair, clothes and face splattered with blood. In her arms was a man, his body limp and bloodied.

'Wake up. Wake up,' she insisted as she wept hysterically and she rocked back and forward. 'Don't do this to me.' She was talking to the man in her arms and paid no attention to the cops and paramedics who slowly entered the room. But they paid attention to everything in the room. It was a scene from a horror film.

The walls, floor and furniture were splashed with blood. On another settee lay the badly mangled body of an older man. Nearby, on the floor, lay another older man. He had horrific wounds covering his head and his flesh and skin were peeling off as if he had been burned. It didn't take long for a paramedic to confirm that both men were dead.

Now they had to check the third man for signs of life, the man the distraught woman was cradling in her arms. Gently she was asked to let the man go. It was if she heard nothing. Again she was asked. She didn't reply at first then turned on the uniforms. 'Fuck off, you bastards. Go on, fuck off.' Then, picking up a bottle, she took a swig from it before throwing it as hard as she could at the dead man on the floor. 'See what you've done,' she wailed, accusing the corpse. But of what?

The two cops decided they had no option but to get the woman away from the man in her arms. He looked badly hurt – dead even

– but he could still be alive with his life ebbing away by the second.

Carefully but firmly, they tried to lift him up and out of her arms. As they did so, she became more frantic, grabbing the man and pulling him, trying to hold him to her chest. The cops had no alternative but to pull him in their direction. A man's life could be at stake. For long seconds, this tug-of-war went on until, at last, the police pulled the man free. But it was all to no avail – he too was dead.

The call to the south-side cop shop had been made by a neighbour, James Sweeney, using a phone in a nearby pub. He had been upset and described what sounded like carnage and three dead men in the flat at 28 Dixon Avenue in the city's Govanhill area. The cops in the south side of Glasgow deal with as much murder and mayhem as any of the city's force but carnage and multiple murder? That was rare. Except not this time.

The Dixon Avenue flat was owned by one of the victims, Ian Mitchell, aged sixty-seven years. The other older victim was his pal and lodger, Anthony Coyle, aged seventy years. The man being cradled on the sofa was forty-two-year-old David Gillespie, the boyfriend of the woman. Maybe that's why she was upset? It would be reason enough for hysterics for most people but, early on, the cops believed this case was different.

The woman was Edith McAlinden, thirty-seven years old, homeless and known to have a drink problem. People who knew her were used to her getting into trouble but minor stuff. Surely not murder?

It didn't take the pathologist long to confirm that all three men had died as a result of incredible and prolonged brutality. They began to list what they believed had been done to the men in their final hours and some list it was: hit with a bottle; stamped on; stabbed; hacked with an axe; smashed with a metal file; thrashed with a belt; and thumped with a hammer, a lump of wood, a golf club and a baseball bat. Finally, they had had boiling water poured over them. It was murder all right but it also sounded like deliberate, cruel torture had taken place.

The murders of the two older dead men were an immediate puzzle to everyone who knew them and to the police. While the bloody deed had happened in their home, there was no sign of theft. The two were popular locally and known as two kindly blokes who enjoyed a quiet sociable drink and never created problems for anyone. They didn't have much and never carried large sums of money. What possible motive could there be for killing such affable characters?

From an early stage Edith McAlinden was in the frame for the murders. Not only was she found at the scene smeared in blood but she had also been the indirect cause of the call to the cops. James Sweeney, who had made the phone call, revealed that she had come to his door that night in a distressed state. Immediately he noticed she had blood on her top and over her training shoes.

'Something has happened, Jim,' she had said and begged him to go with her to Ian Mitchell's flat nearby. He agreed without debate and, when they got there, he noticed that she had the key to the door, using it to let them both in.

The poor unsuspecting man walked into a scene from hell with the three dead men lying in the blood-splattered room.

'What the hell has happened here? Did you do this?' he later recalled demanding, though most people would have used much stronger language. McAlinden said nothing so he told her to wait there. He had to go and phone for help pronto.

'What will I do?' McAlinden wailed. 'Jim, what will I do?'

He didn't respond but hotfooted it to a pub to call the cops. When he returned to the flat, Edith McAlinden was sitting beside Ian Mitchell's corpse, saying nothing, just weeping.

Edith McAlinden was definitely in the frame as far as the police were concerned but, before long, they learned that there had been two other visitors to Ian Mitchell's flat that night – Edith's seventeen-year-old son, John, and his pal, Jamie Gray, who was aged just sixteen.

The three weren't helpful and were denying everything but the murders had caught the public imagination and many people were willing to help find the killers if they could. That's when a breakthrough happened.

John McAlinden lived in a hostel for homeless people. One of the other residents, Bryan Gallagher, had important information for the police. McAlinden had gone to his room one night and chatted too much for his own good.

'Stabbed a guy in the legs, man – there was blood everywhere.' Gallagher had listened as John McAlinden wove his story. 'It was a fella tried to rape my ma so I had to teach him a lesson, eh?'

McAlinden had apparently confessed to beating and torturing one man along with someone he called 'my brother'. They had danced on his body, stabbed him and taken their time hurting him 'to teach him a lesson'. He had added, almost matter-of-factly, 'And I did my ma's boyfriend.'

In May 2005, Edith and John McAlinden, along with young Jamie Gray, all appeared at Glasgow High Court. Each stood accused of murdering all three men. Each pled not guilty.

As they trial proceeded, the three giggled and smiled, not acting as if they were facing life in jail. Nor did they appear worried that they were accused of the most gruesome of murders.

Aside from John McAlinden's confession to Bryan Gallagher in the homeless unit, the Crown case easily established that all three accused had been in the flat that night and were contaminated with forensic evidence that linked them to a point after the murders had been committed. Then came the horror video.

The judge, Lady Dorrian, agreed that a fifteen-minute police film of the flat at 28 Dixon Avenue should be shown. These days it is standard police practice that before a major crime scene is disturbed a detailed video be taken showing the exact position and state of the locale. In this case, the camera had a great deal to capture.

The prosecutor, Sean Murphy QC, warned the court that some of the detail was distressing. He wasn't exaggerating.

The grubby flat had been trashed. There was furniture sprawled this way and that and the floor was littered with bottles of

Buckfast wine and other stuff. The walls ran blood red and around the room lay hammers, a golf club, a baseball bat, lumps of wood and an electric drill. Now and then, the camera zoomed in on individual items. A golf club with a blood-stained head lying across the arm of one victim. A baseball bat, streaked with red. There amongst it all lay the three victims.

It's not known whether any of the jury of nine women and six men looked away at any time. Who could blame them? But there is no doubt that all saw enough to have a major impact on them. They weren't the only ones.

There was a dramatic turnaround. Lawyers for the three accused all offered guilty pleas but only for one murder of one man for each accused. The offer was clearly an endeavour to reduce the possible sentence faced by the accused if found guilty of all three murders.

McAlinden admitted to being in the flat on her own with the three men that night. She had known the flat's owner, Ian Mitchell, for many years and called him 'Pops'.

A lot of drinking was going on and McAlinden, who also had a long-established drugs problem, argued with David Gillespie, her boyfriend, and stabbed him twice in the thigh. He was bleeding badly and she panicked. She phoned her son and his pal, Jamie Gray, to come and help. The trusting Ian Mitchell even paid for the taxi to bring the two young men to his home.

By then, David Gillespie was obviously fading fast and perhaps was already dead. Maybe in some panic, maybe not, the two boys set about assaulting the two older men, as they sat helpless in the flat. Later they'd make some crazy claims to be covering up for the woman, to make it look like someone else murdered the men.

They had started first on Ian Mitchell, 'Pops' to Edith McAlinden. In court John McAlinden alone pled guilty to his murder. The old man was stabbed repeatedly and beaten so badly his brain bled.

It was no surprise that Anthony Coyle was terrified and tried to protect himself by locking himself in his bedroom. The three killers battered at the door, trying to cave it in but failed. Then one fetched an electric drill and removed the locks on the door.

At first, the petrified pensioner was beaten in his bedroom. Then he escaped in terror and fled back into the living room. In court, sixteen-year-old Jamie Gray admitted catching up with Anthony Coyle and smashing his skull in with repeated blows from a golf club.

The three also admitted that water was boiled and poured on the heads of both Coyle and Mitchell. Their explanation? To test if the men were still alive. No wonder the media took to calling this case 'THE HOUSE OF HORRORS'.

There were those in the public benches who thought the Crown should not have accepted the defence's compromise of each accused accepting guilt for only one murder. Not only were these killings of the most exceptional brutality – no understandable motive had been admitted or identified, apart from some booze-riddled argument between Edith McAlinden and David Gillespie. Motiveless, multiple murder deserved to carry serious punishment according to most folk and no way was anything less than that acceptable.

In the event, Edith McAlinden was sentenced to a minimum of thirteen years and each of the young men to a minimum of twelve years – the level of sentences they'd get for one murder.

After sentence was pronounced, the three were led down the stairs from the court leading to the cells – wide grins spread across their faces, laughing and joking with each other. It was rubbing salt in the raw emotional wounds of the three victims' friends and relatives who were packed into the public benches.

Edith McAlinden had been released from prison only a short time before the killings. It transpired that prison was a place the woman enjoyed. While she was held on remand awaiting trial for the murders of the three men, she had embarked on a number of lesbian affairs. According to another female prisoner, 'It was as if she didn't have a care in the world. She was partying and would have sex with any of the women who wanted to – often more than one in a day. She was popular among most of them.'

If McAlinden thought she was going to spend the next thirteen years enjoying more of the same, she was in for a shock. No one follows trials more closely than other convicted prisoners. When the detail of the awful, pointless murders – particularly of the two older men – emerged, popularity turned to disgust for McAlinden at Cornton Vale.

After her sentence, McAlinden was taken aside by a group of the most powerful women prisoners. 'We told her she wasn't wanted here,' said one. 'That she was nothing but a sadistic evil bitch. That she better watch her back or she'd be leaving the jail sooner than she reckoned – feet first.'

Most women would have heeded that warning. Edith McAlinden did for a while but then continued as before – as if she didn't have a care in the world.

When last heard of, she was having a relationship with another prisoner, Pamela Gourlay. In October 1999 in Aberdeen, Gourlay had murdered her downstairs neighbour, twenty-two-year-old care worker, Melanie Sturton. Unsuspecting Melanie had let Gourlay into her home only to be repeatedly stabbed on the head and neck and have her throat cut so deeply she was almost decapitated – all for a few pounds.

Some Cornton Vale prisoners say that McAlinden and Gourlay are well matched. Others that it won't last. Now and then, some women express their disgust at McAlinden's crimes but she doesn't much care. Her stock response is, 'You can't threaten me. Do you know who I am? I'm the woman from the House of Blood.'

PART 3
CHILD
KILLERS

Killing is something most of us can imagine ourselves doing in certain extreme circumstances. Who among us, though, can imagine taking the life of a child?

One night you're lying in bed sleeping the sleep of the innocent. The burglar has been quiet and made his way to your room. You awaken to find him standing over your partner lying there next to you. His knife flashes again and again, ripping into their flesh.

Your hand reaches out under your bed to the golf club or baseball bat you put there for just such a dreaded time that you hoped would never come. You're on your feet and lashing out at him. Once, twice, three times – when do you stop? When you're finished is the answer. Sometimes he'll be finished too.

Is it murder in the eyes of the law? We'll have to leave that one to the wigs. Is it killing? Of course it is. And it could happen to any one of us at any time.

Even then I suspect most of us would be plagued with thoughts, deep doubt and maybe guilt over the terrible deed – even while still believing that the person deserved their fate.

But a child? Who could kill a child? What child deserves to die? That's when the headline writers start using words like PERVO, PSYCHO, EVIL and ANIMAL and most of the public agree. Even the most liberal minded among us struggle to tell them to shut up.

Scotland, and Glasgow in particular, has a nasty heritage of child killing. Ian Brady, the Moors Murderer, was born here and raised in the Gorbals, where he spent a lonely, strange childhood pursuing his favourite hobby of torturing and killing cats. Fred West lived in Glasgow for a while with his first wife and came so close to moving to the city. Robert Black was born and raised in Falkirk though he lived in England by the time he went on his killing spree across Britain. The last woman to be hanged in Scotland, Susan Newell, killed a young paperboy and was caught trying to hide his body in a back close on Glasgow's Duke Street.

It is little surprise then that, in modern times, we still have child killers. What words would you use to describe them? Read on and make up your mind.

A GOOD LITTLE BOY

School summer holidays last forever when you're eight years old. Well, that's how it seems until you grow up and learn otherwise. But some poor kids never get a chance to learn – or grow up.

The concierge at the high-rise block of flats in Royston was conscientious in his work. That's how he found himself about 11 p.m., one night in June 2004, down at the bins clearing them up. It was going to be the worst night of his life.

In those high-rise flats, bags of rubbish could be sent hurtling down towards the massive bins from each floor. The concierge had to make sure the bins hadn't overflowed or, worse, that someone hadn't sent down some flaming bundle. They did that sometimes just for laugh. Big laugh he thought – not.

The school summer holidays had just begun and that meant trouble. There were a lot of kids in Royston and most of them were OK though some were weans from hell. Even the good kids would get bored sooner than they thought possible and then the delinquency would zoom up overnight.

Already one of the kids, just a wee lad, from his block had gone missing. He'd had his mother in that night worried about him because he hadn't come in for his tea. He'd seen the wee boy with his mate playing football as usual out on the grass. His pal had gone home but he hadn't. The concierge had reassured the mammy that the wee fella had probably just wandered off. 'He's probably forgotten the time'. That's what he'd said but it was a worry all right. A big worry. Even the cops were already out searching for him. That was the school holidays for you.

That wee boy was a good wee boy – no trouble at all. Not like some of the wee sods around the scheme. They'd be plotting devilment already and one of the easier targets would be the bins.

The bags of rubbish were different shapes and sizes and landed at different angles. To make sure that as much rubbish as possible got in the bins, he'd sort out the bags, moving them around. It wasn't one of the better jobs but it was necessary just the same.

Down by the bins sometimes it was so quiet you could hear your own breathing and the steady thump of your heart – a bit eerie really. Just as well he wasn't easily spooked. Leaning into the bin, throwing bags this way and that to make more room, he pulled at a big black bin bag that was stuffed full. Christ, it was heavy. He gave it another yank and the plastic ripped, revealing the contents. That's when he almost lost it.

Staring up at him were the dead eyes of a wee boy. Not just any wee boy. A wee boy he knew, who lived in the block. The wee boy whose mammy was looking for him.

Mark Cummings was eight years old. Football and Celtic daft, he'd been out on the grass near the high-rise block he lived in, playing football with a pal. That was as far away from their seventeenth-floor flat as his mother would ever let him go on his own. She was a good mother – a worrier – and now she was heartbroken.

They say that when police officers gets so hard and emotionally wizened that they stop getting upset by the murder of a child, then it's time for them to quit. There were a lot of upset cops at the high flats in Royston that night.

The cops quickly worked out that Mark had been strangled. Worse, he was naked and they knew the likelihood was they were looking for a sexual predator. Given that Mark's body had been found in the bins in the basement of the high-rise, it made sense to check the list of folk living there to see if there were any residents with similar previous convictions.

It didn't take them long to finger Stuart Leggate because they got some help. His father, who he lived with in the same block, had heard about the missing boy. The good man went straight to the police and told them about his own son.

Twenty-eight-year-old, bearded Leggate was on the Sex Offenders' Register for abusing three children when he lived out in Carnwath, Lanarkshire. A quick read of his records revealed that he liked them young – like eight-year-old Mark Cummings.

Leggate had told one of his victims – a boy called Patrick Murray – he was going to kill him and had threatened him with a shotgun and an axe. The boy had only been ten at the time and the abuse had gone on for a whole year until a neighbour sussed out something was wrong with his own child, another child Leggate had been abusing. It all came out then.

His other known victims were girls of seven and three years. This was a dangerous man all right – so dangerous he had already been jailed twice, on one occasion for four years. The cops decided to pull Leggate in for questioning immediately. There was only one problem – he wasn't in and his father didn't know where he was.

The cops suspected that Leggate had panicked and fled. Dumping the boy's body like that was careless. Maybe he had realised that too late and had decided to disappear? They called in the dog teams and a helicopter and were just starting to gear up for a wider search when Stuart Leggate arrived home.

Taken to Baird Street Police Station for questioning, Leggate was confronted by what the cops knew about his previous convictions. Those same cops were more accustomed to dealing with steely-eyed, tight-lipped street players who can sit for days in a stuffy room without saying a cheep. Men who would refuse to cooperate over a parking ticket, never mind murder. Stuart Leggate was a different type altogether. He confessed.

According to Leggate, he had been working on a car in the

parking area near the block of flats that afternoon while Mark Cummings and pal played football nearby. Every now and then Leggate would chat to the boys about computer games. They recognised Leggate as a neighbour and chatted with him. It seems he had some good games – ones they'd be interested in. What the boys couldn't know was that the man had used this ploy before to lure and trap his victims.

Round about 5 p.m. the other boy went home, probably for his tea. Mark had to go in a wee while too but he'd got some grease on his clothes. Leggate offered to help him wash it off so he didn't get into trouble at home.

Mark went into the block with Leggate and travelled up to his sixth-floor flat. Crucially Leggate's father was out at the time. Something, of course, Leggate would have known. If his father had been at home, Mark Cummings might well be alive today.

Leggate took Mark to the bathroom and helped him wash the grease off. Then they went back to the living room and looked at computer games. But Mark Cummings was a well-behaved wee boy and knew his mum would be expecting him. He said cheerio and went to leave but, as he did so, Leggate came up behind him and yanked the boy's jogging bottoms down. This was the moment of no return. Leggate couldn't let the boy go or he'd tell his mum who, in turn, would go straight to the cops. If Leggate had hesitated at that point he was going back to jail.

Leggate lifted Mark bodily up and carried him through to a bedroom, dumping him on the bed and lying across him. Mark was frightened, crying, pleading to go home. Leggate didn't care much. He told Mark what he wanted. He used much cruder terms but what it amounted to was oral sex from the boy.

Mark refused and continued asking to be let go. In Leggate's own words, 'That's when I started losing it.'

He punched Mark hard and repeatedly on the face and body. Maybe ten to fifteen punches went in. Leggate was so furious that he was in a state and couldn't remember all the detail later – probably still can't.

Incensed, Leggate lifted the boy up and threw him on to the bedroom floor. As Leggate later confessed, 'He was really getting to me then and I lost the rag big time.' What he meant was that he just started constantly hitting the wee boy. It became a blur of pummelling him with blows. When asked by the cops why he was hitting the child, Leggate had responded with a puzzled look and said, 'Don't know. No reason.'

If things were bad for wee Mark at that point, they were about to get much worse. Leggate choked him with one hand on his throat. The wee boy was kicking his feet and gasping for air as his face turned blue. When that hand grew tired, Leggate changed to his other hand. Then changed hands again. Finally he took off Marks' jogging bottoms and strangled him with them. Young Mark Cummings was dead.

Leggate's confession is all about what he did to Mark. It's as if he was getting a kick out of talking about it – reliving it in his mind's eye as he spoke the words. What it's short on is information about him. Why did he do it? What did he feel? What state was he in? He had put so much effort into killing Mark that he must have been sweating – tired, exhausted maybe? Then again, maybe he was excited? Maybe he had an orgasm? Maybe more than one?

He did confess to one thought. As he was hitting Mark, he said, 'I kept hearing a voice in my head telling me that I let the last one [meaning Patrick Murray, the ten-year-old boy he had abused in Carnwath] get away – I'm not going to let his one get away.' By 'get away' he meant live.

Stuart Leggate had a perverted desire for sex with kids – that's for sure – but maybe the ultimate sexual experience for him, as with so many serial sexual child abusers, was the act of killing. Maybe he was heading towards that grand finale with the other children he had abused but he had just been caught in time.

With Mark now so obviously dead, Leggate bundled his body in to a black bin bag and threw him down the chute. If this seems careless, it isn't unusual. Some killers do dump their victims in bins – it's as if, by putting them out with the rubbish, they are now gone from them therefore from everyone. It's as if disposing of rubbish is a one-way process with them being the last person who would ever see the bundle. It doesn't work like that, thank God, or Mark Cummings' mum might still be searching for her wee boy.

If Leggate seemed careless about disposing of Mark he went to extraordinary lengths in other regards. He realised the jogging bottoms and a bloodstained towel would incriminate him. Around a city area like Royston, there are thousands of places such small items could be successfully and anonymously destroyed yet Leggate jumped in his car and drove all the way to Berwick-upon-Tweed, on the border with England.

Just south of Berwick-upon-Tweed, Leggate threw the towel and jogging bottoms off cliffs into the North Sea. That's where he had been when his father had gone to the police, after which they were preparing for a wide search for the child killer.

Stuart Leggate was many miles away and had a few hours' start on the cops. He was in an ideal position to go on the run but, thinking he had covered his tracks and not knowing that Mark had been found, he drove right back into their handcuffs.

It was a full and frank confession – almost. Leggate insisted that he had not sexually interfered with Mark. He kept on insisting that he had 'resisted the urge'.

Decent, ordinary people might think that, even if he had simply pulled down the boy's jogging bottoms, then that was an act of sexual abuse in itself. But Leggate was neither decent nor ordinary. Leggate was someone who obsessed about full sexual congress with children and in this case that had not happened. In his confession, it was almost as if he was proud of himself – that, somehow, while admitting murder, the absence of a sexual assault made him a better man. Or maybe that should be a less evil man? Or less mad?

By the day after the murder, the police had enough to convict Stuart Leggate yet they wanted to know why that day and why Mark Cummings. After all Leggate had been living in Royston for a couple of years. There were plenty of kids swarming all over the area all day and most of the night. Leggate thought for a while then answered, saying, 'A bit of the old me came back yesterday.'

Experienced police officers shuddered. It was as if Leggate was describing some beast that lay quietly inside him until it was time to take some prey – some side of him that could rear up, at any minute, and abuse and kill kids.

The cops concluded that Stuart Leggate was a lethal man and always would be. They hoped he would be locked up for a very long time. They were not to be disappointed.

Stuart Leggate pled guilty to murder by strangulation and to sexual assault. Lord Dawson, presiding over sentencing, heard pleas of mitigation from his QC, Donald Findlay, famed for his courtroom rhetoric. For once, Findlay admitted that he was almost speechless, so chilling was Leggate's dossier.

Findlay did claim that his client had intended to drown himself off those cliffs at Berwick-upon-Tweed but had changed his mind. That day, there were those in court and back at Royston who would gladly have thrown Stuart Leggate off those same cliffs.

Lord Dawson was unmoved by any claims of suicidal feelings. 'I regard you as a highly dangerous man and the public must be protected from you for a very long time.' For Stuart Leggate, that will be a minimum of twenty years in jail.

After his trial, there was an understandable outcry from Mark Cummings' mother and supporters that they should have been told there was a dangerous sex abuser living in their midst. Members of the Scottish Parliament of all political parties called for the creation of Mark's Law. Their proposals included not only telling communities if a convicted paedophile has moved into their area but also placing strict limitations on where sex offenders could live. Those found guilty in the future would be given mandatory life sentences even for non-capital offences. Then people like Leggate wouldn't be free to escalate to murder, argued the campaigners.

The public outcry was heightened when Strathclyde Police admitted that, while they supervised known sex offenders as closely as the law allowed, they could not guarantee absolute safety. As one police officer put it, 'Many of these men have developed tactics to pursue their perversion in secrecy. They don't lose those skills just because they are on the Sex Offenders' Register.' If the police admission that other tragedies would happen was bad enough, worse was yet to come.

Stuart Leggate's mother had been a strange fish by all accounts. She had a number of fingers missing and claimed that she had chopped them off herself. Maybe Stuart Leggate had inherited some of her strange ways but he also inherited something else – her name. She was called June Main and died in 1997 of a brain haemorrhage. Shortly after her death, Leggate changed his name to Stuart Main and used the new identity to apply for jobs. And he succeeded.

For two years before the killing, Stewart Leggate worked for a company called SGB as a driver delivering scaffolding. While this might sound safe enough, as well as delivering to the new Scottish Parliament building then being constructed, he also took scaffolding to many schools. It should also be noted that many serial killers – Robert Black and Peter Sutcliffe, the Yorkshire Ripper, among them – sought jobs as drivers because the work offers the opportunity to travel, giving them flexibility in finding targets and then leaving the area. Both were frequent visitors to Glasgow's streets.

Stuart Leggate could have been on the cusp of a killing spree. Instead, poor Mark Cummings was killed and Leggate is looking at twenty years in jail – twenty years he will spend in special units alongside others who are at risk in the mainstream jails from the violent justice that might be administered by other prisoners.

Nicknamed the Nonces and Ponces Units, these places are full of informants, bent coppers, rapists and child abusers. All are hated by other prisoners but near the top of their list comes Stuart Leggate. Do you blame them?

RON AND REG

'Hey you, give us that football.' The shouter was well known locally as trouble – big trouble.

'Naw, get your own baw.' The man in question had a new football and, in an area like Pollok where money was tight, he knew, if he passed the football over, he would never see it again. It was as bad as being mugged.

'Think ye're a wide man, eh? Fucking DO YOU?' The shouter moved forward aggressively. He was young – only fifteen – but he was over six foot tall and built. Behind him stood his brother – his identical twin brother.

'Look fuck off an' leave us alane. We're just having a kick about . . .'

The sentence was never finished. The twins moved in and beat the man to a pulp as others looked on aghast, too terrified to intervene. They knew who was dishing out the violence – knew them only too well. The beating over, the twins moved off victoriously, brandishing their spoils – a new football.

The twins were Stephen and Kevin Stone, known locally as the Pollok Kray Twins and with good reason. Since the age of ten, they had been creating their own hell for neighbours around their home in Linthaugh Road. As they grew into their teens, their physical stature increased and so did their appetite for terrorising.

By the age of fourteen, they had tackled men more than twice their age and had come out top. They didn't just target ordinary, peace-loving citizens going about their business – they went after the street boys who were handy with their fists and boots too. But most were not handy enough for the Pollok Kray Twins.

Whole streets felt under siege. The twins would break into someone's car, rip out the stereo and then set the motor alight. This sort of crime was two-a-penny in most urban schemes – the difference here was that they'd do it in front of the owners or hang around and tell them they were the culprits. Did they fancy doing anything about it? If any complaint was made to the cops, they'd turn up again and throw bricks through the house windows, sometimes followed by a Molotov cocktail, or kick the door in before they kicked the residents up and down their own homes.

One local worthy reported every bit of the twins' badness to the cops – just as good citizens should. At least Stephen and Kevin Stone suspected he was behind it. One day, on the street, they publicly warned him that he was in trouble. That night they torched the roof of his house, then stood out on the road watching the residents panic as they tried to escape the flames.

They were a two-boy crime wave and they caused much of Pollok a lot of grief. Stephen was the more aggressive one and Kevin the follower but it was a fine call – most local people branded one as bad as the other. And the local people were getting fed up.

The twins were legally children and that's how the law treated them. No matter what they did they were processed through the Children's Hearing system, a system that was increasingly having to admit that there were some juvenile offenders they just couldn't cope with – offenders like the Pollok Kray Twins.

Pollok is a large housing scheme on the southern periphery of Glasgow. When it was built, the city mothers and fathers promised local people an area they could be proud of. They were even going to be given wide, tree-lined boulevards – according to the architect, it would be an American-style street layout. The wide, tree-lined boulevards are there and, in the main, the houses are of decent quality but the horrors of poverty and crime haven't magically disappeared.

Pollok has many fine people who are willing to work hard to make their area a better place to live. One night, a community meeting was arranged by those wanting to make Pollok safer. Community activists, local authority officers, local councillors and concerned citizens crammed the place on a sunny night. There was a top football match on the TV and one of those major, much-hyped editions of *Coronation Street* but people attended in their droves – that's how much they cared.

All night they talked about the type of problems they were facing – burglary, car theft, violence, threats – yet there were no names, no pack drills. But, eventually, one of the councillors said, 'Look we all know who we're talking about – it's the Stone twins.' There was an audible gasp round the hall. 'None of us like grassing to the cops,' the councillor went on, 'but there's a difference between grassing and reporting two boys who are making life for the people of this community a misery. They're just two young boys, after all.'

Concerned people at the meeting spoke up for the councillor but warned him that he was taking risks by mentioning the twins. The next day he got a message – if the twins couldn't get at him, they'd get at his parents who lived locally too.

These kids were fifteen years old yet they happily threatened local politicians and had one of the toughest areas of Glasgow on the run. So the scene in the park – beating up the older man for his football – was no big deal compared with the other tricks they got up to. But one of their exploits was going to lead to murder.

Flashing lights from the police vehicles cast ghostly moving shadows in the dull streets. A police cordon was erected and guarded by uniformed cops. Behind them, people in all-over white forensic suits busily moved around. It was the early hours of 2 May 2000 yet locals had spotted the action. They always spotted the polis in Pollok.

People began to congregate, getting as close as they could to the police cordon. Craning their necks to see what was up, some chatted up the uniforms but got nowhere. A couple of the audience had brought out mugs of tea and even more lugged cans of beer. This was better than late-night TV – this was real.

Pollok people had been around enough tragedies on their streets to guess that something serious had gone down. Four hundred yards down the street in Linthaugh Road someone knew even better.

Earlier that evening, a young man had knocked at the door of Margaret Stone's house. Obviously stoned and distraught he'd said, 'I've stabbed Kevin – your son Kevin. I think he's dead.' At that the man had turned and run off.

Seven hours later, Kevin Stone had still not returned home. He was lying on a path, 400 yards from his house – dead. Kevin had been stabbed just once and died where he dropped. On being told of her son's death, his mother couldn't quite grasp it. Stephen was the one who was a bit wild. Kevin was the quieter one. Had they stabbed the wrong twin?

Understandably, Margaret Stone was also upset. She hit out at the cops as not caring about families like hers just because they were poor – just because her boys had been in a bit of trouble. She had seen the lights and the movement of the police search team four hundred yards from her home. They hadn't come near her for four hours. Didn't tell her Kevin was dead for all that time. The cops treated people like her like dogs. Just because they were poor and her boys had been in a bit of trouble.

Pollok people had a different reaction. No one was surprised that one of the twins had met an early and bloody death. Many thought it had simply been a matter of time. Privately, some were pleased that, at last, one less troublemaker was going to plague their lives. Besides, there had been a lot of trouble in the scheme that night, with running battles through the nearby Corkerhill patch, a knifing up in Priesthill and other scraps. It was the kind of night that happened in Pollok – the kind of night when young men were killed.

The cops were facing a standard problem they encounter with the street death of a local hard man – too many suspects. Instead of rounding up the large crew who had reason enough to wish harm on the twins, they tried to investigate what had gone on in their area that night – easier said than done when the source of information was the young street players of Pollok.

On this occasion, tongues were a little looser than usual. It transpired that there had been several incidents that night and the young team had been the target of most of them, with kids of thirteen to fifteen being singled out for rough treatment – kids who associated with Stephen and Kevin Stone. Some folk called them the Teeny Team. Teeny they might have been but they were a lethal mob, especially when led by the twins.

In Glasgow street life, the young teens who want to join the gangs usually have to prove themselves. They do this by acts of derring-do directed towards the cops or some gang from a neighbouring area. At that time and place, the Teeny Team had simply declared independence and they were well out of order in their own backyard – at least someone thought so and had decided to put them in their place.

One group of teenagers were chased by a man who was stoned out of his box and running at them with a long-bladed kitchen knife. Another fifteen-year-old came so close to getting grief he had to defend himself. That he had grabbed a five-foot samurai sword to do so says as much about street life in Pollok as it does about him.

All the kids said the same thing. Their attacker was wearing a Celtic football top, boasting about 'getting Kevin Stone' that night and threatening to get them as well.

The twins' younger brother, fourteen-year-old Gary, had been approached that night by a stoned man carrying a blade. 'Where the fuck's your brothers?' he had demanded.

'Dunno,' replied Gary with a shake of his shoulders.

'Well, I'm looking for them and they're going to come crawling home the night or come home in a box.'

One name kept coming up – that of twenty-year-old Gary Hicks of nearby Templeland Road, Pollok. He was arrested on 4 May 2000, two days after Kevin Stone's death, and charged with his murder.

At his trial in September 2000, Gary Hicks pled not guilty. The old street code dictates that, if someone has been taken out bloodily, no one cooperates with the police or the courts. They say nothing and settle the matter where it happened – on the street. But this was the Teeny Team. All thoughts of any street code had died a long time before they were born.

They all turned up. All the kids who had been threatened that night were there – the boy with the five-foot sword and the ones who had run with the twins, creating havoc around Pollok. Pollok produced enough witnesses to seal Gary Hicks' fate.

Gary Hicks admitted being drunk and stoned on cannabis that night and to the incidents involving other people. Yet he denied killing Kevin Stone – adamantly denied it. The jury were convinced otherwise and found him guilty of murder.

Before Lord Hardie for sentencing, Gary Hicks stood tall and straight, a soldier at attention. The good judge was more used to slouching insolence even as he dealt out the inevitable sentence of life imprisonment.

Lord Hardie said, 'You went looking for your victim and his twin brother. You found one of them and chased and murdered him.' Pausing for effect, letting the word 'murdered' reverberate round the court, Hardie went on, 'Whatever his background, he was a fifteen-year-old boy.'

A child killer in law he may have been but that's not how the people of Pollok saw Gary Hicks. 'The Pollok Kray Twins made our lives a misery for years,' said most.

'They didn't care who they hurt – old or young,' one local said. 'The cops were bloody useless and the system treated them like kids when they were worse than any adult.'

'Murder is never a good thing,' said one Pollok woman, an upstanding citizen with a job, three well-behaved kids and her ancient mother at home to care for. Then she thought a little and went on, 'But somebody had to do something. Maybe Gary Hicks did Pollok a favour.'

SUFFER THE LITTLE CHILDREN

It would be the drains or so she had thought – well, this was Govan and the council spent no money in Govan, especially not on the drains. But she was sure the smell was coming from the wardrobe, not the drains – the wardrobe that had been taped shut. Now why would anyone want to do that? She was about to find out.

The owners of 35 Summertown Road, Govan, were renovating the flat they let out to tenants. They'd tart it up – nothing too expensive, though. But someone had complained about the smell and they were right. They had to get rid of that stench, whatever it was.

Shona Campbell, the daughter of the landlord Angus Campbell, pulled the tape off the wardrobe and opened it. The reek got worse. Inside, on the floor of the wardrobe, lay a mess of black plastic bags. Convinced that whatever was in there was causing the smell, Shona called for her brother-in-law Donald to investigate further. Well, you never know . . . there could be a dead rat in there.

As the man ripped the first bag open, his face turned chalk white, he gagged and ran out into the street. There wasn't much left of it now but it was still unmistakable. It was a dead baby.

On the way down from Pollok cop shop, the police weren't looking forward to the call-out. A dead baby in a bag . . . a wee dead baby . . . totty . . . like a newborn. And there were even more bags that hadn't been touched.

It all sounded like one for the forensic people who pick and probe and test chemicals and samples as if they'd never been human. The chemists and scientists and the sad fucks who couldn't get a ride in a brothel because brothels are full of people. The ones who saw the world as symbols and digits and compounds with this and that. They weren't real people like them – they were the polis and the polis were more comfortable with some bear with two butchers' cleavers and a headache that wouldn't go away . . . not dead babies. To the polis, no matter how rotted, how much flesh had turned to fluid, how short their lives had been, how many bluebottles had laid eggs – no matter what, they were still babies and the polis didn't like it. It made the polis mad. It made the polis want to wreak revenge on the bastard who did it. No, this case wasn't for them. Say what you like about Glasgow cops, whatever else they were, they were human – for good and for ill.

The tenement block on Summertown Road was cordoned off. They might as well have put out invitations to a party. Every wee hard man, underage hairy and their mammies' mammies' sisters and the blokes they called uncle were down there at the ribbon. If the prospect of a dead baby sickened the cops, by Christ, it attracted a crowd of Govan folk. The slashings and shootings and chibbings and legs chopped off were weekly, if not daily, events for them – but a dead baby? This was a new one on them. This was sick. This they had to see.

The scene on Summertown Road was chilling. Word had leaked out that the cops had found the corpse of what looked like a newborn baby and they were still looking. It was a mystery and a horror story all in one for the locals but little did they know . . .

Three dead babies were found in the bottom of that rank wardrobe – all tiny, all long dead but not so long dead that it was ancient history. They didn't have flat-pack wardrobes and plastic bags in ancient history.

One baby might have been the result of some poor woman concealing a birth – a tragedy. But three? Something very bad had happened in that flat.

Outside in the street, rumours circulated that the skeleton of a dead baby had been found by a workman as he demolished a wall – all very mysterious, all very Gothic, all very spooky. Inside the house, detectives were gearing up for a murder investigation.

Over in the west end of Glasgow, the place was jumping as usual. What do you expect of that quarter of Glasgow that serves one of the biggest universities in the country, is home to the BBC headquarters and houses the well-off luvvies from film, TV, publishing and the stage? Of course, the pubs are great.

One of the older ones, Tennents Bar, hadn't changed for years. It didn't need to – traditional pubs were trendy again. Say what you like about Tennents, it was a good bar. People liked it in there and were always made welcome.

Young Susan Macleod, the assistant manager, was popular. OK, she was a bit of a Gaelic heedrum-hodrum but that was popular in the west end where there were more young kids learning to speak that lingo than anywhere else in Scotland. They'd even set up their own private Gaelic school. So young Susan fitted in nicely in the west end.

Susan had moved down from her home in North Bragar on the Isle of Lewis in the remote Western Isles in 1996, about five years earlier. Moving to the city from that small community where everyone knew everyone else was a challenge for anyone. But Susan was bright and hard working and her mother, Myra, and her fisherman father, Malcolm, weren't worried about her. In fact, they'd high hopes she'd do well.

When she'd first moved to Glasgow it was to work as a chef in the Park Bar in the west end of Argyle Street. The pub was a well-known meeting place for Highlanders who lived in the city – a kind of home-from-home for Susan.

She'd made many friends there through her work and enthusiastically joined in the Gaelic scene. A couple of years later, she'd moved on to work at Tennents Bar as assistant manager – a move that was just as successful for her. She made more friends although fewer of them were tied to the Highlanders' social circle.

Susan Macleod was only twenty-four years old but was well settled in the west end of Glasgow. The trouble was that her type of work didn't pay a fortune so living in that trendy but expensive neighbourhood wasn't on. Her Highland associations helped yet again. Ever since she'd moved to the city, she had been renting a flat from a friend of her parents – Flat 2/2, 35 Summertown Road, Govan, to be exact.

After the discovery of the three tiny corpses, it took the cops three long hours to track down Susan Macleod. The bodies had been found in that wardrobe in her bedroom, after all, so it didn't need a genius cop to work that one out. There was just one problem – Susan was saying nothing.

When word broke to the public that not one but three babies' bodies had been found and the cops were continuing the search to see if there were others, the words 'serial killer' were on everyone's lips. In Govan, they were only too used to some poor kid being battered to death by a drunken, drugged-up, violent parent at the end of their tether. That was horrific enough but who kills three children?

Still Susan Macleod wasn't telling the cops much. Could this be the same intelligent, sociable, popular young woman they'd quickly found out about? The police were well used to people who wouldn't talk to them. They were beginning to suspect that, this time, they had someone who *couldn't* talk to them.

However, they had confirmed that the babies were hers and that would have to do for the moment. On 21 April 2001, soon after the babies' bodies had been found, Susan Macleod appeared at Glasgow Sheriff Court and was charged with three counts of murder. She made no plea or declaration – yet again she said nothing.

Given the nature of the victims and concern for the accused person's mental health, the court hearing was held in private. All that was released from the court was the fact that she had been charged and remanded in prison for seven days. The combination of secrecy and Susan being held in prison did little to dispel rumours.

People were beginning to imagine terrible horrors behind those walls at 35 Summertown Road. The TV film footage from outside 25 Cromwell Street, Gloucester – showing the cops searching for and finding more and more victims of Fred and Rose West – had remained in the public psyche. Glaswegians held their collective breath and waited for more tragic news.

In a Catholic church across from the tragic scene, parishioners lit candles and priests said prayers for the wee ones. People flocked to Summertown Road and many laid tributes to the babies. Railings lining the short path to the entrance of the tenement were hung with daffodils, carnations, tulips, teddy bears and dolls.

'In our hearts and minds forever, little ones,' read one card from 'a saddened, shocked family'.

Another simply said, 'Sleep peacefully, little ones.'

As one neighbour said at the time, 'I didn't know the people who lived there but who can help but weep over young babies who are murdered? Who?'

With Susan Macleod still not saying very much, the cops started to interview her friends and associates. First off, no one, not even her GP, had even been aware that she had ever been pregnant, never mind that she'd given birth three times. Yet they were her children – of that the cops were certain.

Gradually the doctors worked out the details of two of the babies. One, a girl, had died sometime between 1 August 1996 and 31 January 1997. A baby boy had died between 30 June 1998 and 30 December 1999. The other, a girl, was proving more difficult to date. The likely cause of death was suffocation. Soon after they had died, all three of the babies were put in black carrier bags and left to rot in the foot of that wardrobe.

Susan Macleod had sought no medical treatment to do with any of the pregnancies. After at least one birth, she was gravely ill and could easily have died but still she didn't seek medical assistance.

Even the most cynical police officers began to suspect that they had something a bit odd here.

Thirty-six days after she had been charged with triple murder, Susan Macleod's lawyers applied on her behalf for bail. Until then, she had been in Cornton Vale, the women's prison – not a good place to be. At the time, Cornton Vale was having severe problems with suicide, self-harming and drug abuse by its prisoners. A former governor had said that a high proportion of the women sent to her were so physically and mentally frail that they had be to given long-term hospital care before they were even fit enough to serve their time. So it was definitely not a good place to be – but that was where women charged with murder were detained until their trial.

The European Convention on Human Rights had, by then, been adopted in Scotland. Under the Convention, every individual must be considered for bail regardless of the charges. Though the Crown opposed her bail, in May 2001 Susan Macleod was released on condition that she resided with her parents on the Isle of Lewis until the trial.

What the court or, indeed, the Crown did not know was that Macleod was pregnant again. She had already been pregnant on the day of her arrest. Macleod apparently had always sworn that she would never take the contraceptive pill in case it reduced her fertility later in life. And it seems she didn't go in much for con-doms, the coil or other methods of contraception either. Now, in spite of the secret pregnancies and untimely deaths of three babies, she had become pregnant again.

What might have happened to that fourth child had a tenant at Summertown Road not complained about the stink? If the three babies had not yet been found? If Macleod had not been arrested?

In August 2001, Macleod left her parents' home on the Isle of Lewis, travelled to Raigmore Hospital in Inverness and had an abortion.

For the next year, Susan Macleod remained on bail and living with her parents on Lewis. Local people started to gossip – not that that's unusual in small rural area – and what was upsetting most of them was that she was behaving as if nothing was wrong.

'She was having a great time at a relative's wedding, popping into local cafes and hanging out with her boyfriend,' said one. 'You'd never think she'd been charged with killing three babies.'

Macleod's boyfriend at the time was called Neil Harper. Though it was clear none of the dead children were his, he openly promised to stick by her. In he middle of all this death and doubt, a young man was playing it straight. Some people might call it love.

Locals on the island spoke of her having had an earlier long-term relationship with an older man over many years – a guy who had been her employer at one time in a hotel before she'd moved off to Glasgow. Their relationship continued off and on for years after she'd left Lewis and, over that period, the three babies had been born.

On several occasions, Macleod's lawyer, Gordon Jackson QC, succeeded in getting more time to prepare the case. Though it can be overruled by a judge, in Scotland there is a strict time limit on the period between when a person is charged and when they have to be taken to court for trial. The rule is designed to guarantee swift justice and that is seen as the right of the accused. In this case, as the trial was delayed and delayed, some peope saw it as entirely to Susan Macleod's good fortune.

The defence and the prosecution agreed that this wasn't an everyday case. Macleod was seen by a range of specialists and through them she claimed to have suffered horrific sexual abuse as a child. This could no longer be proven and how it tied in to the deaths of her babies was never made clear. Doctors also confirmed another of her claims that one of the babies had been stillborn.

Early in 2003, Susan Macleod pled guilty to the culpable homicide of two of her babies. The Crown accepted this plea and dropped the charge of murder concerning the third child, believing that it had been stillborn. The experts' view was that she had suffocated the two children shortly after birth by holding them against her body.

Appearing in front of Lord Bracadale at the High Court Edinburgh, her lawyer Gordon Jackson QC pled with the court not to jail Macleod, saying that she was on a psychological knife-edge and prison could catapult her into mental illness. In mitigation, it was also established that, since being charged, she had changed her stance on never taking chemical contraception and her GP had been giving her regular contraceptive injections that lasted for months at a time.

In a masterful understatement, Lord Bracadale said, 'The circumstances of the births and what you did with the bodies is strange and disturbing.' No one in the court was disagreeing with the judge. 'In each case you kept the whole thing secret. What you did is almost unknown, at least in modern times.'

The good judge decided that he would not jail Susan Macleod but something was troubling him. Some reports still indicated that she was unwilling or unable to talk about the deaths. Before he would sentence her he ordered that she undertake six months of intensive counselling by a psychiatrist or psychologist from the Douglas Inch Centre in Glasgow, a clinic that is world renowned for its work with criminals and murderers.

Susan Macleod sobbed with relief. Yet, if she thought she had just been let off lightly, she was about to be surprised.

'PSYCHOPATH' ran some newspaper headlines. Susan Macleod could be a psychopath, according to Anne Carpenter, a psychologist at the Douglas Inch Centre who had been working with her intensively.

This is not the pscyho of the Hollywood horror movies but a defined psychiatric status where someone is incapable of learning by experience, is unable to tell right from wrong and cannot feel properly for another living being, even babies.

It was February 2004 and Anne Carpenter was reporting to the High Court, Edinburgh, on Susan Macleod after six months' work. Macleod had stuck to her claims of being sexually abused and alleged it had left her able to cut off easily from her surroundings and major life events. Yet, put simply, the psychologist didn't believe her claims of abuse.

The defence team called another psychiatrist, Dr Gillian Mezey from London, who pooh-poohed Carpenter's assessment in the time-honoured way of expert witnesses in court.

Macleod's lawyer, Gordon Jackson QC, claimed that Carpenter was making the mistake of believing that Macleod had somehow been actively involved in the babies' deaths. He was, as ever, supporting his client's position because now Macleod was claiming that the babies died because she failed to get them medical treatment after birth.

Some would say that this argument is too technical for lay people. Others would add that it's beyond the scope of lawyers' expertise. But judges still have to make judgements.

Once again showing his talent for precise understatement, Lord Bracadale, presiding, said that the psychological treatment 'did not appear to be productive'. He then placed Susan Macleod on probation for three years. The order came with teeth. She would have to be sure that, if she became pregnant again, she would obtain the appropriate medical care for the child. Failure to do so would result in jail. The law can't, of course, prevent anyone from having a child. Maybe it should?

Susan Macleod will only be thirty years old when the probation order ends and she's free to live her own life again. That will give her ten, maybe twenty child-bearing years. Some experts are very worried by this prospect. People around Macleod's home on the Isle of Lewis agree. 'Susan always talked about having a family,' said one, reflecting the comments of most of her neighbours. 'As many babies as she could.'

RECKLESS AND WICKED

Heads turned to watch the fire engine race through the streets, its siren screaming. Even with one of the worst records for house fires in Europe, the people of Glasgow have lost none of their fascination for fire engines. But that night there was more trouble afoot than an accidental blaze.

The fire engine and crew were heading through Easterhouse, a sprawling township of a scheme on the north-east edge of Glasgow. Easterhouse had been part of what they used to call the rejuvenation of Glasgow but no more. By March 2005, they had long since acknowledged all the mistakes that had been made and that included Easterhouse – big time.

The houses of Easterhouse had been built and the people moved in before the authorities realised that they'd forgotten shops, doctors, buses – that kind of not-so trivial detail. Almost immediately, it became one of the trouble black spots of the city with razor gangs, murders and drugs, of course.

A few decades on, they'd whittled away at the deficiencies by building facilities, bringing in employment, developing community resources. Now Easterhouse wasn't nearly as wild as it had once been but it still wasn't so peaceful that the fire crew could expect not to be attacked.

Kids used to watch the fires and the firefighters working hard to put them out. That was still enough for many people but not for others. Now the crews went out to calls in certain parts of the city expecting to be met by a hail of stones – as if their job wasn't dangerous enough. Now some crazy people had taken to firing at them with airguns – like people in Easterhouse.

Mark Bonini was a troubled young man some might say – at least the liberal-minded who came across him might. He didn't see himself that way, of course. He was having a ball.

That night, on 2 March 2005, Mark Bonini was planning to stay in at his flat in Cambusdoon Road in the Craigend patch of Easterhouse. Social workers had helped him get the place because of his problems with drugs. The year before he'd turned up in court charged with driving while stoned, no insurance or licence and a whole heap of other naughty things and not for the first time. Instead of jailing him as he expected, they put him on a Drug Treatment and Testing Order (DTTO) – the best thing that had ever happened to him or so Bonini thought.

With DTTOs, the authorities gave you help to deal with your drugs problems rather than jail. The theory was that some folk only stole and committed other crimes because they were hooked. Break the addiction – stop the crimes. It made sense and worked for a hell of a lot of people but not all.

Not that Mark Bonini had cut down on the drugs. What did people think he was? Some kind of sap? But it meant the social workers helped him with houses and stuff and he'd been into big trouble with the law numerous times since and every time he'd walked out free – all because of that order. Best thing that had ever happened to him or so he thought. Other people were about to have a different view.

That night, he was going to stay in. His cousin, Kevin Bonini, was coming round and they were going to watch a Celtic versus Hibs football match on the TV. The thing was that, when Kevin arrived, they couldn't get any reception on the old TV set. That's when trouble started brewing.

Mark Bonini did some drugs then some more. He was bored. Then he got hold of his big, lethal-looking air rifle.

'Tightened the spring up, man,' he boasted to Kevin, holding the gun proudly. 'It's really fucking powerful now.'

Sitting at the open bedroom window at the rear of his first floor flat, Mark Bonini started firing the air gun. First he targeted objects like streetlights and flats across the way. Then he got bored.

Farther up the road, a window cleaner was working at his job. Bonini got him in his sights and fired. Shooting at real people – that was better fun. Next a woman got the treatment and then it was Mark Bonini's lucky day. Someone had left a chip pan too long on the cooker and the fire engine arrived.

As the fire crew tried to do their jobs, high-powered air pellets crashed down among them. Just as well firefighter Alan Lambert was wearing his thick protective clothing. First one slug hit him on the body, then another. Someone had singled him out from all his colleagues to take pot shots at. Someone nearby. The firefighters could tell the direction the shots were coming from and told a copper there on duty. Off he went to investigate.

But fire engines and their crews attract all sorts of honest, decent people. Most of us don't want to see anyone have a fire but, when it happens, there is something so profoundly exciting about it. Then there's the day-to-day heroics of the fire crew. Right there on your street, men and women are risking their lives in front of your very eyes. It doesn't just bring out the child in all of us – it also brings out the children.

As thirteen-year-olds go, Brian McMillan was very fond of his wee toddler brother. When, that evening, Brian's mother had asked him to go for some chips from the local shop, he was happy to take wee Andrew along with him. Andrew took his surname from their mum, Sharon, and Andrew from his dad – Andy Morton – but the boys didn't think of any of that. They were bros, plain and simple.

Andrew was only two years old so Brian carried him. Only a few yards from their home, the fire crew were busy at their work.

'Fire brigade!' called out bright wee Andrew, pointing in the right direction. 'Fire brigade.'

Big brother Brian knew that Andrew had a toy fire engine and some model firemen at home that he loved playing with. Now here was the real thing. Like every good big brother he didn't hesitate but moved up closer to the fire engine to let Andrew watch all the excitement.

One of Brian's pals, Brian Kerr, came up to chat as they watched the crew. Intrigued, young Andrew had shifted in his big brother's arms to get a good view of everything that was going on.

'Ouch,' is all young Andrew said and he put a one small hand up to the right of his head. Big brother Brian immediately saw a trickle of blood coming from small hole there. Clasping Andrew to his chest, his hand on the wound, Brian turned and sprinted the few yards home shouting hysterically for his mum and dad.

Someone got word to the firefighters that a child was hurt nearby. Two of them grabbed a trauma kit and ran to Andrew's home. There they found the wee boy with a small wound to the back right of his head, drifting in and out of consciousness. The trained fire officers could see it was serious and made sure he got the best of treatment pronto.

Doctors rushed Andrew Morton to the Southern General Hospital in the city's Govan area. It is some miles away, right on the other side of Glasgow from Easterhouse, but it has one of the finest neurological units in Britain and that's what the wee boy needed now. Andrew Morton had an air gun pellet lodged in his brain.

The morning after the shooting, Mark Bonini was quickly collared. He had to appear at a court hearing because social workers wanted his Drug Treatment and Testing Order to be ended due to his lack of cooperation. They had applied for this several times before and each time had been unsuccessful. If they had succeeded, he would have been in jail the night he shot Andrew Morton. But, yet again, the sheriff refused to end the order.

Arrested for shooting young Andrew, even Bonini knew he was

in serious trouble this time. The whole scheme was buzzing about the wee boy being shot and critically ill but still he played that well-worn routine he'd been practising most of his life – 'It wasnae me.'

Except the cops knew it was him. His cousin knew it was him. Half his neighbours, fed up for months with him firing that gun, knew it was him. Local taxi drivers he had targeted knew it was him.

Blame life, blame age. Two-year-old Andrew's skull hadn't had the time to develop all of its hard, protective shell. The slug had entered a soft part of the skull at the rear and travelled on, lodging in the front of his brain.

Two days later, Andrew Morton died.

Blame life, blame age. Blame the man who pulled the trigger. Mark Bonini was facing a murder rap.

At the High Court in Glasgow, Mark Bonini caused a problem. He admitted that he fired the shot that killed Andrew but said it had been 'a tragic accident'. Not for nothing had he hired a rising star of the courtroom jousts, Paul McBride, Scotland's youngest QC. McBride addressed the court and offered that Bonini would plead guilty to a reduced charge of culpable homicide. If the deal had been accepted, no evidence would be led, the truth would never emerge and Bonini would probably have been out of jail in no time. But the deal was rejected.

Taxi drivers, fire officers and Andrew Morton's big brother Brian all covered the events of the night leading up to the shooting. When big brother, Brian, spoke of the toddler simply saying 'ouch', eyes filled with tears round the courtroom.

Then Brian McMillan's pal, Brian Kerr, who had been with them at the time of the shooting, took the stand. 'I heard a hollow pop,' he said, 'just like bubblegum bursting. Then wee Andrew said, "Ouch," and put his hand up to the right side of his head. His big brother, Brian, asked him if he was all right and went to rub his head where it was sore. There was blood all over Brian's hand.'

The young boy's plain, simple description of that night was horrifying in its straightforward detail.

Given that Bonini had already conceded that he fired what was to prove the fatal shot, the jury now needed to know the circumstances leading to him pulling the trigger.

According to Kevin Bonini on the stand, Mark Bonini had been high on amphetamine, known as speed, and other drugs that night. In fact, when the police searched Bonini's flat, they found cocaine, speed and a samurai sword. The drugs were found in such quantities that he was also charged with being a drug dealer – something that he denied.

Kevin Bonini described how Mark had been at the first-floor bedroom window taking pot shots. Then Kevin saw the shooter turn his weapon in the direction of Brian McMillan, Andrew's older brother.

'Don't shoot,' Kevin had shouted, 'he's got a kid in his arms.' In spite of the warning, Mark Bonini continued to take aim and Kevin interrupted again with a warning about the child. Both Andrew and his brother Brian were known to the Boninis.

'It's all right,' insisted Mark Bonini, 'I'm going to shoot wee Brian.' As if that was an OK thing to do. 'I'll shoot wee Brian no' the wee boy. I'll shoot Brian.' Then he took aim and fired the fatal shot.

The one thing the cops didn't find in Mark Bonini's house was the air gun itself. Someone had disposed of the weapon. When this emerged, Paul McBride, QC for Mark Bonini, started accusing Kevin of lying about the conversation about the risks of firing that shot. Then he accused him of panicking and getting rid of the gun.

The implication was clear. There had been two people there that night – Mark and Kevin – and maybe the latter had more to hide. Kevin denied all the accusations.

Then the boys' grandmother, Susan Bonini, took the stand as a defence witness. She told how, that night, Mark and Kevin had come into the Barge Pub where she worked. They told her that a kid was shot and Kevin said that Mark had fired the gun. But later, Mark said that it was his younger cousin, Kevin who had fired. Understandably, Mrs Bonini was left not knowing which of her grandsons had fired the fatal shot.

The trial had begun with Mark Bonini facing sixteen charges to do with the gun, drugs and that sword. But, late in the proceedings, prosecutor Sean Murphy QC dropped all other charges apart from murder. Now the jury would have a straightforward decision to make – or would they?

In his charge to the jury before they left the court to make their decision, the judge, Lord Brodie, pointed out that two convictions were possible – murder or culpable homicide.

Mark Bonini was accused of murder through 'wicked carelessness' – a most unusual charge. Lord Brodie offered guidance to the jury, saying that, to convict him of murder, they had to be convinced that Mark Bonini had been so reckless as to have behaved in a wicked and depraved way – in the way of a deliberate killer. If they were not so convinced, then they could find him guilty of the lesser charge.

It took the jury less than three hours to decide that Mark Bonini had been both reckless and wicked. Bonini was the first person in the country to be found guilty of murder with an air gun. Thus he made a little British history but history to be ashamed of.

Even before Mark Bonini was sentenced to a minimum of thirteen years in prison, a public furore was growing over the need to ban or control air guns. Even before the cops called for any weapons to be handed in, hundreds of people flocked to do so, sickened by the murder of wee Andrew Morton. Newspapers had been sensitised to the issue and were reporting other air gun shootings up and down Britain. There seemed to be many more than anyone had imagined. Eventually the politicians caved in. Soon only licensed shops will be allowed to sell air guns, the minimum age of owning one will be raised to eighteen years and it will be an offence to carry one in public.

There are some folk in Glasgow who call this Andrew's Law.

They believe if it saves one eye, one wound, one life, then it will be a fitting memorial for a wee innocent boy who wasn't allowed to grow up.

Meantime, as if they didn't have enough to contend with, Andrew's parents suffered some public embarrassment. In January 2006, relating to an incident back in 2004, both his mother and father were found guilty of dealing in cannabis, one of the substances Mark Bonini was high on the night he shot Andrew.

The charges related to £300-worth of dope – a very small amount – that the parents said had been bought to sell on to their friends. This is a standard approach of cannabis users who don't have a lot of money yet want to fund the purchase of some dope for themselves. It is only cannabis and they only sell to their friends. That doesn't make them junkies or dealers in most people's book.

In jail, Mark Bonini has been feeling sorry for himself. While he was awaiting his trial, he became a father for the first time when his child – a son – was born. Now he'll miss most of his boy's childhood.

Some might say there is justice in that – others that it might help him see the world differently. As a place where people should be neither wicked nor reckless. For the sake of the children. All of the children. Now that it includes his child too.

THE GHOST OF THE FATHER?

There was no warning – the baby just died. Heartbreaking for any family but these parents had suffered the same tragedy twice within four years. But the medics weren't sympathetic. They were suspicious.

When the first baby had died, the family home was a council flat in Inverness Street in what was known as Drumoyne, one of the poorest neighbourhoods in the south side of the city. It was 1995 and, since then, the area has been modernised and redeveloped, with many private houses being built. But, in 1995, it remained untouched and made an ideal setting for Lynne Ramsay's film *Ratcatcher*, based on the strike by binmen that almost paralysed Glasgow in the 1970s.

They were a young couple. Frances was only twenty-two and her man, Darren, twenty-seven when the second baby died in 1999. They had moved to Granton Street, in Oatlands, near the Gorbals, a short time before the second baby was born. Word quickly spread that the new young couple had moved from Drumoyne because a baby had died there. Imagine living with daily reminders that your poor wee babs had died. Locals were sympathetic.

The first baby, Aaron, had only been two months old. He'd had a few health problems but nothing of any greater seriousness than the usual things that rack every new parent and cause even experienced mothers and fathers to fret. The word was that the wee guy just stopped breathing – a kind of cot death, local folk were thinking. These days they call it SIDS – Sudden Infant Death Syndrome. That's how little they know about what causes these terrible events. Mum and Dad put it down to some heart disease running in the family. A real shame, locals in Drumoyne thought.

The Jenkinsons were a nice young couple – steady for an area that had its fair share of winos, junkies and blade-carrying heavies. She'd been a care worker and he had had a few different jobs. One time he worked in a burger joint and another he drove a fork-lift truck. Low-paid, right enough, and he didn't seem able to hang on to a job for long but at least he did work – not like a lot of his neighbours who'd live and die on the welfare.

Frances and Darren seemed close – soft on each other. That was OK. They might have lived in a hard place but the people knew what it was like to be besotted. Besides, they were still young. If you couldn't enjoy each other when you were young, you'd lost your chance. Well, you had in an area when people popped their clogs twenty years before they did in the better-off suburbs.

Frances and Darren were liked well enough in Oatlands. People had been chuffed for them when they had a new baby. So, when word went out that Jacob had died at only three weeks old, much of the neighbourhood went into shock. That hush and depression of communal grief fell on the place like a lead blanket and hung there. How did you ever get over the death of one baby, never mind two?

'These things happen,' locals would say with a shake of their heads. And they did, especially in areas like theirs where newborn babies stood more of a chance of dying early on than soldiers did at war these days. They all lived in a place where, if they were lucky enough to be born alive, too many babies died in the early months. A harsh place but it didn't stop locals from feeling sorry.

The medics were suspicious. The odds against such sudden deaths occurring to two babies in the same family were high – possible but worth looking into further.

When Aaron had died in 1995, the quacks had found nothing that raised any concern. 'Natural Causes' had been put on the death certificate and, not long after he died, the wee boy had been cremated. Now, with Jacob, they took their time and they had the benefit of developments in forensic medicine.

Science aside, there was something else bothering the cops. When each child died, the same pattern was present. Darren, the father, had been feeding them while Frances, the mother, had been in another room or in bed having a sleep. Darren said he'd fed both boys and, a short while later, they'd died. Both times, he'd been on his own with them. The cops didn't like such coincidences. Usually they were worth investigating further.

When the Jenkinsons were first interviewed about the possible sinister death of Jacob, they went through the roof. How dare anyone suggest they were anything less than good, loving parents? They knew what the cops were implying. They didn't need it spelled out. Then the cops got a bit more specific. They wanted to interview Darren. They wanted to know a bit more about what had happened just before Jacob died – and Aaron.

Darren Jenkinson denied that he had done anything wrong, loudly and vociferously. His wife, Frances, supported him. For four years she had believed what he had told her about the time Aaron had died. Why should she doubt her man now? Except, in private, doubt had crept into Frances Jenkinson's mind. Why would the cops go to all these lengths if they didn't have reasons? Cops didn't waste their time, did they?

They didn't this time. Not long after they interviewed him, they charged Darren Jenkinson with the murder of his two baby boys, claiming that he had confessed. To his wife Frances, Darren insisted that he'd been all mixed up . . . that the cops were putting words into his mouth . . . that he was so grief stricken he didn't know if he was coming or going. But he insisted that he hadn't killed Jacob or Aaron. She accepted his word.

That's how things stood when they both entered Glasgow High Court early in August 2001 – Darren pleading not guilty, Frances believing him. Then the prosecution played a tape of his confession. Darren Jenkinson sat with his head bowed as his voice filled the courtroom. There was his voice saying that both babies died four years apart but in almost identical circumstances. That he had been taking care of the babies on each occasion while his wife was sleeping or out. He had suffocated them with one hand while holding their legs with the other. Holding their legs to stop them kicking and struggling.

Male jurors blanched and looked unsteady. Two female jurors burst into deep sobs and were so upset they had to be helped from the courtroom.

The defence team had argued for four days that the tapes should not be allowed in court. Now everyone knew why. It was damning evidence and in the words of the accused.

Darren Jenkinson admitted killing his two babies but claimed diminished responsibility due to mental illness. The issue before the court now wasn't whether or not he'd killed them but whether they would find him guilty of murder and jail him or send him for psychiatric care.

Dr Isobel Hamilton-Campbell, of Dykebar Psychiatric Hospital in nearby Paisley, had been working with Jenkinson and was called to give evidence. In her view, he was suffering from post-traumatic stress disorder, similar to the condition soldiers suffer when they have been in fraught war situations like in Belfast, the Falklands and Iraq. Jenkinson had never been a soldier, of course. The cause of his condition, according to the doctor, was repeated childhood abuse by his father and flashbacks.

It then emerged that Darren Jenkinson had spent most of his childhood in children's and foster homes in England but he claimed that, while he was allowed short periods back with his family, his father had sexually and physically abused him. Dr Hamilton-Campbell went on to say that, until he was the age of about twenty-one, Darren had lived on a cocktail of drugs and he had tried on numerous occasions to commit suicide by cutting his wrists, overdosing on pills and trying to hang himself. Worse than

Friends of Colin McKay lead him away from court in March 1998. McKay was ccused of murdering Christopher McGrory but the jury returned a not proven verdict. ('As Cold as Death')

Here Ricardo Blanco is being taken into Dumbarton Sheriff Court in August 2002 after escaping from custody to visit his wife. Blanco has since been released from prison and is holed up in a secret location in France. ('No Body, No Problem')

This is Tony McGovern's funeral, held in December 2000. Carrying the coffin are his brothers Tommy McGovern (front, right) and Jamie McGovern (left). Did his murder ignite a drugs turf war as the police suggested? ('The Birdman of Possilpark')

Martin Toner was murdered after being granted bail to await trial on drugs trafficking charges. ('Safer in Jail?')

This is Rose Broadley pictured with her common-law husband Robert Butchart. Rose stood trial for the murder of Joanna Colbeck. She was accused of causing Joanna to fall to her death from the window of a twentieth-floor flat. ('Low Life in High Places')

Here Steven Ryan is being led away to start his life sentence for the murder of Marshall Stormonth. But was he really a sex killer or just a robber? ('Dead Lonely')

Dean Ryan seems less camera-shy than his brother Steven (seen behind him). Both were accused of murdering Marshall Stormonth but whether it was a homophobic attack or not remains unclear. ('Dead Lonely')

This is the grief-etched face of Aileen McDermott. She and her sister Marilyn McKenna would look forward to their 'Stress Buster' nights out – until Marilyn was brutally murdered by a man who had terrorised and stalked Marilyn for years. ('Dying on Deaf Ears')

During a reconstruction in June 1986 to try to jog the public's memory, a policewoman follows the path taken by Alison Murray on the day she was killed. ('The Bloody Bluebells')

Iain Murray, Alison Murray's half-brother, and Brian Wilson are led from court handcuffed to each other after being found guilty of Alison's murder. ('The Bloody Bluebells')

This is a picture of Andrew Ferguson in a happy mood. That mood was soon to change when he stood trial as an accomplice to Christopher Hutcheson, who cruelly tortured and murdered his cousin Daniel Hutcheson. ('Life Imitates Art')

This was the scene at the back of the Govan flat where Daniel Hutcheson met a truly gruesome end at the hands of his cousin. ('Life Imitates Art')

Here, Christopher Hutcheson is pictured partying with his girlfriend Donna McLeish (middle) and Andrew Ferguson. Hutcheson would later admit to murdering his cousin Daniel and playing football with his severed head. ('Life Imitates Art')

These attractive gates open on to Cathkin Braes Country Park, a venue where some less than attractive activities go on. This was where ex-cop Gordon Gibson was found murdered. ('Dogging Days and Deadly Nights')

Here is Robert Power in holiday mood on an aeroplane. What started as a missing person case ended with a host of unanswered questions. ('Lost and Found')

Here is top pathologist Doctor Marie Cassidy at a crime scene. A consultant on *Taggart* and the role model for Amanda Burton's character in *Silent Witness*, she still manages to look glamorous in spite of the wellies. ('No Angel But . . .')

Stuart Gair claimed to be watching a film on TV when the man he was found guilty of murdering died. The man he was watching the film with corroborated Gair's story but he was still convicted. Some famous names have got behind the effort to address what is seen as a gross miscarriage of justice. ('No Angel But . . .')

Dr Jim McGregor, who gave up his post as a prison doctor to fight to prove Stuart Gair's innocence, is pictured here with his wife, Maureen. The couple welcomed Gair into their home when he was released pending appeal. ('No Angel But . . .')

Former Home Office pathologist, Professor Bernard Knight, looks in pensive mood here. Sir Bernard brought new evidence to light in the murder of Dorothy Niven . . . or was it murder? ('Nose in the Air')

CHERISHED MEMORIES
OF
OUR LOVING DAUGHTER
AND SISTER
DOROTHY NIVEN
TAKEN FROM US
28th JUNE 1995 AGED 33

R. I. P

William Lynch, Dorothy Niven's boyfriend, arranges flowers on her grave. Dorothy's ex-lover, Richard Karling, was convicted of murdering her but serious doubts about whether her death wa actually murder have arisen. ('Nose in the Air') that, in many respects, she claimed Darren Jenkinson had poured acid over himself. On another occasion, he had insisted on having minor blemishes on his toes and chest removed even though it was quite unnecessary. Most people get depressed from time to time and can almost imagine being sad enough to want to end their lives but pouring acid over your own flesh? Having operations that weren't necessary? People struggled to understand that.

A picture was emerging of a deeply disturbed man – a man whose past horrors haunted him still. On the mantelpiece of his fireplace at his home, there was a photograph of Jenkinson's mother and dead father. At bad times, his father's picture would talk to him, telling him that he was going to be just like him – an abuser. That he, Darren, would sexually and physically abuse his own children.

No surprise then that, at the end of her evidence, Dr Hamilton-Campbell concluded, 'His state of mind at the time of the killings was sufficiently abnormal as to meet the criteria of diminished responsibility.' It looked like Darren Jenkinson didn't know what he was doing at the times he killed his babies. Then he took the stand.

Jenkinson told the judge, Lord McEwan, about his childhood abuse by his father and the flashbacks triggered by the picture of his mother and father. The voice of his father told him that he was going to turn out an abuser just like him and it drove him to distraction, to madness.

On the night Aaron had died he had suffocated him with his plastic bib. Seeing that the baby had gone still, he frantically tried to revive him but failed. He hadn't meant to kill his oldest child. It had been an accident. He didn't know what he was doing.

Over the next four years he and his wife tried to have another child. Eventually they sought medical assistance and it was discovered that she'd need fertility treatment. Frances Jenkinson underwent the treatment and, much to her delight, Jacob was born in 1999. Her husband explained what had happened the night

Jacob died, saying, 'It was my turn to feed him. I put him on the mat to change him. I took his Babygro and nappy off. Seeing him lying on the mat with nothing on, it was as if my dad was there again. He was saying again that I was going to turn out like him. I was going to abuse Jacob.'

He admitted suffocating his three-week-old baby but claimed he hadn't meant to hurt him. As the words left his mouth, in the public benches his wife Frances stood up and staggered towards the door. She fell and had to be grabbed and supported by her mother, Elizabeth. She finally believed her husband had killed both of their children.

Back in court, Anne Smith QC, the prosecutor, accused Jenkinson of fabricating his childhood abuse and hearing his dead father's voice – of 'racking his brains' to find an excuse for the murder, of only having thought of this explanation after he had been charged.

'I couldn't tell anyone about what my father did to me before that,' is all he said in reply.

One week later, the final witness was called. Dr George MacDonald, a forensic psychiatrist from Dykebar Hospital, had a different view of the accused from his colleague at that same hospital, Dr Hamilton-Campbell. Dr MacDonald claimed that Jenkinson was sane, always had been. The prosecutor, Anne Smith QC, was curious that Jenkinson had only mentioned the childhood abuse and the mental problems the month before, when interviewed by a psychiatrist. Did that fit with post-traumatic stress disorder, she wondered?

'In cases of post-traumatic stress disorder, I would expect the symptoms to have a significant influence on their lives,' replied Dr MacDonald. 'So much so that it would be extremely unlikely if they had not told people around them – members of their family, doctors, psychiatrists – that they had such symptoms.'

No one had noticed that Darren Jenkinson was ill and he had told no one, not even his wife, of his alleged suicide attempts, his father's voice or the acid incident. It was punishing expert evidence that said what the prosecutor had been arguing all along – Darren Jenkinson was lying to save his skin. But which psychiatrist would the jury believe?

The jury found Darren Jenkinson guilty of murdering both Aaron and Jacob. Further, they also found him guilty of trying to murder Aaron on three previous occasions and Jacob twice, before succeeding in ending their lives.

Jenkinson had denied all charges but had been found guilty of everything. Now he was about to be labelled the most evil man in Glasgow. One person certainly agreed – his wife.

A month after the guilty verdicts, Darren Jenkinson was brought to back to court to be sentenced and outside the building Frances Jenkinson was happy to talk to the media. She had arranged to meet with her husband in the cells at the courthouse and tell him that their marriage was over and she would hate him for the rest of her life. At the last minute, the High Court security cancelled the meeting. Jenkinson had already collapsed that day. He was so depressed that he was going to take no more part in the proceedings. The court officials feared that, if confronted with his wife, he'd try to kill himself, right there and then.

Inside the courtroom, Lord McEwan gave Darren Jenkinson his colours, telling him, 'On three occasions, you attempted to murder Aaron and you did murder him on the fourth occasion. You attempted to murder Jacob twice and then, on the third occasion, you murdered him. To take one life is terrible but, when it is your baby, it is monstrous. How you could take the life of your second child is beyond any words that I can find to describe it.'

The good judge jailed Jenkinson for life on each count of murder, setting a minimum tariff of fifteen years in jail. He also sentenced him to twelve years in prison for the earlier assaults on his sons. All sentences were to be served concurrently. Jenkinson could apply for parole after fifteen years.

Immediately after the hearing, Jenkinson's lawyer announced his intention to appeal against the sentence. This was the early days of limits being set to life sentences. The lawyers perhaps thought the sentences given were high or at least could be challenged.

In July 2002, ten months after he was sentenced, Jenkinson's appeal was heard. His legal team would have been optimistic about getting some reduction to the minimum of fifteen years in jail. The judge thought differently and decided that he should serve the time given for each of the babies murdered. This would double his sentence, meaning it would be thirty years before he could apply for parole.

After the hearing, his wife Frances said, 'I'm pleased. I want him to have as long as possible to think over the terrible things he's done.'

But the saga didn't end there.

On 1 March 2006, Darren Jenkinson appealed again. His lawyer, Pat Wheatley QC, argued that thirty years was too much – it was the kind of sentence to be expected in a case where someone had been found guilty of multiple murders involving firearms – that only offences at the top level of seriousness were punished so severely, that Darren Jenkinson's offences didn't compare, that killing his two baby boys was not at the top level of seriousness.

Amazingly, Lady Cosgrove and Lord Penrose were persuaded by this argument and reduced Jenkinson's sentence from thirty to twenty-four years. They then reduced it by a further two years because of the good progress he'd made in prison. Good progress? Just like he was seen as a good neighbour at the time he was killing his sons?

Twenty-two years is still a long time. Some people say long enough, others that killers like Jenkinson should never see the light of day again. It's an argument as old as crime, as old as jails.

As he spends day after day in prison, it isn't known if Darren Jenkinson thinks much of his two dead baby boys or if he still hears the voice of his dead father. Or if he ever did.

PART 4
SEX
KILLERS

Rape is not about sex – it's about power. 'Look,' says the rapist, 'I can control you so much and so effortlessly, I can still get an erection and fuck you. Do what I want with you. That's harder than just killing.'

If rape is about power what is sex killing about? Being God?

Rape is to do with sex in some sense, of course. It's about using sex for power but it's the power that's the hit, the turn-on, the drive. With sex killers, that's also true but it's the murder, the taking of life, that they seek.

Too few sex violence cases make it to court for the public to understand what really happens. Hollywood comes along and airbrushes rape and sex killings into some ultimate erotic turn-on. Pure crap.

Glasgow produced one of the most prolific sex killers Britain has seen in modern times. John Duffy, known as 'The Railway Rapist', was born and brought up in Glasgow. After years of preying on women near railway stations circling London with his partner, David Mulcahy, Duffy was jailed for life in 1988 for two murders and a string of brutal rapes. In 2001, he received another seventeen sentences for seventeen other sex attacks.

Duffy has only been sentenced for some of his crimes. It is likely, by his own admission, that he has raped and killed more women. He has committed so many of these crimes, one blurs into another in his memory. When they jailed Duffy, the court made a promise – the serial sex killer and rapist would die behind bars.

Duffy's story isn't covered in this book because he exported his killing elsewhere. The people in this book are in Glasgow and commit their crimes in the city.

Nor, with regret, is another set of important sex cases covered – the seven Glasgow prostitutes murdered in the early 1990s. Jacqueline Gallagher, Tracey Wylde, Margo Lafferty, Marjorie Roberts, Karen McGregor, Leona McGovern, Diane McInally – I salute them all. Poor working women who died horribly. If anyone deserves to be written about these women do. I have views about who might well have been involved but must hold my tongue – or my pen. They're not names that you will have read in the press. But my limits are this – in such a case, if the cops look like they are pursuing some suspect, I must back off. Justice for the women and their loved ones comes first.

The police tell us they are pursuing a convicted sex killer and multiple rapist, a Glasgow man, Angus Sinclair, for some of these deaths. So be it. Justice for the women – and for Sinclair – must come first.

But it's not as if it's difficult to find other sex killers from Glasgow. Tragically, we are spoiled for choice.

Sex killers aren't just the infamous serial killers who haunt human consciousness through fiction and, sadly, fact. They can be motivated by jealousy, loneliness, being caught out, outrage, lust and a hundred other reasons. Sex killers can be women as well as men and they can be old, young, any age.

We take a look at some of those who have walked Glasgow's streets over the past twenty years. The message is – choose your husband, your wife, your partner, your lover and your special friend very, very carefully. It could be a matter of life or death. Your life or death.

A GOOD DAY TO KILL

It was 13 April 1998 and the Holy Day of Baisakhi – a very special day in the Sikh calendar – a day for revenge. By the last years of the twentieth century, it was meant to be symbolic revenge but someone was about to take it literally.

Rajwinder Bassi lay in drenched in her own blood. The thirty-two-year-old had been stabbed repeatedly and had her throat slashed more than once. Worse than that, even the rookie cops on the scene noticed right away that she was pregnant, very pregnant. In fact, she was a few short weeks away from giving birth. This wasn't a symbolic act of revenge. This was a hate killing.

As ever, the cops were first suspicious of Rajwinder's husband, Harbej Bassi for no other reason than that he was her husband. The two had been married just the year before in the Punjab and she had travelled to Glasgow to be with him. But they heard things about Harbej they didn't like – things that were worth looking into.

Harbej had been married before to a woman called Gurmit Bassi. He had met her on a flight to India in the 1980s when he had been deported from Britain as an illegal immigrant. After a short romance, they had been married in 1987 and, since his new bride was a British citizen, that allowed him back into Britain. That's how it seemed with Harbej Bassi, the cops thought – he was always looking for something in it for him.

In 1992, after they had two sons together, Harbej had divorced Gurmit. Was his use for her now over, the cops wondered? He had done well since they moved to Scotland. At first, he had worked as a waiter in curry restaurants and then opened his own place, the Royal Ashoka Restaurant in Bridge of Allan, Stirlingshire, about twenty-five miles from Glasgow. He was doing well and now could legally live in Scotland as long as he wanted.

In 1997, he met the murder victim Rajwinder Bassi. When he married her, he received a substantial dowry from her family, to take her out of the grinding poverty of the Punjab. Again the cops wondered if the money rather than the bride was the attraction for Harbej.

Rajwinder and Harbej set up home in Woodlands Drive, Charing Cross, near Glasgow's city centre. That's where she was found with her throat cut and her body full of stab wounds on 13 April 1998 – the Holy Day of Baisakhi – the day for revenge.

Harbej Bassi wasn't best pleased at being asked awkward questions. He knew, by the way the cops were treating him, that he was under suspicion. His was not an unusual situation. In such murders, the cops know that, in a high percentage of cases, the killer knows the victim very well. How much closer can you be than husband and wife? But, for the innocent, it's a hard one to take. You're no sooner facing up to the horror of a loved one's murder, than cops are suggesting you are the killer. Harbej Bassi swore he was innocent.

A neighbour – an Asian woman – living near to the murder scene had some information for the police. She had heard a commotion coming from that house that night. She had heard Rajwinder call out in Punjabi, 'Leave me alone, you dog. I am going to die. Save me.' Even more interesting was the phrase for 'you dog'. In Punjabi it only referred to males not females.

Husband Harbej Bassi's position was looking dodgier by the minute. Just one problem for the cops – he had a watertight alibi. That night he had been working at his restaurant, the Royal Ashoka in Bridge of Allan. Plenty of staff and customers saw him there. The police were going to have widen their search.

* * *

The more the police spoke with Harbej, the more interested they became in his ex-wife, Gurmit Bassi. Harbej claimed that his former wife suffered from depression and that's why he had divorced her. Depression was putting it mildly, if what he said was accurate. Harbej admitted that, after he had divorced Gurmit, he continued to have sex with her. And, even after he had married Rajwinder, he continued his affair with his first wife. When he eventually told Gurmit that Rajwinder was pregnant and broke off with her, she went ballistic.

Sectioned by law to be detained at Leverndale Psychiatric Hospital in the city's south side, Gurmit told doctors that her former husband was a mass murderer and named names – none of which could possibly be true. She said she had a small animal living inside her body and that she fed it snakes at her home in Cambuslang. The poor woman was very ill.

But Leverndale Hospital is one of those large Victorian institutions with expansive grounds and many hundreds of patients. Apart from a few in the locked wards, the patients can wander around the grounds and get whatever they want. In Gurmit's case, this included large quantities of cider – not the most therapeutic of medications. As is the way in these days of Care in the Community, though drinking heavily and still obviously unwell, Gurmit was released after only five weeks.

Being mentally ill didn't make the woman a killer but the cops had another witness who pointed towards Gurmit Bassi. This witness they believed entirely. It was her own fourteen-year-old son, Steven.

Harbej and Gurmit's two sons had moved in with their father and his new wife just weeks before. On the day of the murder, the fourteen-year-old reported how his mother had phoned him while he was at home and asked him to come down to the street with the house keys.

Downstairs, the boy duly handed over the keys to his mother. With her there was a man, a white man he'd never seen before. When he asked his mother what she wanted with the keys, she told him that she'd paid the man £1,000 to kill Rajwinder's unborn baby. In telling the police this, the poor boy broke down and sobbed. If he hadn't handed over the keys, would Rajwinder still be alive? Was he as guilty as the ones who plunged the knife into her again and again?

Out at Gurmit's house in Cambuslang, the police heard another tale. Sure, she had been at the house in Woodlands Drive. Yes, she had called her son to come down with the keys but the man she was with had been paid by her former husband to kill his new wife. Her man loved her, Gurmit, not that pregnant devil.

The man with Gurmit that day was a former butcher, twenty-five-year old Christopher Jones, also from Cambuslang. They had met a couple of years earlier through Jones working in a shop near her home. To the cops, Jones was clearly a bit gullible, suggestible, easily led – not the standard photo-fit of a knife-killer hit man.

Eventually Jones agreed he had been at the house that day but was insistent that he knew nothing of any murder. He had gone with Gurmit to the flat to see a lawyer who she'd promised would help his lover, Anne McBarron, get a divorce from her estranged husband. But there was going to be a different story from an unexpected source – Anne McBarron herself.

The night Rajwinder was killed, Jones had returned home late to the flat he shared with McBarron. She noticed that he had blood on both hands and asked him how that had happened.

'I must've left a guy for dead,' he replied, going on to give an account of a street fight he'd just had with two men. She noticed that he had a substantial cut on each hand – like blade cuts, not the scraped knuckles and swollen fingers she'd expect to see from a street fight.

That was enough for the cops. Gurmit Bassi and Christopher Jones were formally arrested and charged with the murder of Rajwinder Bassi.

At their trial in Glasgow High Court in December 1998, both the accused pled not guilty. Gurmit's counsel, Gordon Jackson QC, submitted on her behalf a special alibi of incriminating two others.

Put simply, Gurmit claimed that her former husband, Harbej, had hired Christopher Jones as a hit man to kill his pregnant wife. That her husband had arranged with their son, Steven, to let the hit man in. The mother was blaming her own son.

The prosecution set about establishing the basis of the relationships between all key parties. The cops had been doing their job and had found local people – especially taxi drivers – from Cambuslang who testified that Gurmit had been asking around about how she could hire a hit man.

When Gurmit and Harbej's fourteen-year-old son, Steven, was called to give evidence the poor boy was upset, crying. Gently the prosecution took him through the events of that night.

The teenager confirmed that, around 9.30 p.m. when it was dark, his mother had phoned him at the Woodlands Drive flat he shared with his younger brother, his father and Rajwinder. The building and area were quiet since most folk were at the temple celebrating the Sikh New Year, the Holy Day for revenge.

Being a good kid, Steven did as his mother asked. Downstairs, he met her and the man he now knew to be Christopher Jones. Then the boy changed his story. Christopher Jones had gone into the flat on his own, he claimed. Was he telling the truth? Or was he just reacting out of loyalty to his mother? The same mother who was blaming him as part of her own alibi? Or had he been pressured? And, if so, by whom?

The prosecution was having none of it and gently but firmly reminded Steven what he had said earlier. With more tears streaming down his cheeks, he admitted that his mother had gone into the house with Jones while he had stayed on his own outside the house. And that, before she had gone inside, his mother had said Jones had a knife and explained he was going to help her get rid of Rajwinder's baby.

A short while later, Gurmit and Jones had emerged from the home. According to young Steven, Jones was puffing and panting, sweating and out of breath.

Then two police photographers were called to show what the

cops found inside the flat that night. Before the pictures were shown the jury were warned that some of them were 'distressing'. It was an understatement. Blood stained the walls. Clothing lay scattered on the floor soaked in blood. Rajwinder Bassi lay face down. Stab wounds peppered her back. Lower down there was a deeper wound and the angle showed that her throat had been slit so severely that her head hung on a thread of gristle and tendon.

As the photographs were shown, jury members shook. Some held their heads down trying to deal with the horror of the images. For all the world, it looked like a film set from some gory piece of movie fiction. But they knew that, just a short time before, the body had been a vivacious young woman expecting her first child in just a few short weeks and with her life to look forward to. They weren't looking at Hollywood but at Hell.

The police photographers had some other snaps to show, of Christopher Jones's hands. They showed a cut like a knife slash on his left hand and another on the palm of his right. Although not nearly as gruesome as the other pictures, these would prove crucial to the jury in making up their minds.

Pathologist Jean McFarlane took the stand at the High Court in Glasgow. With professional clarity and detachment she described the injuries to Rajwinder Bassi's body. There were at least thirty wounds to her neck and back. A blade had carved criss-cross wounds across her back. Her throat had been slashed so severely that her windpipe and gullet had been cut right down to her spine. The blade had been pushed through her back into where her womb and unborn baby lay.

Those were the hard facts but the doctor needed to add something else, something personal. 'I have never seen injuries like that before,' she said.

Christopher Jones took the stand and stuck to his story. He had gone along with Gurmit Bassi to the flat that night and been paid £500 and some jewellery for his pains. But, he insisted, he didn't know what was going to happen.

If that was the case, how did he have blood on his hands and clothes that night, the prosecution wanted to know. Because, when Gurmit Bassi started slashing and stabbing Rajwinder, he had fainted and collapsed beside the body, Jones claimed.

What was it the Asian neighbour had overheard?

'Leave me alone, you dog.' She had been quite clear. The Punjabi word used for 'you dog' applied to males only. Even in her panic and terror, Rajwinder would never have used the wrong gender if it was a woman she was appealing to. If it had been Gurmit Bassi. What else had the neighbour heard Rajwinder crying out? 'I am going to die. Save me.' Christopher Jones admitted being in the house but he hadn't saved Rajwinder Bassi, had he?

In his final speech to the jury, Donald Findlay QC, defending Christopher Jones, painted a picture of Gurmit Bassi as a murdering she-devil who systematically destroyed a young woman's life, in utter jealous rage, simply because her former husband had taken a new wife.

'You lost the place and you kept cutting and cutting at her and butchered and murdered her,' he said. 'The final degradation was when you cut at her back at a spot where her unborn baby would have been if she had been lying face up.' As ever Findlay's rhetoric was graphic and convincing. However, when it came to his own client, the same could not perhaps be said to be true – Findlay described him as 'an immature young man, susceptible to exploitation by others'. That description is one Christopher Jones's family would also use to describe him. As Findlay pointed out to the jury, Jones hadn't even been in any trouble before. Now he was facing a horrific murder charge.

In his concluding statement, Gurmit Bassi's lawyer, Gordon Jackson QC, blamed Jones, of course, and described his own client as having lived in a 'cauldron of mental pressure' because of her divorce and the messy after-effects of her continuing sexual relationship with her former husband.

Two of the top QCs of their time had tried their best for their clients yet the majority of the jury were persuaded otherwise by the case presented by Advocate Depute Samuel Cathcart for the prosecution. Both Gurmit Bassi and Christopher Jones were found guilty of murder.

It was the type of murder where, before the abolition of hanging, the judge would have donned the black cap with the approval of most of the public. Instead, in December 1998, Lord Marnoch spoke about the particular brutality of the killing and added, 'The crime was one which would turn the stomach of any decent citizen.' He then sentenced Bassi and Jones to the mandatory period of life imprisonment.

After the trial, Christopher Jones's brother, the landlord of The Sun pub in Cambuslang, said, 'Anyone who knows Christopher knows he isn't capable of such a terrible crime. He's been the fall guy here – sucked into this by that evil woman.'

Rajwinder Bassi's mother had travelled the 4,000 miles from India for the trial. When asked why, all she would say was, 'I want to see the face of the woman who murdered my daughter.'

Maybe both families are right. Maybe not. After sentencing neither Jones nor Bassi wanted to talk about the murder. Maybe we'll never know exactly what happened in that flat that night.

A short while later, Harbej Bassi took his sons to live in Bridge of Allan near his restaurant. During the trial, lawyers and his ex-wife had accused him of somehow being involved in the killing. Rightly, he believed the trial and verdict had cleared his name. Yet he still had to move out of Glasgow – a city now filled with all-too painful memories for him and his boys. In that they are not alone.

GREEN-EYED MONSTERS AND RED MISTS

It wasn't just anyone who could stroll through the streets of Drumchapel at 1 a.m. on a Sunday morning. But John Munro wasn't just anyone – he was a local and wasn't scared of anyone. Munro could handle anything. Or so he thought.

He'd had a few drinks with friends then he decided to head up the road – up to his girlfriend's house where he sometimes stayed over. She wasn't expecting him but that was OK. It would be a wee surprise. It was going to be more than that.

John Munro had been out of prison for one short month. Not that he was a crook. He'd got into a fight and was done for assault to severe injury. He'd been jailed for two years – one hefty sentence for assault that reflected the damage he had inflicted.

Most people who knew him said he wasn't a bad guy – he just had a hell of a temper and knew how to inflict the pain. But then he lived in Drumchapel, that big scheme on Glasgow's north-west periphery that Billy Connolly described as a concrete desert with windows. A lot of the windows were metal, indicating that those homes had been deserted or the tenants evicted and the places had been boarded up.

Drumchapel was one tough scheme and hard men like John Munro carried some status. Having spent time in jail for assault as he had wasn't taken as a bad thing by a lot of folk. It sent out a message, 'Don't mess with me.'

That night, Munro wasn't in the mood for being messed with.

He hadn't had just a few drinks but been out drinking for many hours and was now heading to the house of his girlfriend, Teresa McRobert, up in Fettercairn Drive in Drumchapel. Teresa lived quite near to his own folks' place where he stayed – too close some might say.

Since he'd come out of jail, he had been staying with Teresa once or maybe twice a week. She was a thirty-four-year old divorcee. Attractive in some people's opinion, she was a bit older than twenty-nine-year-old John but that didn't matter much. But some folk who knew Teresa would say that she was full of life and looking for a good time after her divorce. That's what worried John Munro.

They hadn't been getting on too well since he'd come out of the jail – nothing that he could put his finger on but things just weren't right between them. He'd watched guys in the jail eating themselves up emotionally over the same feelings – the suspicions that their women were seeing somebody else. Well, it wasn't going to happen to him. He was nobody's mug.

He'd had a bellyful of booze, it was one in the morning and he was going to pay Teresa a surprise visit. That's when he saw the man coming out of her house. At one in the morning? Teresa was there, saying cheerio to the man. It wasn't so much what she did but how she did it. John Munro could just tell that she'd been seeing that guy, having sex with him. Munro saw red.

By the time he was in Teresa's house, he was shouting the odds but Teresa wasn't cowed by him – no matter how tough he was – and she shouted right back. A next-door neighbour was disturbed by the noise and it went on for half an hour. She said she mainly heard Teresa screaming and then suddenly it stopped. And with good reason.

John Munro had smashed an axe down on his lover's skull, stabbed her and then throttled her with his bare hands.

What the neighbour had heard wasn't Teresa and John arguing. It was Teresa pleading for her life, crying out in agony. She'd heard Teresa McRobert's death throes.

Sitting there panting from his efforts, the adrenalin turning to acid in his gut, the white fury calmed and John Munro realised what he'd done. He tried desperately to give his lover the kiss of life. He wasn't even sure he was doing the right thing – just panicking, copying what he'd seen on TV.

A short while later, John Munro turned up at his parents' house, upset, weeping, almost distraught. His family weren't used to seeing John that way.

'I've killed Teresa,' he told his brother Robert.

At his trial, John Munro was defended by Donald Findlay QC who, for once, pulled no magic tricks out of the box. All he could suggest was that the terrible events of the night had all started over that other man who had been in Teresa's house. That it was all about jealousy – mad, raging, blind, lethal jealousy.

In 1993, Munro was jailed for life. A man cast into prison for much that remained of his adult life, living with the ghosts and nightmares of the terrible thing he had done to a woman he wanted to live with. That might well have been the end of the story. But it wasn't.

In September 2001, John Munro was found dead in his cell at Glenochil Prison. There was no sign of suicide or an attack on the thirty-seven-year-old's life. He had died in his sleep.

His family will mourn him. Teresa's friends and family will feel somewhat different. There are those who knew him a little during his prison years who reckon that his death was no surprise.

'Eaten up by guilt,' was how one ex-con put it. 'The night he killed that lassie, he killed a bit of himself.'

DEAD LONELY

It had been a pleasant night out with good company. The talented lawyer attracted people like that – sharp brains and witty minds like his. But, as they waved him away into the busy night streets, little did they know it was the last time they'd see him alive.

Even in daylight, the buildings have a Gothic feel to them. The old steeples and the twists and curves in the stonework make them more suited to ancient, rural Romania than the centre of a modern city. But that's where the Tron Theatre is on the far east end of Argyle Street, surrounded by big stores and streams of busy shoppers. A thriving, buzzing, energetic place. Except at night. That's when the Tron comes into its own.

The Tron was an old church but has since been converted into a theatre, restaurant and bar. Its conversion was the beginning of a plan to make that quarter of the city centre into something a little arty, a little bohemian, a little special. They call it the Merchant City and, in earlier times, it dripped with death.

A short walk from the Tron is the tower of the Trongate, an ancient doorway of original Glasgow. Once upon a time, they hanged people there, out in the open. These days they chib people there, out in the open.

The middle of Argyle Street is bright, new and bustling but it gets shabbier the farther west or east you travel. The Trongate end borders on to the Barras and a long street called Gallowgate, named because it was the way to the gallows. Gallowgate has a special place in the history of Glasgow's bloody streets. It wasn't just the hunting ground for serial killer Bible John – it was a place full of hard, bloody pubs and even harder, bloodier men. A chronicle of the murders of that part of the city on their own would fill several books. They were mainly drunken, petty, violent deaths – the way Glasgow's street deaths often are.

Gallows has also given us the Scots word 'gallus'. It originally meant 'fit to be hanged' but extended its meaning to 'wild' and would be applied to a rascal who was heading for the gallows for sure. These days it means 'confident, daring, stylish, impressive, cheeky'. Maybe that's how Marshall Stormonth was feeling that night – he was certainly on top of the world and with good reason.

Stormonth was only thirty years old but he was already acknowledged as one of the top legal brains of his generation. That is no mean compliment in Scotland, with its rich tradition of high-quality law faculties at its ancient universities where some of the finest talent of all social classes work hard to join that profession. Marshall Stormonth was one of the best.

Born in the picturesque coastal town of Oban in the West Highlands, as soon as he could, Stormonth headed to the University of Edinburgh to study law and he flew through the course. The brightest talents in the legal profession usually chase private practice. Those who wish to work in criminal justice aim for one of the large city firms who attract the high-profile cases and pay the largest salaries. Stormonth wanted to work with law-breakers in the courts but he didn't want to defend them – he wanted to prosecute them. He became a Procurator Fiscal.

The Procurator Fiscal service in Hamilton must have been delighted to recruit such a bright young man. It was a busy enough court but not a patch on its near neighbour, Glasgow, whose high crime rates produced the busiest courts in Europe. Marshall Stormonth knew that, of course, and, before long, he had moved to Glasgow, becoming one its youngest Depute Fiscals ever.

Not that Stormonth was all work and no play. No dull boy he.

With a lifelong commitment to Gaelic and a sweet singing voice, he was recognised as a top performer. In 1993, he had won a gold medal at the Mod. It's the Gaelic equivalent of an Olympic medal. Love or hate the language and the songs, Marshall Stormonth was good, very good.

Stormonth didn't rest on his laurels but worked hard behind the scenes. In the 1980s, when still student, he was a founder member of Lothian Gaelic Choir, which is still going strong to this day. In the early 1990s, he formed a folk group, which was filmed performing at the Edinburgh Festival. Somehow he even found time to be a member of Glasgow's famous Phoenix Choir. All that and a busy career yet he always had time for a night out with friends.

That's what he was up to one night in November 1993. A meal and some drinks at the Tron Theatre with pals – just his kind of place. Feeling well refreshed and in good spirits, he left his friends late that night and headed for home – or so he said.

Stormonth had other thoughts on his mind though. The brilliant, popular Procurator Fiscal, Mod gold medal winner, bright spark with a glittering future ahead of him had a secret. It wasn't that he was gay – though it wouldn't have helped his career much if he had made song and dance over it. All his friends and associates knew that he was gay but what they didn't know was that he liked rough trade – very rough.

Marshall Stormonth knew the various places where he could pick up male prostitutes in the city and headed there straight from the Tron. When he met the two young men looking for trade, maybe he stopped and considered their ages. One looked very young. In fact he was seventeen years of age and at that time sex with a young man of that age was illegal, even without money exchanging hands. The brilliant young lawyer was risking every-thing. Why? Maybe, even with all that was going on in his life, Marshall Stormonth was lonely.

It was a money deal – extra because the boys were offering to double up on him. Without haggling or hesitation, Stormonth paid for a taxi to take them back to his place in the well-off middle-class quarter of the west end.

There was another attraction in the night's offering – the young men were brothers. Judge this any way you want – that is for each to decide – but, for men like Marshall Stormonth who enjoy their gay sex rough and sleazy, it was a night to look forward to.

The older of the pair, Steven Ryan, was aged twenty. Dean Ryan was just seventeen and looked younger. They came from a poor background and had little prospects of jobs or success. They had tried their hands at a number of enterprises from robbery to housebreaking but they just didn't have those skills. Besides, they'd found an easier, safer way to raise some dough – gay mugging.

They had carried it off successfully a few times before. Their early modus operandi was to use Dean as the bait. The men who prey on the gay prostitute market tend to like their meat young – chickens, they call them. After dark, Queen's Park on the south side, the Botanic Gardens off Great Western Road in the west end and the expanse of Glasgow Green were regular bases for the 'chicken runs'. Still are.

So, in the early days, Dean would hang around in the chosen place as if on his own. They soon worked out the signals by watching others. As you walk past a potential client, turn abruptly and stare them in the eye as you do. Then you give a quick smile as you rub your crotch. Or you can hang about near a designated bandstand or public toilets. In those places, at that hour, such signals were as obvious as five-foot-high letters in neon lights.

Inevitably some punter would approach Dean and ask him if he was looking for trade. They'd go to some secluded part of the park but, before anything could happen, older brother Steven would appear. He'd be irate and intent on physical damage. He'd rant on about his brother being underage, saying he was just fifteen years old. The pair would demand money from the sole punter or they'd beat him up. Sometimes they'd give him a punch or two prove their sincerity but most times it wasn't necessary. They'd take all

his money, his watch and whatever else they fancied then sometimes give him a kicking from hell just for good measure.

Steven and Dean Ryan hated gays. The gays they hated most
were the ones who fell for their ambush. The ones who dared
think that they really were gay. Now those they detested.

Such attacks on lonely homosexual men have been going on
forever. They rarely get reported. Often the men cruising for male
prostitutes are secretly gay with wives at home. Or they have male
partners who don't know they're paying prostitutes. Or they have
good careers that would be ruined if word about what they were
up to were to leak out – good careers like the one Marshall
Stormonth had.

Back at Stormonth's flat in the comfy west end, the Procurator
Fiscal relaxed and poured some drinks. He was a young man of
taste and refinement and was going to take his time. Steven and
Dean Ryan played along. Looking round the flat everything they
saw spelled out one thing – M O N E Y.

All they needed to do is what they usually did – bide their time
till Stormonth started coming on for sex then confront him.
Threaten him. Hurt him a bit. Then rob him.

Usually all they could steal was what the punter had on him.
Sometimes they'd rifle through his pockets just to make sure they
had everything valuable. But it was never that much. This time
they could take the bloke's stereo and maybe his TV. Maybe he
had a stash of money in the house. Well-off people did that type
of thing, they reckoned. It was going to be a bigger-than-usual
payday. Then something went wrong.

Maybe it was something in Marshall Stormonth's manner.
Maybe he was too polite, too much good company. Or maybe he
was pawing at them, eyeing them up, getting ready for the fun
he thought he was going to have. Or maybe it was just that hate
boiling inside the Ryan brothers. That hate for gay men. A hate
so fierce a psychiatrist might suggest they were hiding behind it
from their own homosexuality. Or maybe from some childhood
experience in which a man had abused them.

One of them picked up a champagne bottle and smashed it down on Marshall Stormonth's skull. They could have left it at that. Left him moaning and half-conscious on the floor, robbed his flat and been out of the door in a flash. What was he going to do? Go to the cops? But they weren't finished.

They found some string and trussed the young lawyer up. With no discussion, no plan, they got hold of a tie and a belt, wrapped them round their victim's necked and slowly throttled him to death.

Then they were out of there. They could run but they couldn't hide. The cops had been watching the rent boys on the chicken runs. They had been watching the Ryans and, on other nights with other boy prostitutes, Marshall Stormonth. The two were arrested and gave away enough clues to be charged with murder.

He had made no secret of it. All his short but outstanding professional life, Marshall Stormonth dreamed of performing at the highest level. Prosecuting in terrible murder cases. Persuading and convincing juries to convict by the sheer brilliance of his logic and rhetoric. Of course, it would have to be in the highest court in the land. As far as he was concerned, that wasn't in Edinburgh but Glasgow High Court. That was where most murders were tried after all.

His final court appearance ever was at that very court, in the North Court that had witnessed more high-profile murder cases than any other court in Europe. Marshall Stormonth had finally made it – not as prosecutor but as victim.

Steven and Dean Ryan were found guilty of his murder. Steven was sentenced to life imprisonment and Dean, because of his age, was sentenced without limit of time. But neither was going to jail. Not to start with anyway. Such was their mental condition that both were shipped off to the State Hospital, Carstairs. They would stay there till psychiatrists decided they were well enough to move to prison.

These were two very ill and dangerous young men. It was

Marshall Stormonth's bad luck that he ran into them that night. The night they finally lost the place.

Ten years after the murder, a killer was on the loose. The Ryan brothers had made good progress and been moved to mainstream prison. Steven Ryan had served his time well and by 2003 was put on Training for Freedom status at Saughton Prison, Edinburgh, as was his brother, Dean. In Steven's case, this meant that he was allowed out, unescorted, every day to attend a work placement. The idea is that it helps long-term prisoners acclimatise to life in the outside world. All was going well till one day he didn't come back.

The authorities weren't too keen to tell the public that one of the Ryan boys was on the run. One month later, without incident, Steven Ryan handed himself in at a Glasgow cop shop. When asked why he had escaped from jail at a time he was so close to freedom he said that he was afraid. Not of freedom but of other prisoners who had been threatening him unless he brought drugs back to jail from his trips out.

The prison believed him enough to put him back on the Training for Freedom programme. Then, in 2004, someone made a call to the press. Someone in the know, probably someone from Saughton Prison itself, decided that they didn't like convicted prisoners being free to roam the streets.

At that time in that jail, the Ryan brothers and another inmate were being allowed out on a daily basis to work in soup kitchens and cafes run by the Church of Scotland. Nothing unusual there – not even that they were all convicted killers.

There was 'Scythe Killer', Roderick McPhee. Back in November 1987 he had slaughtered his girlfriend, Jeanette Balmer, at her home in Beith, Ayrshire, by hitting her on the head with a scythe. Jailed for life, he too had escaped from the prison the previous year within weeks of Steven Ryan.

Then, within twelve months of those escapes, the three men were being given their bus fares every morning and allowed out the gates. To the media it didn't matter that McPhee had spent seventeen years in the system and the Ryans ten. Or that they had changed and developed enough for the cynical screws to decide that they were ready to cope safely in the big bad world. Once a killer, always a killer. The media wasn't going to forget Dean and Steven Ryan or allow them to forget the night they killed a promising young lawman. Some people see public naming and shaming as a kind of justice. But would Marshall Stormonth – the young lawyer who believed in the legal system with all its faults – would he have approved? Doubtful, very doubtful indeed.

DYING ON DEAF EARS

'I've got a new man,' Marilyn McKenna said. She was excited. She couldn't wait for her sister Aileen McDermott to come back from holiday to tell her the news. 'He's wonderful.' But was he a man to die for?

Aileen wasn't just Marilyn's older sister – she was also her best pal, her confidante, the one she shared everything with. As her special person, Marilyn couldn't wait for Aileen to meet her new boyfriend. They arranged it right away.

Stuart Drury was the man. A couple of years younger than Marilyn the pair were in their early thirties – old enough to have made a few mistakes and old enough to have learned from them. Drury seemed to be the perfect gentleman. Now that was something you didn't find every day in a pub in Glasgow.

Marilyn was keen to extol Stuart's virtues to her older sister. Seems that Stuart wasn't just looking for good time, a one-night stand, like most blokes, or even a few dates. Almost from the time they met, he had offered to lend a hand around Marilyn's house and to help with her three kids from a previous relationship. Not many would do that, Marilyn had argued, and Aileen had to concede that she was right. Trouble was that, when she met Stuart, she took an instant dislike to him. He couldn't take his eyes off her sister – that was good – but it felt like he wanted to control her, own her. He just gave Aileen the creeps.

Aileen was as good a friend to Marilyn as she was a sister. She knew that she shouldn't interfere. She didn't like the man but what had that to do with her younger sister's choice of partners? Nothing.

Stuart Drury moved into Marilyn's home. She continued to go out to work at her three jobs. No slouch, she worked so hard to give her three kids the best life she could. She worked in a local chip shop, as an auxiliary in a school and as a dinner lady. It was an exhausting routine and the help that Stuart gave, not just with the kids but doing the housework, the dishes and all the domestic chores, took a huge load off Marilyn's shoulders.

To anyone who knew her, it was clear that the strongly built, six-foot-two man who didn't mind doing the hoovering had bowled Marilyn over. In the early months of the relationship, she was one very happy lady and it glowed from her, like some inner light.

One thing that Marilyn didn't change after Stuart came into her life was what she called her Friday Night Stress Buster – a night out with Aileen and their women friends. They'd just go to some pub, have a few drinks, gossip a lot and then go home – the perfect way for all of them to let their hair down a wee bit and revive their batteries after a hard week's work. And no one worked harder than Marilyn. Then she stopped coming.

The other women joked that she'd be too busy in bed with Stuart. Marilyn had raved about her love life with her new man – three or four times a day wasn't unusual. They could use some of that, her pals had joked, and Marilyn had beamed. But older sister Aileen wasn't so sure.

When the two met up, Marilyn was looking a bit stressed and tired. Soon she was sharing all with her sister. Stuart had started becoming a bit . . . well, paranoid. He had suggested that, when the girls went out on a Friday night, they were going out to pull blokes. She'd put him straight, of course, but he just kept going on and on and, in the end, it had been easier to stop going out on Friday nights. But that wasn't the half of it.

They'd been together for a good few months by this time and sometimes she'd come home from her hard work routine absolutely exhausted and Stuart would insist on having sex – no matter how tired she was. If she put her foot down and said no, he'd go off on one, accusing her of having affairs at her work with one of her bosses, some guy she worked with or even some of the women.

It was easier for Marilyn just to let him get on with it but it felt horrible – almost like rape. Then he'd accuse her of not putting any feeling into their lovemaking. Like her mind was elsewhere. Worse, once was never enough. When he started accusing her of having affairs, he started demanding sex again and again. Even if she just went along with it, they'd no sooner finish than he'd start on her again, accusing her of seeing other people.

Marilyn McKenna went from being deliriously happy to totally miserable within months. Something or someone was going to crack.

Marilyn stuck it out for two years of constant nagging and utter paranoia. Stuart Drury had taken over her life and not for the best. She'd had enough and, one night, she ordered him out of her home and her life.

His answer was to punch her in the face, shattering her nose and sending the seven stone, petite woman flying into a wall. She went to the cops and Drury ended up being ordered to pay her £400 compensation – as if that would help Marilyn get her life back. But the whole episode had the desired effect. Drury disappeared – forever, Marilyn hoped. Some hope.

A few weeks of peace later, Drury was back. On the phone, at her door, waiting for her outside one of her work places. In the two years they'd been together, he'd learned too much about her life for her to hide from him.

'Please take me back, Marilyn,' he begged. 'I'm so sorry about what happened. It was wrong of me – terrible – but I just got scared when you said we were finished. It'll no' happen again.'

She told him no and walked off. Till the next time he turned up begging, pleading, apologising. This time, they sat in Marilyn's front room talking. Her three kids were in the room. They were one of the reasons she had to end the relationship. Their lives had been a misery those past two years. Then she put into words her foremost reason why they couldn't go on. 'I will not stay in a violent relationship, Stuart,' she said as clearly and calmly as she could. 'It's as simple as that.'

Stuart Drury pulled a knife out of his waistband and slit both wrists. Right there in front of Marilyn and the three young children. It doesn't take a psychiatrist to feel the power and desperation of that act. Stuart Drury was telling Marilyn McKenna that he, not her, would have the last word – that he would have the last word whatever it took.

Drury was admitted to hospital but soon recovered and returned to his own place as well as his old ways. Soon pizzas she hadn't ordered started arriving at Marilyn's home. Then taxis, clothes catalogues, emergency plumbers and just about every other hoax nuisance you can think of. She didn't need to guess who was behind this lark. Stuart Drury in the meantime had been sending her a letter every day, sometimes more. Phoning morning, noon and night – always begging her to let him return. She said no and he upped the ante.

Returning home one day she was terrified to see that her door had been kicked in. Her first though was burglars but it was worse than that. Sitting in her front room was Drury. His way of persuading her that they should reconcile was to threaten her with violence, accuse her of sleeping around and warn her that she'd never get rid of him.

Marilyn went to the cops, of course, but they were useless. They didn't want to interfere in what they saw as a lovers' tiff, a domestic dispute that would blow over.

'I'm looking for some business,' the unfamiliar man's voice said down the phone.

'What?' replied Marilyn McKenna.

'How much do you charge?' the man went on.

'Charge for what?' She had been making her kids' tea, listening to the events of their day, her mind on other things. This call flummoxed her and she was struggling to work it out. 'I think you've got the wrong number.'

'Is that . . . ?' and the man rattled off Marilyn's home phone number.

'Aye but . . .'

'Well that's what it says in your advert,' the man interrupted, beginning to show signs of annoyance.

'What advert?'

'In the newspapers, saying you're open for business. "All Desires Met" it says here.'

Finally the penny dropped for Marilyn McKenna. Someone had placed an advert in a newspaper under her name, advertising sex for sale. No guesses who. From that night on, other phone calls came and, worse, men started turning up at her door.

God knows who these men were. All she knew was that they were the type to read the papers looking for sex for sale. What if one of her kids answered the phone to a particularly foul-mouthed man – or if they answered the door to one?

Again Marilyn went back to the cops. Again they didn't help.

When Drury kicked her door in one more time to be sitting waiting for her, Marilyn went straight to the police yet again. But they advised her to go the Housing Department and get a move. Housing weren't willing to flit her but they did offer an iron door.

The final act of attention-seeking came when Drury started waiting for Marilyn after work. Absolutely driven to distraction, she hailed a taxi and clambered in to make her escape. She was too late. Drury jumped in beside her and, once there, calmly slit his own throat.

There are those who'd say that it was a great pity that Stuart Drury didn't do a better job cutting his throat. Rushed to hospital, he survived, only to be referred to a psychiatrist, perhaps exactly what he needed. Amazingly, after months of sessions, the psychiatrist had to conclude that Drury was not mentally ill. But did that make him sane?

The so-called sane man upped his pressure on Marilyn. One of his constant accusations was that she was on the phone to other men, arranging meetings to have sex. Either that or that she was on the phone to her friends and her sister, Aileen, talking about him, Drury. So he cut her phone line. It was time for Marilyn to get out of her home.

Like many women before her, Marilyn took her kids and got shelter and protection at her parents' house. Still it didn't work. For almost a year Drury kept up his pestering and annoyance. He didn't care who else saw what he was up to, insisting everything that had happened, from slitting his throat to breaking Marilyn's nose, happened because he loved her so deeply.

Exhausted, seeing no end to Drury's stalking and threats and worried that his behaviour would have an impact on her parents' health, Marilyn agreed to move back in with him. It was 1997 and Marilyn was praying that their new start would bring an end to Drury's obsessive behaviour. He just got worse.

After a year of practically no contact with her sister because Drury had banned it, one night Aileen McDermott got a call at her home from Marilyn's twelve-year-old son, Brian. 'Help my mum – Stuart is going off his head,' the boy screamed.

When Aileen and her husband arrived at the house, they found Marilyn and the kids barefoot, outside on the street, in their nightwear, terrified of Drury.

That night, in spite of offers from the family, Marilyn insisted on taking her kids to a safe hostel run by Women's Aid for victims of domestic violence. She thought that, if she asked for help in this way, at last someone would take her seriously and help her.

The unit she was staying at was a refuge and its location and phone number were kept strictly confidential. That had been the case for years till Stuart Drury phoned it one night. 'You can't hide from me,' he said calmly down the line. 'You won't ever get away from me.'

Marilyn had no option but to return to her own home only to find the windows smashed, her clothes ripped up and dog excrement smeared all over the place. She had hardly begun to clean the place up when the phone rang, 'You bitch,' howled Drury. 'You're dead.'

At other times, when she'd answer the phone and realise it was him, she'd put it down, leaving it off the hook, knowing that, if she hung up, he'd keep phoning back all night. Trouble was she could still hear him scream, 'Pick up the phone, you fucking bitch. Pick up the fucking phone or you're a dead woman.' If she hung up and let his calls go on to the answering machine the same type of message would be left time after time.

Then he'd taken to watching her from outside the house. She'd phone the cops and they'd move him on but, one night, she was sure he was there, watching her from some place she couldn't see him. Eventually reluctant cops arrived and had a look round the area. Sure enough, there was Stuart Drury crouching behind some bushes. After that incident she had her windows boarded up and got her oldest boy Brian to help her barricade the door with furniture. They were living in perpetual dark, under siege, all because of one man.

It got so bad that Marilyn went to a lawyer. She had reported Drury often enough to the cops that it was relatively easy to obtain a court order banning him from going near her. But then her lawyer warned that there was a catch. Because they weren't married, it could take weeks, if not months, to have the order enforced if Drury started up his games again. It seemed almost everything Marilyn tried to do to protect herself turned into dust.

That Marilyn McKenna didn't lose her sanity is a tribute to her emotional strength and love for her three children. She just had to keep going for their sake. Then, one night, she just couldn't take any more. 'He's been calling again,' she told her sister Aileen on the phone.

'A lot?'

'Every ten minutes – threatening me and screaming.'

'You need to go back to the police.'

'What for?' Marilyn asked. 'They do nothing. Just nothing. One day, I'm going to be left in a pool of blood. Then maybe we'll get some attention.'

Two days later, on 4 September 1998, Marilyn and Aileen went out for one of their Stress Busters. A quiet drink at a nice pub. A blether. Some good company. God knows Marilyn needed those therapeutic sessions more than ever before.

A handsome guy nearby was paying a lot of attention to Marilyn. Eventually he picked up the nerve to go over to the women and offered to buy them a drink. It was just the boost Marilyn needed – some normal guy paying her attention for all the right reasons. Aileen could see that and was pleased for her younger sister. Not wanting to play the gooseberry, she made her excuses and left after a short time. If only she'd stayed.

Marilyn and her new suitor got on so well she invited him back to her place in Gorebridge Street, Carntyne, for coffee. For once Marilyn wasn't worried about the deranged Stuart Drury. For once she felt safe. That night she had a man to protect her. Drury wasn't that brave or that mad. Was he?

They had hardly settled down when Stuart Drury appeared at the door. He was raging, his eyes popping out of their sockets. He told the other bloke in no uncertain terms that Marilyn was his woman. The new bloke took to his heels.

Terrified, Marilyn ran out of the house and away. She only got as far as nearby Abbeyhill Street when she was caught by Drury waving a claw hammer. She tried to protect herself but she was short and petite compared to his towering six foot plus. It was hopeless. He smashed her on the face again and again. When her head slumped over, he crunched the hammer into her neck. A dozen blows had rained in. It only took a matter of a minute. Then Drury was off, leaving Marilyn McKenna lying there, in a pool of her own blood.

Her jugular vein had been severed, her skull cracked in several places and her jaw ripped out. The ambulance crew who quickly arrived at the scene had to remove the woman's smashed teeth from her airways just to help her breathe. Marilyn McKenna was alive – but only barely alive.

A few hours later, Stuart Drury was arrested. Not surprisingly, his clothes were still splattered with Marilyn's blood. When the cops removed his possessions at the police station to take him into custody, they discovered that he was carrying a photograph of Marilyn – a photograph he'd slashed in two with a knife.

Later that day, in the Southern General Hospital, Marilyn McKenna's family said their last, tearful farewells to her. Then her life support machine was switched off.

Marilyn McKenna was thirty-seven years old. Vivacious, energetic and attractive, she was the loving mother of three young kids. The kids would now be separated – two went to live with different aunties and the other one went to stay with their natural father. They had been a happy, loving family till Stuart Drury had come into their lives.

In February 1999, Stuart Drury appeared in court charged with murder. It then emerged that Marilyn had made sixty-four formal reports to the police over the four years she had known Drury. An even more worrying fact emerged from his earlier life – for two years Drury had also relentlessly stalked Anne Govan, a former girlfriend of his. That had culminated in him attacking her in the close of the tenement where she lived. Drury had left her battered, bloody and unconscious. The cops had nabbed him and he went to trial but was jailed for only sixty days. A few weeks after being released from prison, Drury took up with Marilyn whose hell was about to begin.

There are those who ask if the police checked up on Stuart Drury's background. Marilyn had been to the police so often and they knew he was stalking and threatening her so did they check him out? Did they know of his previous offence? They should have.

Stuart Drury was jailed for life for the murder of Marilyn McKenna in February 1999 at Glasgow High Court. Most people entering the Scottish prison system, guilty of a high-profile and terrible murder of an innocent woman, would keep their heads down – Drury appealed.

The grounds of his appeal were two edged. His lawyers claimed the original judge, Lord Kirkwood, should have addressed the jury differently on two points. That he didn't acknowledge the relationship between Drury and Marilyn or the prospect that Drury might have been provoked. And that was what Stuart Drury now claimed – that Marilyn McKenna had provoked him.

Drury's lawyers won the technical points and his conviction was quashed. Poor Marilyn's kids and family – they must have felt their loved one's killer had escaped justice. But the Crown and the cops weren't going to let that happen and he was sent for a retrial at Edinburgh High Court in August 2001.

Yet again, Drury was found guilty of murder and sentenced to life. Escorted to the cells in the bowels of the High Court to await the prison van, Drury pulled a makeshift knife from his trousers and slit his own throat. It wasn't the first time he'd pulled this move, of course. This time he wasn't any more successful than the earlier occasions. After having fifteen stitches inserted in the wound on his throat, Drury was escorted to Saughton Prison in Edinburgh that night to serve life in prison.

Some folk might say that Drury is clearly insane and should be in psychiatric care not jail. But the psychiatrists judged him sane and the cops believed him to be just a nuisance – before he committed that terrible murder, of course. Others would say that Stuart Drury is mad but mad with jealousy and deserves every slow minute of punishment the courts have doled out.

What is for sure is that Drury is the stalker from hell. The women of Glasgow will never be safe if he walks the streets again. *If* he walks the streets again . . . there are those who intend that that will never happen.

Marilyn McKenna had so much going for her. She'd still be alive now, with her children, her jobs and meeting her big sister for a Stress Buster on a Friday night. Still be here if only those who are paid to protect had listened . . .

THE BLOODY BLUEBELLS

They called it the Bluebell Woods or just The Bluebells to locals. At a certain time of the year, those fragile little flowers would spring from the earth, covering the ground with their bruised blue heads swaying in the most gentle of breezes. Being so close to one of the most populated parts of the city, it was a good place to go to relax, to catch your breath – or to kill.

They found her there on the ground. Alison Murray was only twenty years old but she was going places. A bright young woman, she was a biology undergraduate and no one doubted she would get her degree and live a life of middle-class comfort and academic challenge – not bad for a lassie from a struggling family in the Drumchapel scheme, a neighbourhood of Glasgow more accustomed to junkies and violent deaths than educational success.

Alison Murray was going places till they found her there in The Bluebells. Lying on the ground. Dead.

The young woman had fought and struggled for her life but she was almost naked and had been sexually assaulted. Even if she had been totally overpowered by her killer or killers, this would have taken time. Long minutes of terror and pain. Then she had been strangled with her own bra and all her hope and life were snuffed out.

It was 1986 and the people of Glasgow were appalled by this killing. She had been an innocent young woman – a serious girl who was studying hard. Just minding her own business one minute and raped and strangled the next. It was a sex killing – something we all dread because it could happen to you or yours.

It didn't take the police long to arrest two suspects – local man Brian Wilson, who was only eighteen, and Iain Murray, Alison's seventeen-year-old half-brother. A relative being accused of the murder added to the public indignation. Decent citizens struggle to comprehend men who rape and kill. To contemplate that a brother – even a half-brother – would do that to a young woman he had grown up with was well beyond the pale.

At their trial at the High Court in Glasgow in 1986, the case against both men rested on their own confessions. The cops claimed that Iain Murray, in front of his own father, Iain Murray Senior, had said, 'I done it and that's it.'

The police admitted that Iain Murray Senior had said that he couldn't remember those words but, instead, he had offered further confessional material. After Iain Murray had been arrested he had apparently said to his father, 'Brian and I were playing with each other in the woods and Alison came along and it just sort of happened.'

Brian Wilson, in a separate interview with the police, had apparently declared, 'There is nothing more I can say. We did it. She caught us playing with each other and we strangled her.'

Both of the accused had admitted the murder and the motive in almost the same terms – one to his father, the other to the cops. It was damning evidence indeed.

By 'playing with each other' Murray and Wilson had meant sexually. The two boys were masturbating each other when young Alison chanced upon them. The Bluebells wasn't just known as a breath of the country in the city. Young folk from the nearby streets such as Cloan Avenue and Southdeen Road, where Murray and Wilson stayed, would go there to drink booze, smoke drugs, sniff glue and have sex. The Bluebells was well known for it and, according to the evidence of their own statements, Murray and Wilson had gone there for sex that day.

Big sister Alison had stumbled upon Iain and Brian in a homosexual clinch. At that time and place, two young men having sex would have been deemed much worse than a man and woman having sex. To many of the public, gay encounters were still considered dirty, sleazy, something to be ashamed of. Alison Murray had threatened to tell the families of both boys. That they couldn't allow. Anything was better than being thought of as homosexual. But murder?

With such damning confessions, there was no defence possible and the trial more or less collapsed with both men being found guilty of murder on a majority verdict. Iain Murray, because of his youth, was sentenced to imprisonment without limit of time – as was the rightful sentence in 1986. Brian Wilson, being eighteen, was treated as an adult and sentenced to life.

One year later, in 1987, the two were back at court – this time on appeal. Both claimed they had confessed to the police under duress. Brian Wilson claimed that the cops had totally fabricated a statement in his name and then put him under constant pressure to sign it. Exhausted, worn out, he had eventually put his signature to the statement. 'It wasn't true – that statement,' Wilson said at the time. 'I only signed it to get the polis off my back.'

Iain Murray had famous representation that day in Ian Hamilton QC. In 1950, Hamilton had made his name as a young man when, with others, he had liberated the Stone of Destiny from underneath the Coronation Throne in Westminster Abbey.

The Stone had eventually been returned. Or had it? Controversy rages to this day about the whereabouts of real the Stone of Destiny, a potent symbol of Scottish independence. Those who know him see Ian Hamilton as being just as fiercely independent as the Scots nation has ever been.

In court in 1987, Hamilton argued that his client, Iain Murray, had been constantly provoked by the cops over whether or not he was gay. Poof, pervert, shirt-tail lifter, homo and Nancy Boy were just some of the names the police had thrown at him again and again.

'My client was questioned repeatedly on homosexual matters just to soften him up for the main event – which was to get him to confess,' claimed Hamilton. At that time and in that place, with the deep-rooted prejudices against all things gay, it made sense as a threat to any young man, apart from the most liberated.

Yet it was an audacious appeal. The common wisdom of all those appearing professionally before the courts in the 1980s was that they should never accuse the police of corruption or underhand practices, even if there was evidence – the criminal justice system in Scotland would always choose to believe the police. Some say not much has changed.

Lord Justice General Emslie, Lord Grieve and Lord Brand, hearing the appeal, judged that Murray and Wilson had made confessional statements to different police officers in different police stations at different times; and that, when compared, those statements described the same events, the same timing, the same motive.

The good judges chose not to make a judgement on the accusations against the police. Even if such pressure had been put on both Murray and Wilson, how come they both came out with confessions that matched so well? That seemed to be the point the Law Lords were making when they announced that Murray and Wilson's appeal had failed.

The two men went back to jail, probably resigned to spend much of their adult years in the protection units for 'nonces and ponces'. Then, out in Drumchapel in 1997, events took a turn for the worse.

Iain Murray Senior shot himself. Much pop psychology is spouted about suicide being a cry for help. Murray took a shotgun and blasted himself at close range. Not only did he mean to kill himself, he succeeded. Through suicide, Iain Murray Senior had avoided a scandal. His oldest son, Kenneth Murray, had accused him of sexually abusing him when a child – and not only him but his sister Alison and her half-brother Iain as well.

On their own, those facts make for another modern-day tragedy but there was more. If the original trial of Iain Murray and Brian Wilson had not gone as it did, if their confessions were accepted as having been forced out of them, if Murray Senior had been called as a witness and the allegations of him abusing his children had come out, if all that had happened, perhaps the court, the judge and the jury would have taken a different view of Alison Murray's death. Iain Murray Senior was scheduled to appear as a witness but, as was the case with many others who had been cited, he was never called. It took his suicide, eleven years later, for a crucial aspect of the truth to emerge.

Iain Murray and Brian Wilson have since served their sentences and been released from prison. At the time of writing, they have an application for an appeal before the Scottish Criminal Cases Review Commission.

The final piece of the jigsaw that was the Bluebells Murder may emerge soon. Finally, we may learn how the life of a promising and energetic young woman was ended there, the day she took a walk in the fresh air.

But The Bluebells weren't finished with murder. Not yet.

PART 5
KIDS WHO
KILL

In February 1993 – the month wee James Bulger was murdered down south – an eleven-year-old child in Aberdeen was caught trying to kill a baby in pram. The public have never heard of the Scottish case and for very good reasons.

Every year children in Scotland turn killers but there is a problem in writing about such cases. Since the Social Work (Scotland) Act was introduced in 1969, it has been deemed that children in trouble, including those who commit offences, are better treated not through the adult court system but at Children's Hearings heard by members of the Children's Panel.

A Children's Hearing is a more informal setting and Panel members are lay people, supported by professionals, who are empowered to investigate child and family issues and to make legal orders as necessary. Implicit in this law is the right of the child and his family to confidentiality.

Even murderers can be dealt with by Children's Panels. For example, if poor James Bulger had lived in Scotland, Jon Venables and Robert Thompson, the kids who killed him, would probably have been tried in court but in a court closed to the public and the media. The court's task would have been to determine guilt or innocence. Having decided the pair were guilty, they could have been referred to the Children's Panel to determine what action would be taken, such as being sent to a locked top-security residential school. Alternatively, they may have been bound over without limit of time, meaning they should be compulsorily held in a regime till it was decided that they were safe to be released. In both options the child would spend their initial time in custody in the same locked secure residential school. Either way, they would be regarded not as murderers but as children who needed care and help. They would also have certain legal rights, including the right to confidentiality.

Whether we agree with this stance or not, it means that certain murders by children cannot legally be written about to any great satisfaction since nothing about their personalities, background, motives or problems can be revealed.

The accounts that have been chosen, therefore, are of kids who killed but who are now adults – people who are now grown up, often going about their business but hiding a secret from their past – their past as kids who kill.

WASTED WARNINGS AND IDLE THREATS?

Bright eyes and a lovely laugh, the wee three-year-old was a right darling. Everyone thought so. Sometimes a handful, like all three-year-olds, but mainly a joy, like all three-year-olds. But life hadn't always been that good to him.

It was the worst of starts in life. When he was only eleven weeks old, his mother was killed in a fire. Life owed Jamie Campbell a break. Everyone thought so. Well, almost everyone.

Jamie Campbell was lucky in that he had a loving family. When his mother died in 1987, his aunt and uncle, Kim and Robert Campbell, took him to live with them and Kim became his legal guardian. With that loving care and his granny who lived near the family home in Drumchapel, life should have been good for a wee boy with the worst start in life.

Granny's garden was always a safe place for Jamie to play. It was 1990 and he was three years old, an energetic, curious, sociable wee boy. When the older boy started chatting to him and joining in his games, Jamie didn't have a problem. Why should he?

Looking out her window, Jamie's granny didn't panic when she didn't spot him first time. He'd be near the edge or chatting to some kids next door. He was a good wee boy who didn't wander. Anyway, the garden was safe place. She knew he'd be there.

Craning her neck, peering from the side of the window, she still couldn't see Jamie. Repeating the exercise at the other side of the frame, still no sign. Now she was worried.

Outside there was no sign of the boy. Now she was panicking. The best she could get from folk in the area was that he'd been playing with another boy, a good bit older than him. Just playing away happily the way Jamie did.

It wasn't long before they were searching the Bluebell Woods nearby. A lot of parents had warned heir children, especially the young ones and the daughters, from going there. Some folk thought that place was evil.

They had warned the kids ever since the day young Alison Murray's almost naked body was found. It didn't matter if it was 1990 and Alison's convicted killers had been locked up in jail for three years – that horrible sex killing had reminded the good parents of Drumchapel just what a dangerous place The Bluebells could be.

Young Jamie Campbell wouldn't go to The Bluebells. Not on his own. Everyone knew that. But that's where they found him – battered and bloody, lying underwater in a burn in the Bluebell Woods. Jamie Campbell deserved better than that. All children do.

If, four years earlier, the murder of Alison Murray had outraged the people of Drumchapel, the killing of Jamie Campbell horrified them. Who kills a sweet young toddler?

Locals feared the worst. In their opinions it had to be some sick psycho – some sleazebag of a paedophile who got his kicks from hurting wee kids. Dodgy types like that hung out at The Bluebells spying on teenagers having their first sexual fondles, flashing their penises at any female and sometimes any male. They imagined a grown man, in a manky coat, hanging around in the bushes waiting for some vulnerable wee one. No one suspected an eleven-year-old child.

The community's horror at the murder resulted in everyone racking their brains to think of anything that could help. Soon reports emerged that Jamie had been seen with a boy, who had led him out of his granny's garden. No one thought anything of it. The boy was local and Jamie seemed happy enough. They'd just thought maybe Granny had asked the kid to take Jamie up to the ice-cream van or whatever. Come to think of it now, they had been heading towards The Bluebells. They hadn't thought anything of it. Nobody blamed the silent witnesses except themselves.

The eleven-year-old was soon identified as local boy, Richard Keith. Richard was seen as a difficult child, a loner and prone to acting out. But, in an area that produced its fair share of hardened criminals even by that tender age, no one had marked Keith down as a potential killer – well, almost no one.

The cops and social workers wanted to know the how and why of the killing. How was the easiest answer to get – Richard Keith had deliberately led wee Jamie away from his grandmother's garden. When they got into the Bluebell Woods, Jamie had asked to go home. Keith had smashed his head and body with the largest boulders he could lift, thrown his body into a burn and then gone back into the housing scheme as if nothing had happened.

Richard Keith had no reason for killing Jamie. Even with the benefit of hindsight, time and gentle interviewing by experts, the boy could give no reason why he had killed the toddler.

At the High Court in Edinburgh, Richard Keith was found guilty of the culpable homicide of Jamie Campbell. The lesser conviction applied because of Keith's young age and everyone's acceptance that there was no motive in this killing. That the boy must have been behaving in a manner akin to being mentally ill – behaving in a disturbed way, beyond his control.

Only then was it revealed that, three days before, Keith had attacked another three-year-old Drumchapel child, Thomas Garrity. He had stripped Thomas, cut his body with a penknife and beaten him senseless. If that had been a warning sign that the authorities missed, there had been others. Given the personal and family problems he faced, Keith was known to social workers. Although she has never gone public and never will, one of his social workers was deeply worried about Richard Keith – so much so that she had written to her managers, drawing their attention to the inherent dangers she saw in the boy becoming violent, particularly towards much younger children.

Months before Jamie Campbell was killed, the social worker had written a report strongly recommending that Richard Keith be urgently taken into care and that he should be seen by child psychiatrists. She urged her department to send Keith to a closed residential unit in order to protect the public from him. It was a most unusual set of recommendations. Rarely will social workers pursue such restricted care arrangements for a child so young when he or she hasn't been involved in some serious offence. This worker was also known to be a radical liberal in her approach to children and was most reluctant ever to recommend that any child be removed from home. You'd think her bosses would have paid attention but, as Jamie Campbell was pulled out of the burn in the Bluebell Woods, the social worker was still waiting for a response from her department.

At eleven years of age, Richard Keith became Scotland's youngest convicted killer. Describing the murder as 'sheer wickedness', Lord Sutherland sentenced him to be detained without limit of time as befitted his age. In reality, this meant that Keith was sent to a locked residential school, Kerelaw Secure Unit in Stevenston, Ayrshire – the very same school he would have been sent to had the earlier pleas of the social worker been acted on.

Kerelaw Secure Unit contained some of the most dangerous and disturbed children in Scotland. It was what it says – a closed unit, locked. Some people saw it as little more than a jail for kids but it was a jail that tried to meet their needs while making sure the unit remained secure. Thus it had school classes, keep fit, games and films for leisure time. It had staff who were trained in child care though they carried big sets of keys on chains, much as prison officers do. Hard as the staff may have tried, it was a bleak, depressing place. What else could a place be that housed kids who have become killers, arsonists or blade merchants?

When the laws governing the sentence 'without limit of time' were changed so that a minimum time limit must be set, the trial judge, Lord Sutherland, was called on again. This time in secret.

The task of child-care units such as Kerelaw is to prepare their charges for life in the community as good citizens. As children, they have a right to privacy, regardless of what they've done. So, in secret, Lord Sutherland set Keith's minimum sentence at eight years, a figure that was likely to have been met with horror had it been announced in open court after the murder trial.

Richard Keith, meantime, was afforded privacy on other counts. In 1990, when he was nineteen, the Kerelaw Secure Unit psychologist, John Jamieson, arranged for him to carry out work placements away from Kerelaw. The idea was to help him prepare for life in the community and give the psychologist an opportunity to test his readiness for freedom.

On eight separate occasions, Richard Keith spent time in the home of Russell and Sharon Anderson. On most occasions, he played with their children, seven-year-old Kyle and four-year-old Kahli. The Andersons were good people, happy to help a young man 'who'd been in a bit of trouble'. That's all they were told – not that their guest had been a child-killing child and Scotland's youngest murderer.

In January 1999, the Parole Board, who deal with children who have committed the most serious offences as well as with adult prisoners, made a quiet decision. Richard Keith was released. Concerned members of Kerelaw staff alerted the media anonymously. They didn't break their professional code of confidentiality lightly.

'Richard Keith is a very dangerous young man,' said one. 'Most staff believe we didn't change him at all. Richard Keith will kill again.'

As is the way for people convicted of a killing, Richard Keith will be supervised for the rest of his life by social work departments. They call it life licence and failure to cooperate or falling into further trouble can result in that licence being revoked –

meaning a swift return to jail. But having the power to supervise is one thing, how it is used is another question entirely.

Months after Richard Keith was released, he proudly told friends that his girlfriend was pregnant. She was a girl he'd met while he had been in Kerelaw Secure Unit – someone who had problems of her own. They wouldn't be allowed to live together till she was eighteen but that wasn't too far away.

Three years later, it was discovered that, with the support of his supervising social workers, Richard Keith had got a job in Ardentinny Outdoor Centre, Dunoon. The centre attracts thousands of visitors a year, mainly school parties, mainly children. It is also based in the middle of a vast tract of hills, lochs and forest. Everywhere you look you see trees and, at the right time of year, bluebells abound – the kind of place someone could get lost, accidentally or deliberately.

Back in Glasgow, a young man struggles to sleep most nights and, when he does, the nightmares come. He is eighteen years old now but Thomas Garrity was only three when he last saw Richard Keith. When Keith left him naked, stabbed and beaten on the ground. Bad as the memory of that beating remains, it's the words that haunt young Thomas.

As Keith walked away he had turned to the barely conscious toddler and warned, 'I'm going to come back. Come back and finish you off.'

THE REVOLVING DOOR
TO HELL

It was the hottest day of the summer and Jimmy and Elizabeth Currie intended to take full advantage of it. They'd been married for forty-seven years and still loved each other's company. A stroll into the city centre for some shopping would be lovely. Or would it?

Glasgow in the sun is wondrous. Especially the city centre where the old stone buildings with their ornate carvings compete with high spires and steeples so beautiful you catch even locals shading their eyes to look up again for the umpteenth time.

One whiff of the sun and Glasgow folk ditch the drab cold-weather gear and transform into brightly coloured butterflies floating around, sucking in the rays. The mood lightens, camaraderie hangs in the air and you can almost hear a collective sigh that it's good to be alive and even better to be in Glasgow.

Down by the River Clyde as it slices through the city is best. Jewels glitter in the magic detail of the old stone bridges up and down river, winking at you and whispering, 'Are we no' just the bee's knees?' And they are.

On the riverbank walkways, sweat-damp joggers dodge round courting couples strolling hand-in-hand oblivious that there's anyone else in the world. The break-out teams from the offices sitting on the grass. Men with their ties and jackets cast off, sleeves rolled up. Women, their top buttons undone, shoes off and skirts pulled high. Giving the sun every chance to give their skin a friendly kiss, add a little happy colour to match their mood. Sipping cool drinks and nibbling at sandwiches, wishing every lunchtime could be just like this.

Then there's the river itself. Rolling slowly by to the sea. No need to hurry. It knows where it's going. It has always known where it's going. Besides it's too hot to rush. The experience of age.

Just like Jimmy and Elizabeth Currie. Him sixty-eight, her sixty-seven strolling through their city, as familiar to them as their own faces. As familiar as each other's faces, they'd been together that long. Yet, after all those years, Jimmy and Elizabeth were insepa-rable. They went everywhere together by choice, not force of habit. On the odd occasion, they'd do something separately – like Elizabeth going to the bingo – but Jimmy would get the family pet dog on the lead and stroll down with her to the bingo hall. When it was finished, there he'd be waiting for her and he'd get a big smile for his efforts.

Jimmy and Elizabeth didn't make a big song and dance about it but it was plain to anyone who knew them that theirs was a very special love story. A love that had lasted almost half a century.

They'd had a good day's shopping in the city centre and were heading for their home at Waddell Court in the Gorbals. No bus for them. They'd just walk down to the River Clyde and cross the narrow suspension bridge and after that it would be a short stroll to their home.

As ever, Jimmy was being the gentleman and carrying the heavy carrier bag full of their shopping. Maybe they'd stopped halfway across the bridge and stood and looked down the river. On a sunny day like that, the big crane down river looked magnificent on the blue skyline. Sometimes, a bit farther down, small foreign ships would dock. Then there was the berth for the steamship *The Waverley*. Older Glaswegians never tired of seeing that old girl. Maybe they just kept going. The suspension bridge did attract some characters all the time – and more so when the weather was good. Just jakies drinking their fortified wine or maybe a homeless guy or two looking for a couple of coins. All harmless really but it was always wise to watch out for trouble.

They had crossed the bridge and decided to take the Clyde Walkway home along the river. It's something they'd never do after dark when dangerous characters would hang around but it was sunny and there were plenty of people around so it had to be safe.

Jimmy Currie kept an eye out for any worrying signs in front of him. You never knew when some drunk was going to appear and pester you. But he didn't have eyes in the back of his head.

Behind the Curries, a small-built, skinny young man was attracting the attention of others. Weaving from side to side, bumping into pedestrians, he was clearly drunk, drugged or probably both. In spite of the hot weather, he was wearing a canary-yellow anorak with the zip and the hood up. In the sweltering heat of that peaceful afternoon he stuck out like a rain cloud.

As the Curries reached some steps, they let go of each other's hands so, ever the gentleman, Jimmy could set off up in front, lugging the shopping. That's when he heard the shouting and turned.

There was his wife Elizabeth struggling with a young guy in a yellow anorak who was yanking at her handbag with one hand and waving a knife in the other. Elizabeth was having none of it and was holding on fast. Before Jimmy Currie could get to Elizabeth to help, her attacker stuck the knife into her temple. A second later, Jimmy was there swinging his carrier bag at his wife's attacker. The carrier split, spilling the shopping and the man in the yellow anorak was sprinting off, Elizabeth Currie's handbag in his mitt. Jimmy was on his tail but the younger man soon left him trailing and he gave up the chase to help his wife. A passing off-duty nurse was already there tending to her.

Rushed to hospital, Elizabeth Currie was found to be in a coma. A scan revealed that she had bled extensively into her brain. There was nothing the doctors could do. Two days later, on 21 June 2000, Elizabeth Currie died from her injuries.

Murder hunt on.

Elizabeth Currie had been robbed of her life for a mere £30. Cut down in broad daylight on a happy summer's day as her constant companion of forty-seven years looked on in helpless horror.

Cops are meant to be impartial but they are only human. There are certain crimes and victims that make them feel as we feel – disgusted and outraged. Certain crimes and victims that move them to make extra-special efforts. This was one of those crimes, Elizabeth Currie was one of those victims.

In fact, they didn't need to pull out too many stops. The mugger turned murderer had drawn a great deal of attention as he had run away. That canary-yellow anorak wasn't exactly great camouflage. Nor was the knife he kept in his hand as he sprinted. Nor the fact that he ran weaving, stoned out of his box.

The first cops on the scene were given pointers by a number of people. The trail led to nearby Ballater Street, to the front of an office belonging to – of all organisations – the Procurator Fiscal, the prosecution service in Scotland. There on the ground, they found the murder knife still covered in Elizabeth Currie's blood. A little farther on, in a lane, they found Elizabeth's handbag – minus the £30, of course.

The knife would prove to have some of the killer's blood as well as the victim's and the handbag would be covered with his DNA, fingerprints and other forensic evidence. The cops had solid evidence against the killer. All they had to do now was catch him and, as it turned out, it didn't take long.

One group who had seen the running, obviously intoxicated young guy had approached him. He had explained his distressed, blood-smeared state by saying, 'A've been involved in an incident.' Accurate, for sure, but, if the witnesses had only known what kind of incident, they might well have nabbed him right there and then.

As it was the cops soon tracked down the guy in the canary-yellow anorak. He turned out to be Gary McGowan, a fifteen-year-old child.

By the time Gary McGowan was called to trial he had turned sixteen years of age and would be dealt with by the adult criminal justice system. There are those, especially among the police, who would have been pleased at that. At least now he'd be punished properly for a terrible crime, they'd reckon.

Gary McGowan's trial in January 2001 was a quick affair because he pled guilty to the charges of murder, robbery and assault. Under these circumstances, no evidence or witnesses are necessary. It's straight to sentencing.

The prosecution wanted the heaviest possible punishment, citing the horror and cruelty of the murder. McGowan's own lawyer, the youngest QC in Scotland, Paul McBride, acknowledged that he wouldn't, indeed couldn't, plead much in mitigation for his client such was the awful nature of his crime – although he did add that McGowan had taken vodka, Valium and fortified wine on the day of the murder and that he owed drug dealers £1,000.

Then the judge, Lord Johnstone, made an unprecedented apology to the victim's family. Sentencing guidelines for people McGowan's age had been laid down in 1999. That meant the maximum he could sentence the young killer to was twelve years, meaning that McGowan would likely be free after only six years.

Having passed sentence, Lord Johnstone then said that he hoped no one would think the pre-determined maximum sentence was his 'idea of an appropriate sentence'. The message was clear – he would have locked him up for decades if he could.

Not surprisingly, Elizabeth Currie's family were outraged and angered by how short the period of imprisonment was to be. McGowan might well have been legally a child at the time of the offences but a lethal child nevertheless and now a legal adult. Jimmy Currie later said, 'He knew what he was doing that day. Why didn't he just cut her fingers to make her let go of the handbag? He knew what he was doing. I hope he dies in jail.'

The Crown agreed that the sentence was too light and took the rare step of appealing against it. We have become used to appeals being made by those who believe they have been unjustly convicted or too severely punished. Appeals to increase a sentence are also possible but not nearly as common.

In July 2001, the Appeal Court decided that McGowan should spend a minimum of ten years in prison. It was in the right direction for the grieving family but it seems sure that they'd still not consider it enough.

Only after McGowan's trial did details emerge about his past. He'd been a troubled child from infancy. At the age of only four years old, he had stabbed a nurse for no apparent reason. From then on, his behaviour had become increasingly unpredictable and violent.

In spite of being taken into care and spending much of his childhood in residential schools, he slipped deeper and deeper into trouble. By the age of eleven, he was hooked on drugs and booze and was associating with dangerous low-life types in his home patch of the Gorbals.

It was then revealed that McGowan had been in a secure residential school but had been released in March 2000, just months before the murder. When challenged, the Social Work Department admitted that this was true. Then they revealed that they had strongly recommended that he be kept on in secure accommodation, for fear that he would become involved in some serious offence.

Three lay members of the Children's Panel had decided otherwise and set Gary McGowan free. Back home, he was now heavily addicted to drugs and booze and totally out of control. He had told Dorothy McGowan, his despairing mother, 'Someone is going to die.'

Gary McGowan didn't start his sentence for murder in adult prison. Because of his age and his problems, he was sent to a secure school – the very type of place he had been freed from a short time before. Freed to commit murder.

After trying and failing for all his childhood to make him into a good citizen, it has to be asked if the system will work for Gary McGowan this time?

THE CARING KIND

Coping with disability is difficult enough, even with the support of a husband or wife, grown-up kids or a large, but close, extended family. Living on your own with disability can be exhausting, lonely and dangerous. Luckily, Catriona McLean had neighbours who cared. Catriona, a fifty-five-year-old unmarried woman, suffered from cerebral palsy. In almost constant pain, she was a small, brave woman who rarely complained but, over the years, her condition had got worse. Now she walked with a Zimmer frame and, for most of the time, she was a prisoner in her home.

. Her world was a small flat in Muiryfauld Drive, Parkhead, an area better known for Celtic Football Club and their stadium which is also known as Parkhead – though followers often preferred to call it Paradise. The football stadium could have been on the dark side of the moon as far as Catriona was concerned – as could the shops, the chemist and her doctor's surgery. That's where her friends and neighbours came in.

Want an example of how caring and selfless the good folk of Glasgow can be? Look no further than the life of Catriona McLean. Look at the ordinary, working-class, often poor and struggling people around her who, in spite of their own problems and pressures, gave her help. Gave her their time. A wee bit of their hearts. Without fuss, without pity. Never looking for thanks.

These good folks knew how hard it was just to get by. How

much harder must it be with cerebral palsy, nagging pain and a Zimmer frame? Simple as that.

Some of them thought that Catriona's life expectancy wasn't good. With all her health problems, they wouldn't be surprised if, one day, they'd walk in on bad news – their friend still in her bed, eyes staring wide open but lifeless, her pain over, her struggle to move a few feet ended forever. They half-expected the worst every day. What they didn't expect was murder.

Three days after Christmas 2001, a female neighbour found her on the floor of her home. This had happened before, when Catriona had tumbled and couldn't get back up. But, this time, she wasn't looking up with tears of frustration glistening in her eyes. She was sprawled flat out, quite still, with a duvet and pillow covering her head. Dead.

Scene-of-crime cops and forensic staff ascertained that Catriona had been stabbed and probably smothered. Also some kind of liquid had been thrown over her. More thorough tests over time confirmed that, although she had been stabbed, it was smothering that had been the cause of death. But they also revealed something else – Catriona's genital area had been damaged. She had been raped or at least sexually assulted.

The cops were looking for a sex killer – someone sick enough to rape and kill a lonely disabled women.

The cops had problems. Numerous local people were known to go in and out of Catriona's home to help her. As they did door-to-door interviews, names came up of the people who had been seen going into her home. But then they had a reason to – they were helping the woman. Nevertheless, the police had to consider the prospect that it was someone known to Catriona. Overnight, all her good Samaritans became suspects in her murder.

The cops' other problem was that the victim's state of incapacity was well known in the area. Anyone out there with the inclination would know she was a sitting target for their sick lusts. Also, Parkhead is a large, densely populated area – that was a hell of a lot of potential suspects.

Yet the cops also had a strength. Catriona was practically housebound. No one was going to take her out of her home, murder her then bring her back – always a highly disorientating influence on any murder inquiry and a sure way to get caught. Anyway, why bother? She was trapped in her home and practically defenceless. So her small flat had to hold some clues to identify the murderer.

The scene-of-crime and forensic folk went through that flat even more thoroughly than usual – and that was saying something. They were convinced the killer's identity was there, some place in that flat. All they had to do was find it.

As expected, fingerprints were found in the flat belonging to different people but one set drew their attention more than most because of their position through the house and near where Catriona's body was found.

As the forensic folk were working their magic, detectives were talking to the good-Samaritans-turned-suspects. One who was beginning to draw their attention was Richard Clark, the nephew of the woman who had found Catriona dead. Only fourteen years old, outwardly, Clark was an unremarkable teenager in every respect. From nearby Caroline Street, Clark was a kid who some local people thought highly of because he did help Catriona on a regular basis. Not many teenagers make the time to care for others. He'd been in trouble a couple of times for fights and referred for background reports but they appeared to be minor incidents. Besides, compared with the guys his age who ran with the local gangs, his fights were nothing at all. He appeared to be just an average teenager – not one rolling fast towards a career in crime.

But then, the cops knew that sex killers are very often mundane in every other aspect of life and, sure enough, the worrying set of prints matched Clark's. When questioned about this, Clark denied being in the flat on the day of the murder but he didn't deny being in the flat plenty of times before. He was one of Ms McLean's helpers and often ran errands for her. His explanation was perfectly valid, of course, but the detectives were left with a bad feeling. They call it suspicion.

Then the forensic bods made another breakthrough. From early on, they had been intrigued by the fluid over Catriona's corpse. Tests indicated that it had been sprayed over the body and surrounding floor area. What it was and why someone should do that were still questions they couldn't answer. All they knew for sure was that it had occurred after Catriona had been killed. Then they spotted the footprint.

Close to the body, on a linoleum-covered area of the floor that had been caught by the sprayed fluid, they found the print of a training shoe. With modern lights and photographic techniques, they were able to take accurate images of that print and they were in luck.

Shoes can throw up all sorts of unique features. We all walk differently, putting more weight on different parts of the feet, rolling on our heels, leaning down on the ball or whatever. The longer a shoe has been worn by the same person, the more distinctive the print it produces. This training shoe had been worn long enough. The footprint was in a position that the killer would have stepped on to leave the flat. It was a crucial clue.

Going back to the fingerprints, the cops were now particularly interested in one set on a doorframe. Close to where Catriona's body had lain, the fingerprints' position was exactly right if the killer had grabbed the doorframe to support himself as he had stepped over the corpse on the floor. It was another crucial clue.

It didn't take long for the cops to confirm that the finger- and footprints belonged to same person – fourteen-year-old Richard Clark.

Charged with murder, Clark denied killing Catriona McLean. His repeated explanation that he had been in her flat often to run errands for her didn't wash any more. Now they had evidence that he had been in there after she had been killed. He had no explanation for that.

By the time Richard Clark went on trial in 2003, he was sixteen years of age. Facing not only a murder charge but also one of rape, he continued to declare his innocence on all counts.

The case against him leaned very heavily on the foot- and fingerprints. In the courtroom, the cops carried out a re-enactment of the murder scene, indicating how they believed the prints were made by the killer as Catriona lay dead on the floor. That was impressive but Clark had another problem of his own making – his mouth.

Since being charged, social workers had been working with him closely. They reported that, on two separate occasions when discussing the murder charges, he had said, 'I'll no' do it again.'

When confronted with this at the trial, Clark simply denied ever saying it.

Friends of Clark's also gave testimony that he had told them that he had been in the flat the day of the killing. He denied that this was true; and denied saying it to others..

With no murder weapon, no witness, no history of motive and an average teenage kid in the dock, the jury was faced with a difficult decision. Though the rape charges had since been reduced to indecent assault, with the murder charge of a frail, disabled woman, the jury was facing one of the weightiest civic duties imaginable. Perhaps the words of the prosecutor, Murdo McLeod, rang in their ears as they debated the evidence for and against. 'It would be too much of a coincidence if someone else was the killer,' McLeod had said.

When the jury of fifteen people returned, they were not all of the same mind but this is allowed in Scots Law. By a majority verdict, Richard Clark was found guilty of being a fourteen-year-old sex killer. As the verdict hung in the air, Clark groaned, put his head in his hands and promptly collapsed.

By the time of sentencing one month after the guilty verdict, Richard Clark was still declaring his innocence. Normally his lawyer would, at that stage, make some plea in mitigation in an attempt to have the judge give a lesser sentence than he might otherwise. To do that effectively, his client has to accept guilt. Not in this case. Clark's QC, Jack Davidson, did his best but was more or less left telling the judge that Clark didn't see himself as having any problems.

Lord Wheatley sentenced Clark without limit of time, the appropriate sentence for a child found guilty of murder in Scotland. However, he was also obliged to set a minimum period of incarceration and in this case decided on eight years.

The sentence wasn't warmly welcomed by some folk back in Clark's home patch of Parkhead – particularly not among those who knew Catriona McLean well. One of her elderly friends said, 'Life was never easy for Catriona. Then someone she trusted made her death hell as well. Richard Clark should rot in jail forever.'

Richard Clark could be back in Glasgow a free man by the age of twenty-four years.

CHILD'S PLAY

Curry – the favourite food in Glasgow. Ask any Glaswegian to list what is good about their city and most will claim it has the best curry houses in the land. Whether that's true or not, you'll have to decide for yourself. But what is for certain is that even curries can be dangerous sometimes.

All he wanted was some takeaway grub – curry, of course. It was only a short walk from his house so he'd nip down there and pick some up, bring it back home and eat it front of the TV – a quiet night in.

Other people, outsiders, might think twice of walking through Possil – not him. It was his area, after all, and, if you can't feel safe on your own patch, where can you feel safe? After all, Stephen Mulhall wasn't a troublemaker and he wasn't a kid. He was thirty-seven years old and all he wanted was a curry for his evening meal. Not that he was naïve – far from it. His family had suffered on Glasgow's violent streets.

Five years before, in 1999, his younger brother Derek, only twenty-two, had been knifed to death. Just some stupid argument on the street and someone had stuck a blade into Derek's heart. Twenty-two? His whole life ahead of him one minute and snatched away the next. What a waste.

You can't live in Possil and not know how violent the streets could be, that's for sure. But Stephen was thirty-seven years old – a grown man almost at that middle-aged mark of forty and he

179

didn't have any truck with any of that street crap. It was mainly the druggies and their dealers sorting out their disputes. Or young kids, hanging around in the pretend gangs that seemed to have flourished again lately. But that was child's play – nothing to do with him.

All Stephen Mulhall went out for that night in January 2005 was a curry. One minute he was walking up the road minding his own business, the next he heard a shout, 'YOUNG POSSO FLEET.'

Then they came at him, team-handed, out of nowhere – young guys, skinny wee kids. No threat really but there was just too many of them. Swarming into him. Thumping him with things. Mulhall hit the deck, knocked over by the weight of bodies. They just kept coming at him. Hitting him with objects. Knocking him back down when he tried to get up. One kid lifted his silver scooter smashing it down on to Stephen's skull. A scooter – that's how young they were.

It was just too much and he passed out.

Somehow, he managed to stagger back home – bruised and bleeding but safe. He'd got a hell of a rap on the skull though and his head ached. Nothing for it but to lie down in bed. Maybe sleep. Maybe feel better in the morning.

They were just kids after all.

The next day, Stephen Mulhall was found dead on the floor of his bedroom. A post-mortem would show that his skull had been fractured in the attack. During the night, he had suffered a massive blood clot on the brain and died.

Four youths were originally charged with his murder. Charges have been dropped against three of the accused. One boy alone now faces sentencing. At the time of writing, he is fifteen years of age.

Gangs and Glasgow go hand in hand – have done ever since the late nineteenth century up to the present day. There are some who would romanticise this connection as in the good old Billy Boys and the Norman Conks. Those two teams are ancient history from before World War Two so it's safe for us to look back on them as we do on all bloody history. But that's all it is – history.

Stephen Mulhall's life and death are the true face of gangs in Glasgow today. We don't look back at that – we look over our shoulder and we look out. That's what he'd warn us to do.

MASTER HYDE?

What is it about buses? Never arriving on time. Usually late but occasionally so early they're gone by the time we go to catch them. How often do we end up waiting at a bus stop when we should have been long gone on our way? How often are we grateful for some friendly chat to while away the boring, wasted minutes?

That's what James Herd was doing on Gartloch Road around 8 p.m. one day in March 2003 on his home patch of Garthamlock. Garthamlock is in the east end of Glasgow and part of that sector some people call the Bandit Lands. The highest crime and poverty levels in the city and among the highest in Europe are there. Not the kind of place you'd choose to move to but locals love it. Locals feel safe.

Twenty-seven-year-old James Herd was chatting to two women at the bus stop. Relaxed, unperturbed, he was just being friendly. It isn't on record what they were talking about. They were just passing the time of day so it probably wasn't important. It was about to become even less important.

The metal pole came crashing down on the back of his skull. Herd's knees buckled and he fell flat on the ground. He didn't have a chance. The women screamed and saw a boy they recognised from Gartloch Road. It was Thomas Shields, who lived nearby, and he was only fifteen years old. Shields raised the pole high into the air and smashed it down on James Herd's head again.

'STOP!' One of the terrified women somehow managed to find her voice.

The attacker didn't even look at her or hesitate but lifted the pole high and smashed it down on James Herd's head again.

'YOU'RE GOING TO KILL HIM! STOP. PLEASE STOP,' screamed the woman.

He didn't.

Each thud made a dull, sickening thump as the pole battered into James Herd's prone and broken body. Then, just as suddenly as the attack had started, it stopped.

Thomas Shields, the young assailant, walked off. Farther up the road he threw the pole away and continued walking. Looking down at the bloody and still body of the young man they had just been chatting to a few minutes before, the women were in shocked panic. They didn't notice the attacker stop, turn and head back their way.

Shields walked quickly up to James Herd still lying on the ground where he had left him. Standing up close with his feet together, Shields jumped high in the air landing his full weight on James Herd's head. Still not finished, he stepped up for another leap.

Just then a bus arrived. As the driver approached he saw the small group of people at the bus stop and a young guy jumping on what appeared to be a bundle of rubbish.

'Bloody vandals!' is what the driver might well have thought. 'Scattering rubbish in their own neighbourhood. How stupid can you get?' Then he saw that the 'rubbish' was a human being.

In all, Thomas Shields jumped four times on James Herd's head before he was stopped. But the damage had been done – James Herd was already dead.

In the Bandit Lands, many people are reluctant to go to court as witnesses – particularly for the prosecution. The view is that they shouldn't help the police ever – that such matters should be sorted out between themselves on the street. Not this time. At his trial for murder in February 2004, the two women, the bus driver and other witnesses came forward – such was the horror and outrage of this motiveless killing.

Shields was found guilty of murder and was held on remand for a few weeks in order that background reports be prepared. Such reports are required by law when someone is about to be sentenced to prison for the first time and are usually called for whenever someone is convicted of a serious offence. In the eyes of the law, nothing is more serious than murder.

At the High Court in Edinburgh, the formidable former Lord Advocate, Lord Hardie presided over the sentencing. He was not a happy man. The social work background report on Thomas Shields concluded that probation or community service would be an appropriate disposal for that bloody, unprovoked murder. No surprise that Lord Hardie slated the report as 'a waste of public money' and reminded the court that Shields had been found guilt of a 'vicious, brutal, persistent and unprovoked attack on an innocent man'. Besides, the law demanded that there was only one sentence that could be given for murder – prison.

Shields' lawyer Kirsty Hood QC then pled in mitigation. It seems that, by the age of fifteen, the boy had a serious addiction to alcohol. On the day in question, he had drunk a large amount of vodka and claimed he now realised that booze changed his personality, inclining him towards mindless violence. He also publicly stated his regret at murdering James Herd.

Kirsty Hood then urged Lord Hardie not to give her client such a long sentence that he would think he had been 'written off by society'. Lord Hardie sentenced Thomas Shields to a minimum of eighteen years in prison. It is a long sentence and will be a hard road for Thomas Shields, rife with the dangers of violence and drug addiction. Yet Thomas Shields could be free by the age of thirty-four years. Still a young man, he'll be just a little older than James Herd on the day he was chatting at a bus stop – the day he battered him to death.

PART 6
THRILL
KILLERS

Killers kill for all sorts of reasons. Anger, fear, lust, greed, power –
the list goes on and on – but the ones we all fear most, the ones
who cause most dread, are those who kill for thrills.

Some of the murders covered elsewhere in this book were
worthy of consideration for this section. Certain players in organised crime were infamous for not only using violence for business
but also enjoying perpetrating the violence as well. These are
fewer in number than the stereotypes created in fiction would
have us believe.

Robbers, gang members, femmes fatales, kids who kill – all
these categories include some murderers who were thrilled by
their ultimate act. Most had other motives for the murders,
though, even if that was simply behaviour most of us would consider deranged. The thrill killers that truly frighten people are
those who simply kill for that thrill.

Here are a few examples of just those folk and their victims, who
found themselves in the wrong place at the wrong time with the
wrong people – the thrill killers.

DOGGING DAYS
AND DEADLY NIGHTS

It was a chilly night and a total loss. Up there on the isolated countryside of the Cathkin Braes, it could be lonely and bleak. That's why they went there, of course – the men and women willing to put on sex shows in one of the car parks. But no one had shown that night. He was the only watcher with nothing to watch. Then he found the corpse.

It was a man, tall and heavily built. That much was obvious even as he lay flat out on the ground on his back. His eyes were staring wide open and he was drenched in blood. He was dead all right.

James McLanaghan knew what he was – a voyeur. He'd got into the habit a few years earlier through an internet club that arranged such meetings when he was working in London. It was all about consenting adults, sometimes even husbands and wives. Nothing illegal about it and nothing to be ashamed of. Nothing to hide as far as he was concerned. James McLanaghan knew what he was – a voyeur – but that didn't make him a bad man. He didn't hesitate to contact the cops.

If McLanaghan had taken a more secretive approach to his hobby, then it might have been days, maybe even weeks, before they discovered the body. As it was, the cops were on the scene not long after they reckoned the man had been killed. They spotted another clue on the way up the long, winding, hilly road to the Cathkin Braes. Smoke was belching from nearby – maybe four or five miles away – but the flames and grey-white billows of smoke could be clearly seen from high on the braes. A radio call to colleagues and they'd deal with it. Probably just some kids torching a bin, the cops thought. It will have nothing to do with the body.

They quickly ascertained that the man was dead and that it looked like he'd been stabbed more than once. As they waited for more suits and the scene-of-crime guys to arrive, they turned their attention to James McLanaghan. Just because the guy had reported the crime, it didn't mean he was above suspicion. Being up at Cathkin Braes late at night was a bit suspicious to say the least. The cops knew that was where the so-called doggers met. It was a place for thrill-seekers with particular tastes. As well as the watchers, people wanting to have secretive sex would also use it as a meeting place – men and women, women and women and, especially, men and men. Had that been the reason those two were there? The victim and the reporter of the crime? The cops wondered if it was the result of a lovers' tiff.

Their colleagues who were checking the fire radioed in to say that it was a car – a red Hyundai Accent – in a cemetery near Cambuslang and it looked like it had been torched. That usually meant it had been stolen for a joyride by some kids who had then set it ablaze to cover the evidence or, more likely, out of sheer badness. At most, it might have been stolen for some robbery then set on fire to destroy fingerprint and DNA evidence.

When the police carried out the routine checks on the ID of the body, the dead man was found to be one Gordon Gibson, a forty-four-year-old operations manager for a security firm, Westguard Securities. That set the cops thinking right away. According to the newspapers, there had been a turf war going on in some sectors of that business. The police didn't have much evidence of that and had written it off as imaginative journalists just trying to sell more papers but maybe they'd been right all along.

McLanaghan, who had reported the body, claimed not to know the dead man and the police had to admit he was convincing, giving off all the right signals. He openly admitted to having gone up to Cathkin Braes that night on the off-chance he'd see some dogging. There were quite number of bored housewives from the south side of Glasgow and nearby Paisley who'd often turn up and happily strip off. Then they'd have sex with some man, sometimes more than one, and didn't care who was watching. Cathkin Braes was the top venue for that kind of thrill.

The cops might not approve of McLanaghan's sexual habits but they were becoming convinced that he knew nothing about the dead man. Just then they got a call from their colleagues about the car. It hadn't been reported stolen as they first assumed. It was registered to a Glasgow company, Westguard Securities and was the car of their operations manager, the selfsame Gordon Gibson. A short while later, just as the pathologist informed them that he had been stabbed twenty-one times in the back, the arms and the face, they found out that Gibson was an ex-cop. This case wasn't as straightforward as they'd first thought.

It was November 2001 and Gibson had left the police almost ten years earlier. Married for eighteen years and the father of two kids, it seemed a strange move. He had only been a beat bobby but the wages were good and he could have retired on a decent pension when he was still young enough to take on another job.

An examination of his old police file indicated that there had been some personal problems just before Gibson had left the cops. There had been some kind of snooping incident, a peeping Tom. Not that Gibson had been found guilty of that but apparently some of his bosses thought he was.

Police forces everywhere are the leakiest, most vindictive bunch of men you'll ever find. It was no different with Strathclyde Police. A couple of days after Gibson's body was found, newspapers splashed with headlines about 'GAY COP KILLED BY LOVER', quoting an unnamed police source. They went on to call Gibson a 'disgraced ex-cop'. No one seemed to give a thought to his grieving wife and two teenage daughters who were bereft at the death of a man they loved and, on top of that, had to cope with headlines like those.

Reports came in that Gibson's car, distinctive because of the Westguard Securities logo on the side, was seen in Cathkin Road close to where he had been found earlier that night. There was an argument going on between him and somebody in a larger car – a 4 x 4, the witness thought. Gordon Gibson had left work that night at 10.30 p.m. and was found dead forty minutes later. Had the witness seen Gibson with his killer?

The cops thought so. They soon tracked down the car and found that three Glasgow men had been in it that night. William Wilson, Stephen Bates and Carl Anderson, all twenty-one years old, were in trouble.

By the time of their trial in late spring 2002, the three accused had turned on each other. Carl Anderson turned Queen's evidence and was granted immunity from prosecution for murder. Even a charge of attempting to pervert the course of justice by torching Gibson's car was dropped. With immunity from prosecution, Anderson gave his account of the events of that night. He claimed that there had been an argument between Gibson and the other two from their cars. The three of them had followed Gibson into the car park at Cathkin Braes.

According to Anderson, when Gibson parked his car, Bates got out of his and, pulling a knife from a pocket in the car door, he slashed one of the tyres of Gibson's motor. Gibson leapt from his car, argued with Bates and grabbed him in a bear hug. Then, Anderson claimed, William Wilson came up behind Gibson and stabbed him repeatedly.

Gordon Gibson was a big man. Standing at six foot six and weighing in at twenty-two stones, he fought for his life and took a lot of killing. Whoever had killed Gibson had ferociously stabbed him many times.

Dr Marjory Black, the pathologist who had examined Gordon Gibson's body, confirmed his struggle for life. He had nine wounds to his stomach and chest. Five wounds to his arm – one here was so fierce it had gone right through as he had tried in vain to defend himself. But the final horror was that he had a total of seven knife wounds to his head and face. Gordon Gibson had fought for life all right.

A deep wound to his heart had done for Gordon Gibson – he died within minutes of the attack ending. The pathologist was clear that he had struggled manfully, fending off blows with his left arm – the side that had suffered most of the damage. When asked if this indicated how he had been attacked or by how many men, Dr Black said, 'It seems clear that these wounds were consistent with him trying to defend himself as he was being attacked from behind and from his left side.'

The good doctor's report was consistent with what QE (Queen's evidence) witness Carl Anderson had said but it wasn't good enough. When an accused turns QE and is granted immunity from prosecution, it leaves the way open for his former co-accused to take the line of blaming him for the crime. That's exactly what Stephen Bates did so it was his word against Anderson's.

In the event, the trial judge intervened and determined that there was insufficient evidence against Bates. All charges against him were dropped. If that wasn't a big enough calamity for the prosecution case, a problem was identified with one juror and the judge decided that trial had to be abandoned.

Two months later, they reconvened at the High Court but this time only William Wilson stood accused of murder. In the dock, Wilson looked frail and ill – as well he might. If he was found guilty, it was more than likely that he'd be looking at a minimum of twenty years in jail. The criminal justice system in Scotland doesn't take kindly to anyone killing cops – even ex-cops.

McLanaghan took the stand again, openly admitting his sexual peccadilloes and describing how he found Gordon Gibson's body that night.

Gordon Gibson's widow, Susan, also took the stand. Now was her chance to set the record straight. Her husband had been depressed in his last days at the police. It had been brought on by working at the mortuary at the time when the victims of the Lockerbie massacre were brought in. In 1989, Pan Am Flight 103 had been bombed over Lockerbie, killing 270 people. For weeks, the victims' remains had been being scraped off the ground. That was the horror Gordon Gibson had to cope with. He wasn't the only public servant to pay a hefty price for helping in the aftermath of those mass murders. Heroes all.

According to Susan Gibson, her husband had been clinically depressed and remained so for some time later. Even at the time of his murder, he had been on medication for depression and often felt tired. Sometimes he stopped off on the way home from a long hard day at work to 'refresh himself'. The Cathkin Braes was en route from his work in Glasgow to their home in East Kilbride.

Represented by the bold Donald Findlay QC, William Wilson denied all the allegations against him. Instead, he now claimed he saw the other two men – Bates and Anderson – fighting with Gibson. It was a good defence. Anderson had immunity from prosecution so couldn't be charged. Bates had been tried and found not guilty and couldn't be charged again either. It came down to a simple judgement at the end of the day – Wilson's word against Anderson's word.

When the jury returned with a verdict of not guilty, Wilson turned, beaming and winking at his friends and family. Close to them sat Susan Gibson and her two teenage daughters, weeping their eyes out.

There is no closure in a murder case. The killer of your loved one being jailed for life doesn't bring the pain and hollowness of grief to an end. But it is a sense of progress to know that callous murderers haven't been allowed to take the life of one you hold dear and just walk away. Susan Gibson and her girls will never be allowed even that feeling.

After the trial, Gordon Gibson's father, Jack Gibson, spoke out angrily. He may have been seventy-seven years old but he'd lost none of his fight or his sense of injustice. Outside the High Court he said, 'There has been a complete miscarriage of justice and I blame the Crown.' He meant the prosecutors, the administration, the ones who do deals with the accused and grant them immunity from prosecution.

'The Crown should have put all three of them on trial together instead of using one to try to convict the other two,' he went on. 'There is something fundamentally wrong in this case.'

Gordon Gibson's murder will go unpunished forever.

LIFE IMITATES ART

It took a great deal to shock William Beggs – after all, he was the 'Limbs in the Loch Killer' who had raped young Barry Wallace then killed him, chopping up his body and scattering it in different places. But, sitting in his cell at Peterhead Prison, the letter shocked him all right.

The letter was from a young guy serving four years in Glenochil Prison for drug dealing. It said that his crime was 'far superior' to that committed by Beggs. That was a first for The Limbs in the Loch Killer.

The week before, a limbless, headless torso had been found on the banks of the River Clyde at Erskine, a few miles downstream from Glasgow. The letter boasted of the killing and pointed out that the victim's head had not been found. That made him a better killer than Beggs so the gay psychopath should acknowledge that, admit it and pay homage to him – just like other serial killers did to Hannibal Lecter in *The Silence of the Lambs*. It was a clue about the mind of the writer.

The letter writer in question hadn't been charged with any murder . . . yet. It was March 2002 and the Glasgow cops had just realised there had been a gruesome killing on their patch. They were finding body parts around Glasgow as well as on the banks of the River Clyde near Erskine, where a massive bridge spans the river. This type of thing meant only one thing – the forensic bods had to do their job first.

The body was eventually identified as that of Daniel Hutcheson from Govan in Glasgow. They would have been in real difficulties if they knew nothing about the dead man but they knew a hell of a lot about twenty-three-year-old Daniel and his family – especially his cousin, Christopher Hutcheson.

Christopher Hutcheson had been a hard man and a drug dealer from an early age. Though only twenty-two in 2002, he had forged a fierce reputation for himself around Ibrox, where he lived, and in nearby Govan – two areas that crawled with hard men.

At first glance, Hutcheson came across as a wannabe gangster. He wore the right gear, had a tattoo on his arm declaring 'Thug for Life', talked the talk and walked the walk. Pure wannabe with one difference – he delivered on his threats. He was known to be obsessed with gangster movies like *The Godfather* trilogy, *Gangster No. 1* and *Goodfellas* but he didn't stop at hours of endless viewing. He copied the characters and their violent ways.

The police knew that Christopher Hutcheson had chopped a few junkies who owed him money. On each occasion, he'd used a machete – just like one of his favourite fictional gangsters. They also knew that he lived in Woodville Street, Ibrox, in a manky-looking flat – at least it looked run-down from the outside. When they'd hit his place to arrest him for drug dealing early in 2002, they were amazed at what they found inside. The place dripped with expensive furniture and designer clothes and he had his own fully equipped personal gym, which he used regularly to maintain his powerful build. If they thought about it a little harder, they would have grasped that almost everything Christopher Hutcheson had was in imitation of something he'd seen in his favourite movies – all financed by his drug dealing, of course.

When the police realised that it was Daniel Hutcheson's body they had found, they went in search of people who knew his cousin, Christopher. With his profession and reputation, it was no bad place to start.

Early on they tackled Andrew Ferguson, an eighteen-year-old

known to be a sidekick of Hutcheson. Ferguson was a different type entirely from his pal. Quiet, almost timid, he was seen as a follower not a leader but he might also be a weak spot.

By the time the cops left Ferguson, they knew they were on to something. Now they went out to find other friends of Hutcheson who might want to talk. Who better than straight people, non-criminals? And there were a few.

One of the young drug dealer's weaknesses was for good-looking blondes and he seemed to collect them like he collected designer-label shirts. Three or four interviews later, the cops not only had enough details to charge Christopher Hutcheson with murder, they even had someone who had witnessed his confession. Not some street player who may have an agenda of his own but a frightened sixteen-year-old girl.

In such a situation, the cops would hesitate for a while. It was one thing having people tell them crucial details but another to make sure they'd actually turn up in court and give the same evidence under oath. Hutcheson would try to intimidate all the witnesses – that was for sure – but he was locked up in jail on drugs offences. Other street players would call on allies and associates to help warn off the witnesses. Hutcheson had a problem though – no pals.

As far as the cops were concerned, because he'd threatened and chopped so many people, Christopher Hutcheson had lynched himself with his own rope. Confident that the women and some others would come through with the evidence at trial, they charged Hutcheson and his sidekick, Andrew Ferguson, with murder.

In March 2003, the trial started at the High Court in Glasgow with Lord Bracadale presiding. Hutcheson and Ferguson were charged with murdering Daniel and along with a co-accused, Scott McAulay, of attempting to pervert the curse of justice by chopping up his corpse. Early in the trial the charges against McAulay were dropped, as were two accusations of drug dealing. As soon as the Crown made that decision, the police whisked McAulay away for interview. One minute he was an accused, the next a potential witness.

There was no deal for Christopher Hutcheson or Andrew Ferguson. Between them, they faced nineteen charges, including murder, assaults, drug dealing and threatening behaviour. Then there was another small matter for Hutcheson. He was charged with a second murder.

Out in the lovely rural arena of Lanarkshire, near the small town of Strathaven in September 2001, the body of a man had been discovered, lying under a bridge. At first, the authorities had thought the man might have committed suicide by jumping. Then the pathologist found marks of a struggle, including bruising to his neck. The dead man was John Mitchell from Brighton Street in Ibrox. He was a close neighbour of Christopher Hutcheson.

Then the courtroom fell deadly silent as Samuel Burgoyne told how he and his pal Stephen Baird had found Daniel Hutcheson's torso while hunting rabbits on the banks of the Clyde down by Erskine. They had spotted the bundle wrapped in a black bin bag, a tent and sheet. Stephen Baird pulled a knife and started to cut into the washed-up package.

'As soon as I got a whiff of the stink I knew exactly what we had,' Samuel Burgoyne related. (The poor man had found another dead body when he was just a child.) It had been a full five months since Daniel Hutcheson had gone missing and presumably been killed. Everyone in that courtroom imagined the stench and felt for the two men.

People were lining up to give evidence against Christopher Hutcheson and with good reason. Many had owed him money for drugs, often just small sums, and he had threatened them with death. They included Scott Connolly, who told how Hutcheson had turned up at his house looking for a debt to be paid and pulled out a crossbow, threatening to kill him in front of his wife and kids.

Connolly admitted weeping and pleading for his life. Regardless, Hutcheson had shot a bolt into his thigh. With Connolly in agony, Hutcheson had continued to threaten him. 'He was pointing it to my head, telling me that I was making him out to be a daftie,' Connolly told the court. 'I thought he was going to shoot me in the brain after that.' Connolly pulled the bolt out of his leg and promised on his kids' lives that he would pay the debt. 'I was sobbing and pleading with him asking him no' to kill me.' Eventually Hutcheson left after making more threats. Connolly and his family were so terrified that his wife went straight to her grandmother and borrowed the money to pay an instalment to the drug dealer.

But Connolly still owed money so then, in fear of his life, he agreed to sell a large consignment of heroin for Hutcheson. But still Hutcheson wasn't finished with him. Around November 2001, he was ambushed by Hutcheson and Ferguson and bundled into the back seat of a car. Unable to escape, he was carried helplessly along until they reached Duntocher, a town a few miles to the west of Glasgow. There someone hit him hard and he was pulled out of the motor. The men set about beating him with heavy objects till someone cried out that they should leave him – that he was finished.

A former soldier by the name of Blair McCallum had a similar tale to tell. Twenty-eight-year-old McCallum admitted working for Hutcheson by selling smack and Blues, as Valium is known. He had been short on his money one time so Hutcheson and some others bundled him into a car and drove him to wasteland. There he had a gun stuck into his mouth, was beaten to a pulp and then a rope snaked round his neck. As the air was strangled out of him, McCallum was sure he was going to die. Then suddenly they let go of the rope and left him lying there bloody and gasping on the ground.

These were just some of the familiar stories among many about how Hutcheson and his people collected debts. All such witnesses agreed on one other point – they were convinced Christopher Hutcheson would kill them. Could kill if he decided to. Never mind the offences being detailed, as character witnesses they were describing Hutcheson as a violent psychopath capable of anything. But next came the most damning evidence of how he had killed his cousin, Daniel Hutcheson, and disposed of his body.

The main witnesses in these matters were female friends, girl-friends and ex-girlfriends. To at least two, he had made long, sweeping, unsolicited confessions as if he couldn't help himself from talking about his crime – as if he was gloating, proud.

Later in the trial, another witness to these events turned out to be Andrew Ferguson, his co-accused. Like Hutcheson, Ferguson was pleading not guilty of murdering Daniel. Ferguson's defence was that Hutcheson had been the killer, not him – he had just watched. No doubt under the advice of his lawyer Edgar Prais QC, Andrew Ferguson decided to reveal exactly what he had watched that day. All the witnesses' accounts were remarkably consistent.

Daniel Hutcheson had owed his younger cousin Christopher £30 in a drugs debt and he had little chance of finding the cash. He was tricked into going to his cousin Christopher's flat in Woodville Street, Ibrox, and there he broke down in terrified tears, sobbing that he couldn't raise the cash. He was given a stark ultimatum – have his hand cut off or be killed. With Daniel weeping and distraught, Hutcheson forced him into the bath, making him kneel. Hutcheson was going to cut his cousin's hand off but, at some point, he suddenly changed his mind for his own perverse reasons. 'Fuck it,' he spat, 'I'm just going to kill you anyway.'

Later he'd tell a girlfriend that he 'just fancied going further to see what it was like'.

Christopher Hutcheson left the room, ordering Andrew Ferguson to watch Daniel.

'What can I do?' the sobbing, terrified Daniel had asked Ferguson.

Ferguson didn't know. No-one knew how to stop Christopher Hutcheson doing anything.

Ferguson claimed in evidence that Daniel then said to him, 'I know if you could help me you would.' They would be his last words.

Christopher Hutcheson came back into the bathroom with a rope, strung it round Daniel's neck and pulled. Andrew Ferguson admitted in court he had to look away. When he looked back, there was Daniel Hutcheson's body kneeling in the bath, his fingers stuck behind the rope wrapped tightly round his neck, his face purple, his swollen tongue sticking out of his mouth, blood dripping from his eyes and nose.

'Let him go. He's going purple,' Ferguson claims to have said.

'Fuck it. He killed Mark so I'm killing this bastard,' Hutcheson is alleged to have replied.

Mark was Christopher's older brother who had died from a seizure brought on by illegal drugs. It was well known that Christopher Hutcheson held Daniel responsible for Mark's death but the statement, if true, is the closest we get to motive in this killing – apart from his later statement to a girlfriend, 'Just fancied going further to see what it was like.'

With Daniel slumped over, stock-still and not breathing, Hutcheson pushed his head underwater just to make sure he was dead. Later, when Hutcheson took off the ligature, Daniel gave a loud sigh. It sounded like a deep breath to Hutcheson so he shoved his victim's head under the water again – making doubly sure.

With Daniel Hutcheson's body not yet cold, his cousin Christopher came up with a plan. If the corpse was ever found, he and Ferguson would need an alibi. No problem: they went straight out to a club, drinking heavily in company, laughing and joking. Folk would remember that they were there – if they had to. But Christopher intended that that would never be necessary.

Next day, he had to dispose of the body and Christopher Hutcheson's perverse idea of fun was about to start.

Later, to a variety of people, he had boasted about gouging out his cousin's eyes with a spoon . . . of slicing the tattoos off his arms . . . of cutting his head off and leaving it on a shelf at his flat for two days . . . of sawing off his limbs with a hacksaw then, finding that too slow, he bought a chainsaw. Later, having dumped the torso in the Clyde, he sat by an oil drum in the back close of a tenement and burned his cousin's limbs. The process of burning alone took five days. Bored, at one point, he had played football with his cousin Daniel Hutcheson's skull.

During all this evidence that would disgust even strong people, Christopher Hutcheson appeared calm and unmoved. He even arranged to buy new suits to look smart at the trial. No Ralph Slater special deals for him but three Versace numbers costing well over £1,000 each. Sometimes he smiled at some particularly gruesome evidence. Twice he wasn't too happy about what his co-defendant Andrew Ferguson had said in the witness stand so he assaulted him as they were taken downstairs to the cells, appearing not to care that they were surrounded by guards in uniform.

Ferguson was pleading not guilty to the murder but he was happy to give evidence implicating Hutcheson. Yet he also admitted that he had helped to dispose of the man's body and he wasn't alone in that.

Derek Scanlon, twenty-two, had bumped into Christopher Hutcheson on the day of the killing. He wished he hadn't.

'I've just murdered my cousin Daniel,' Hutcheson had told him. 'No' believe me? Come and have a look.' From the witness stand, Scanlon described going into Hutcheson's flat and seeing Daniel's clothed body lying in the bath. Scanlon then helped in disposing and burning the body parts, wrapped in plastic bags before they were taken out to be barbecued in an oil drum in the back close. After all the parts had been burned they were taken away in wheelbarrows, dumped and scattered in various places.

'I helped through pure fear,' he admitted. 'I'm ashamed of myself.'

The case of murdering his cousin was as strong as could be imagined but there was another major accusation Christopher Hutcheson had to answer – murdering John Mitchell, the man whose corpse had been found under a bridge out in rural Lanarkshire, near Strathaven.

The girlfriend he had confessed to about killing Daniel had asked Christopher Hutcheson, 'Have you ever tortured or killed anyone else?'

He almost proudly said he had and filled in the details.

There had been two other men who owed him money for drugs – it was always about drugs debts with him – and he had tortured them in his flat. Then there was 'John the Beggar'. That was his name for John Mitchell, who started out by owing him £300 but, because of late payments and the interest Hutcheson added for this, he was nowhere near clearing his debt.

They had tortured Mitchell before, him and Ferguson, but it didn't help to produce the money. Mitchell was homeless and in a mess. With no job, a drugs habit and no friends, the man was reduced to begging on the streets to raise some cash – thus the nickname of John the Beggar.

Eventually Hutcheson's patience had run out so, in September 2001, he and Ferguson had got hold of Mitchell, cut him up, smashed his fingers and hands with a heavy metal bar then poured boiling water over them. Later that day, they sliced his head like an overripe tomato – again copying some scene from a film. After that, they'd driven out into the country, to a remote place near Strathaven, and thrown him off a high bridge. But Hutcheson wasn't happy.

'He was disappointed that the man didn't go "Aaarrrgh!" as he fell,' his former girlfriend said. According to her, Ferguson had confirmed everything about both murders later.

By the time they retired to make their minds up, it had been three weeks of gruesome, bloody detail for the jury, but reaching their verdict only took them four hours. They found Hutcheson and Ferguson guilty of Daniel's murder and of disposing of his corpse. Hutcheson was also found guilty of murdering John Mitchell while Ferguson was convicted of his attempted murder and assault.

Before sentencing on 8 April 2003, Lord Bracadale spoke with calm reserve, describing the crimes as 'grotesque' and adding, 'People everywhere will be horrified to hear of such barbarous acts committed in their midst.'

As Lord Bracadale spoke, relatives of Daniel Hutcheson clapped, cheered and wept. Christopher Hutcheson turned and stared at them. Smiling widely, he raised his hands above his head and applauded. It could've been straight from some Mafia film and it probably was. Hutcheson was acting the part right to the end.

It ended when both the men were sentenced to life, with Hutcheson being given a minimum of twenty-five years in jail and Ferguson seventeen. Again applause broke out from the victim's relatives. It must be remembered that most of these people were also related to Christopher Hutcheson, the murderer. Again he turned and smiled at them, raised his hands in the air and clapped. Beside him, his partner in murder, Andrew Ferguson, held his head in his hands.

Shortly after the men were sentenced, Andrew Ferguson announced that he intended to appeal. He had only become involved in the murders through fear of Christopher Hutcheson, he argued. If he hadn't complied, maybe he too would be a dead man. He didn't kill anyone. He watched but watching isn't murder, he argued. At the time of writing, the outcome of his appeal action is not yet concluded.

Up in Peterhead Prison, William Beggs, the Limbs in the Loch Killer, wasn't happy. He didn't like the treatment he was getting in the special unit for sex killers. The diet wasn't good and it was affecting his health. He wanted to complain to the Scottish Prison Service on a number of counts but he wasn't getting access to a computer. In the meantime, he had a cushy job, as prison barber.

It isn't known if Beggs ever responded to Christopher Hutcheson about his 'superior crime' or indeed if they write to each other. What is known is that Beggs never handed that first letter from Hutcheson – the one written before he was charged, in which he boasted about the murder of Daniel – on to the authorities. Why would he? He is the Limbs in the Loch Killer.

Back when he was a free man, Christopher Hutcheson used to say to one of his girlfriends that he would commit a crime that everyone would notice – a crime that everyone would remember.

'One day,' he said, 'I'll be on the front pages of every newspaper.' In that, he wasn't wrong.

PART 7
WHODUNNIT?

Everyone loves a mystery. Working out the facts, the characters, the personalities, the action and then deciding, before the final scene or the last chapter, exactly whodunnit. Crime is one of the bestselling genres of books and movies for those very reasons. What could be better than real-life mysteries, though?

There are plenty around. The shortest murder trial in Scottish legal history saw Mark Clinton walk away free in 2004 but it left us with one question – if Clinton didn't do it, then who did knife down The Licensee's equaliser Billy McPhee? Alexander Blue was a businessman who was beaten to death on the street – who could possibly have wanted him dead? TC Campbell and Joe Steele successfully appealed against their conviction for killing the six members of the Doyle Family in the Ice-Cream Wars – so, if it wasn't them, who did torch the Doyles' home? The list goes go on and on.

None of the above cases are included here because they have already been adequately covered in books or by the newspapers. We cover three true-life tales – one of murder unsolved, one of cause of death unknown and one a case of suicide or murder. You decide.

The difference between these tales and fiction is that they are real. Real cases have real victims and, usually, real grieving loved ones – human beings who have lost someone dear to them and who need to know how, why and who.

Closure is an overused, awkward term that, for most bereaved victims, never happens. But knowing what happened to their loved ones does help them move on with their lives, as does knowing whodunnit.

NO ANGEL BUT . . .

The woman was worried. Her son was on one of his trips to Glasgow and he was late. She was right to fret.

One time before he had ended up in trouble. The police had found him in the city centre late at night disorientated and without his shoes. Later he told her he thought his drink had been spiked. Anything could happen to him if he was drugged and if, as she suspected, he was in bad company. It was worse than she feared.

Peter Smith had never told his mother what he got up to in Glasgow but he suspected she knew. Ever since he had confided in her that he was gay, that it was their secret, she thought he went there to pick up men. She knew nothing about that scene – why would she? But she worried all the same.

Fifty-two-year-old Peter Smith was an ex-soldier who managed a big store. He'd experienced life, was good company and had a large circle of friends. He was unmarried and living with his mother near Stirling so maybe those friends suspected he was gay but he wasn't for telling them. He had only told his mother when he got upset after being diagnosed as having a sexually transmitted disease.

It was impossible to keep anything secret in his small village of West Plean near Stirling. Everyone knew everyone else and saw everything you got up to. Even in the larger town of Stirling, just up the road, there was little privacy. So, for fun, adventures and thrills, Peter Smith headed down the road to the big city of

Glasgow. There you could get anything you wanted and some-times things you didn't want.

It was Tuesday, 11 April 1989, just after 11 p.m. Peter Smith lay at the bottom of steep steps leading into the public toilets below pavement level on St Vincent Street. He had one stab wound to his chest and was bleeding heavily. Alive but unconscious when they found him, he was rushed to the Royal Infirmary nearby.

Back in Stirling, his mother worried for him. Soon she was going to have her heart broken.

As Smith lay in hospital fighting for life, the cops surveyed the scene of the knifing and, more importantly, the people who hung around there. The St Vincent Street toilets have been known for many years as a place for gay pick-ups for casual sex – cottaging as it is now known. Open all hours, as it was in 1989, men of all ages would be hanging around at any time night or day. With staff alert to the toilet cubicles being used for sex as well as junkies shooting up, the surrounding dark lanes and alleyways were used for encounters. So the cops extended their search there and found what they expected to find – vulnerable, desperate men with secrets.

Soon the cops had decided Peter Smith had been mugged for money and it had gone too far. They also identified North Court Lane, running parallel to St Vincent Street, as the scene of the stab-bing. Blood had been found there and they surmised that Smith had been stabbed in the dark lane and had staggered out on to St Vincent Street before collapsing, ironically, down the steps of the main cottaging venue in Glasgow's city centre.

They had two witnesses. Young men who said they saw two men stab Smith. All they needed now were the names. It wasn't going to take them long.

The morning after the stabbing, twenty-six-year-old Stuart Gair was up early and heading out to collect his welfare giro. It was only two days since he'd been released from jail for possession of drugs and he was skint. Cashing in the £150, he bought some food and, of course, some smack. Going to a nearby cafe, he locked himself in the toilets to shoot up. The monkey off his back, he came out and right into the arms of the police. He was lifted for possession of drugs, taken to Barlinnie Prison and held on remand to await a court appearance – but things were about to take a more serious turn.

A week after the stabbing, Gair was told he was going on an ID parade, suspected of the stabbing and attempted murder of Peter Smith. It was a name he'd read about in the papers. It was a name that was going to haunt him the rest of his life.

Tall and slim, Gair complained that all the other guys on the ID line-up were much shorter. The cops proceeded anyway. Two of the young men who had been hanging around St Vincent Street toilets that night and had told the cops they'd seen two guys stab Smith were called in, one by one. Neither picked out Stuart Gair but both chose other volunteers on the line-up. However, a third man who had responded to a police appeal for information did finger him. Gair was now the main suspect in stabbing Peter Smith.

Gair declared that he was innocent right from the off. His alibi was that he'd been in bed and breakfast digs in Glasgow some distance away, watching a Clint Eastwood cowboy movie. He'd watched the film in the room of a fellow-lodger called Hector Wood and another lodger had looked in a few times and had seen them. But the cops clearly didn't believe him. A few days later, he was put on another ID parade. A third man who had been on St Vincent Street that night was called in and he too picked out one of the civilians rather than Gair. Then they brought in two uniformed cops who did pick out Stuart Gair.

The public are notoriously unreliable in identity parades. Our memories are less efficient than we imagine in recalling what would have been mundane detail on a night two weeks before. The events of that night would have appeared mundane and routine to most folk. After all, they didn't know there had been a stabbing or that they should be on the lookout for a killer. Yet now they were expected to recall just that everyday detail. Cops, on the other hand, are trained to remember faces – or so they'd have us believe. Stuart Gair remained number one suspect.

The cops needed a second suspect since witnesses said two men stabbed Smith. A beat bobby who'd been around St Vincent Street that night said he recognised two guys who had been hanging around that area. From that and the civilian witnesses the cops made up photofits of the two suspects and handed them around. Then, on 29 April, over a fortnight after being stabbed, Peter Smith, suffering from bronchopneumonia caused by the knife wound, died in hospital. Now it was murder.

Immediately, the cops charged Stuart Gair with murder. A few days later, they arrested their second suspect. Willie McLeod is one of life's loners. Unsure, uncertain, suggestible, he struggles with the day-to-day challenges of everyday life. Now he was going to have to cope with a murder accusation.

Arrested at Buchanan Street bus station, a few blocks away from St Vincent Street, McLeod denied any involvement in the murder. Held in police custody, McLeod was put on an ID parade a couple of days later. The three young guys who had been on St Vincent Street that night – the ones who had failed to identify Gair – were called in. They failed to identify McLeod as well. Then the two cops came in – the ones who had fingered Gair – and picked McLeod out of the line-up as someone they'd seen near the murder scene on that night. McLeod was in deep trouble.

The police accused McLeod of killing Smith and named his accomplice as Stuart Gair. He told them again and again that he didn't know anyone called Stuart Gair and had nothing to with any stabbing. The cops kept on at him for days, demanding to know if it was Gair or maybe it was him who had shoved the blade into Peter Smith.

The hapless man now panicked and told the cops it was Stuart Gair who had killed Smith. The following day, he was taken to court for a pleading diet. This is where the charges are put formally and the accused can declare himself guilty or not guilty or say nothing. McLeod said a lot – mainly that he had made up the story about Stuart Gair being the murderer. He said he didn't know Gair – had never met him – he was nowhere near St Vincent Street on the night of the killing and he had only made up the tale under pressure from the police. But it was all too little, too late. Charged with murder, Willie McLeod was jailed on remand.

In August 1989, the murder trial took off in Glasgow High Court with Stuart Gair still pleading not guilty. For Willie McLeod, the whole process became a bit messy.

The day before the trial started, he had somehow managed to broker a deal with the Crown that, in return for giving evidence against Gair, they would drop charges against him. The following day, he was put immediately into the witness box. He was now the main man whose testimony alone would be enough to convict Gair. The trouble was he was now retracting everything he'd told the cops. With his voice shaking and tears welling up in his eyes, he even stated that he had never met Stuart Gair – had never heard of him till the police arrested him and mentioned Gair's name.

The judge wasn't pleased. He decided to charge McLeod with perjury and had him thrown into the court cells. The trial proceeded without him but then McLeod, terrified of prison, changed his mind again and was brought up to give evidence. Yet again, he retracted, telling the judge that the cops were threatening him, putting him under pressure to incriminate Gair. Back to the cells he was sent.

This yo-yo effect went on several times, with McLeod promising to give the evidence then changing his mind when back on the stand. Exasperated and probably fed up with running up and down stairs, the Crown representatives allowed McLeod to sit in the body of the court as other witnesses gave their evidence.

With Willie McLeod watching from the public gallery, four men who had been in the area that night all gave evidence that Gair was the killer. All of them were on the gay scene. One admitted being a prostitute, another was just fifteen years old and a third was a successful businessman who persuaded the court to keep his identity secret.

Three of these men had failed to pick Gair or McLeod out in earlier ID parades but now they all pointed out one or the other in court. It's not difficult to spot the accused man in any trial. But now, months later, they were also saying that they recognised Stuart Gair whereas they had been unable to do so only days after the killing.

Pathologist Dr Marie Cassidy, one of the top people in her profession, was an adviser on *Taggart* and would later become the role model for the BBC drama series *Silent Witness* starring Amanda Burton. She took the stand and the most crucial part of her evidence related to the knife. Was it the knife that killed Peter Smith? The knife in question was a skean-dhu, a short-bladed, double-edged, ornamental affair that male Scots wear tucked into a sock when dressed in the kilt. The skean-dhu had been found among the belongings of Gair's girlfriend, Julie Porter. The knife hadn't offered up any forensic evidence so the crucial question was, could it have been the murder knife? The wound on Peter Smith's chest was caused by a double-edged blade just as the skean-dhu was. So the answer was yes.

They had witnesses and a possible murder weapon. All they needed now was someone who saw the murder. Willie McLeod finally gave the evidence the cops wanted. Game, set and match for the Crown – apart, that is, from Stuart Gair's defence case.

The defence lasted thirteen minutes. In a murder trial, where the accused was adamantly and consistently pleading not guilty, it must be one of the quickest defences ever. Even Hector Wood, the man who swore that Gair was with him that night watching TV, wasn't called. He and another alibi witness were available in court – they just weren't called to give evidence.

The jury found Stuart Gair guilty of murder and he was sentenced to life in prison. As the verdict was read out, several members of the jury were crying though the reason for this is not clear. Someone else in that court – Stuart Gair – was also weeping but on the inside. This wasn't the end as far as he was concerned.

Five years later, in Glenochil Prison, Alloa, in 1994, Jim

McGregor, the prison doctor, was tending to his morning clinic. It was the usual queue of guys with bad backs, sore heads, hurt hands, looking for pain relief and a docket to get off work duties. There were also the hypochondriacs that every prison has and the worst among the cons are the fittest, the hardest. Then a genuinely hurt man hobbled in.

'How did this happen?' Jim asked the prisoner, examining ribs that were obviously cracked and a mess of bruises and cuts.

'The screws did it to me,' the con replied, 'though they're saying I slipped and fell.'

Jim McGregor had heard every sob story in the book, every kind of paranoia that prison seems to breed, had listened to the best conmen and the worst. If he had ever been a soft touch that had long since been worked out of him through his contact with the cons.

'Why did they do that?' McGregor asked.

So, in a calm, intelligent, articulate manner, with no temper tantrums or emotional demands, Stuart Gair told him. Jail staff don't like the prisoners who protest their innocence. It's all right at the start of their sentence but the ones who go on and on for years get on the system's collective nerves. Stuart Gair had kept it up for five years. Five years of beatings and punishments and the worst conditions and still he kept it up.

By the time Gair had left the surgery, Jim McGregor was thinking. The man had impressed him not by his power or force but by his genuineness. He was going to make a point of seeing Gair regularly and find out more about his case. As Stuart Gair returned to his wing, nursing his ribs carefully, he didn't know it but his life had just turned around.

At first, Stuart Gair couldn't believe it that someone, a prison doctor even, believed him. Prison doctors get a mixed press from the cons. There are those who misuse their power to punish and neglect the men. There are others who take to drink and leave the medical care to untrained screws in white jackets. And then there are the diamonds like Jim McGregor.

Dr Jim McGregor became Stuart Gair's voice and legs. Correction – Jim McGregor, his wife, Maureen, and their three children, Julie, Fiona and Jamie, took Stuart Gair to their hearts. Not that they felt sorry for him. In fact, Maureen was wary at first because of his continuing involvement with heroin and his petty offending in the past. But they became convinced of his innocence and supported Jim in working hard to find out the truth. That meant they hardly saw him or, when he was at home, he'd be stuck on the phone for hours. Inevitably, some of the screws at Glenochil started to give him a bad time. A brave family.

Jim McGregor had demanded to know how Stuart Gair had slipped on a wet floor. He was a tall, slim, reasonably fit young man. OK, he still had his drug habit and looked wan and spaced out some of the time but he wasn't the type to just slip. That stayed the official explanation but Jim McGregor's persistent challenge to the system won the confidence of Gair. Soon he was meeting with Jim McGregor regularly, telling him more and more about his case – the one thing he was a expert on.

As Jim McGregor dug into the details and chased up key players, so more and more information came to him, convincing him of Gair's innocence. He wasn't alone in his efforts.

Gair also had a new lawyer, John MacAulay. Years before, MacAulay had been a police officer who left the force because he couldn't stand the brutality and the corruption. The police's loss was criminal justice's gain in that he became one of the most respected and sought-after criminal layers in Glasgow. There was an added bonus. His experience in the police left him, unlike many of his profession, perfectly willing to consider that miscarriages of justice occur. MacAulay was intrepid and tireless and soon he was taking sworn statements from key witnesses in Gair's case – from people like Willie McLeod, the reluctant and hapless witness, who had tried to kill himself twice since the trial. He spelled out that the cops had simply threatened him over and over again and he felt as guilty as hell. He was willing to testify at any appeal.

Hector Wood, the man who had been willing to testify that Gair had been watching a Clint Eastwood film with him in his room that night, had a worse story to tell. After he had made his statements to the cops, they had come back time after time, trying to convince him to change his story. He refused so they threatened him. Wood had an outstanding fine of £48.

'We can make that disappear if you change your mind,' one cop had offered.

Wood refused. The next day he was arrested and thrown into jail for the paltry fine.

'Your life can become very difficult,' another cop had told him, 'unless you change your tune. Then everything will be sweet.'

He refused. They hassled him every day.

Wood turned up at the trial still adamant that Gair had been with him that night watching telly. For a long time, he sat and waited in the witness room. Then some court official came and told him that he wouldn't be required. He went home still not knowing why he wasn't called.

The men who had been near the scene of the murder that night had a similar tale to tell. 'They kept threatening to tell my folks and newspaper reporters that I was gay,' said one. 'I didn't want my parents to find out that way. They're old and very straight – strict Christians. It would've killed them.' There was a price for police silence. 'All I had to do was say that I saw Gair up that lane that night.'

'They threatened to out me publicly,' said another. 'I'm married and she doesn't know. Besides, if they had, I would've lost my job. I know I would and I can't afford that, what with the kids and the mortgage. I just had to give the evidence against Stuart Gair. I'm heart sorry for him but I just had to.'

'They said they'd put it into the newspapers that I was a homo prostitute,' said another. 'I was ashamed of what I was. Don't do it any more but, back then, I'd tell any lies rather than be exposed.'

It was looking much better for Stuart Gair but then personal disaster struck Jim McGregor. Maureen, his wife, had a heart attack.

His energy would now be needed to look after her. There was a hard choice to be made – either he could go on working at the prison or continue with Gair's campaign.

At the age of fifty-one years, Dr Jim McGregor resigned from the work he loved. He had his wife to care for and a man to free from an unjust imprisonment. How lucky was Stuart Gair the day the screws smashed his ribs in Glenochil Prison?

On 29 September 2000, after eleven years in jail, Stuart Gair was released pending an appeal against his conviction. The McGregor family, who had already given Gair so much, then took him into their home. For six years, all of them had lived day-to-day with their father's struggle to prove Gair innocent. But Stuart Gair was still a drug user though, by this time, he was on the methadone programme. The danger was that he'd go back on smack and reach out to crime to pay for his drugs. This was a nice, middle-class family. How could they take that risk? Because he was innocent, they believed, and he needed their help.

A few months later, Gair left the McGregor household. Cynical journalists suspected a fall-out and asked them why. They refused to answer. Why should they? Gair was innocent of murder in their view and that was the most important point. But Stuart Gair had returned to his old ways. Jail hadn't helped his heroin problem but made it worse.

Now out on his own, Gair visited his elderly mother who had moved into a nursing home. He loved his mother and had always said that he hoped he could prove his innocence while she was still alive. Now that he was free, he visited her most days because he wanted to and because he could. But the cops were watching him very closely.

Every person involved in a high-profile campaign of a miscarriage of justice reports that they attract special attention from the police while their appeal is pending. Catch the sods out on something else and that will influence the appeal court, seems to be the rationale. It was no different for Stuart Gair except that he shot himself in the foot.

In 2001, a year after he was released pending appeal, the local council offered him temporary housing and he accepted. His mother, by then seventy-one years old, had suffered a brain haemorrhage and had had part of one leg amputated. She was living in Westerlands Nursing Home in Stirling. Gair visited frequently and staff got used to seeing him around. The trouble was that, by then, members of the public knew who he was. They were familiar with his murder conviction and knew a little about the man himself. Then one day, he asked the staff to lock his mother's room. Explaining the reason for this request, he said, 'There's something valuable in there. I want to be sure it's safe.'

Staff phoned the police. Local cops were then running Operation Overlord, aimed at catching the bigger drug traffickers. When they searched Gair's mother's room, they found £3,000 worth of very pure heroin – not a huge amount but enough. Later, at his flat, they unearthed a factory for cutting and bagging smack, as well as more drugs.

Stuart Gair claimed to be innocent of murder but he didn't claim to be an angel. The High Court in Glasgow agreed and jailed him for two years for the drugs. Sentencing him, Lord Clarke said, 'It is a particularly stupid and reckless thing to get involved in.' A lot of people agreed. Others, however, stuck by Gair even though they felt let down.

Among his supporters were some new ones including Peter Mullan, the film actor and director, who was considering making a film starring Ewan McGregor of Gair's story. John Hannah, the film actor, Tommy Sheridan, the Member of the Scottish Parliament and others of a radical persuasion all supported him but, most surprising of all, were victim Peter Smith's own brother and sister, David and Ann.

Gair had written to Ann in 1991, just two years after he was convicted. The pair had kept up a correspondence and slowly she became convinced that he was innocent. Moreover, along with everyone else who looked into the case, she believed the cops had lied to secure his conviction. In Ann's case, this had particular complications since she had started a relationship with a Strathclyde Police officer. Sadly, the more she became convinced of Gair's innocence, the less feasible her relationship with the cop became and it ended.

A major support to Gair was his lawyer, John MacAulay, who worked tirelessly on the case. He had established that all the witnesses were willing to be called to an appeal. All the men, none of whom knew each other before or after the trial, were willing to say that the police threatened and pressurised them to finger Stuart Gair. Then there was another breakthrough – this time on forensics.

MacAulay had not been convinced by the evidence regarding the skean-dhu as the murder weapon. Smith's wound had only been one centimetre wide and the skean-dhu was too broad. Two independent experts agreed. Then there was an approach to Dr Marie Cassidy, the pathologist who had reported to the murder trial. She had since left Glasgow to become Irish Deputy State Pathologist – a very senior position.

Dr Cassidy agreed with the other experts and went public, saying that she had misled the trial. Worse than that, she claimed that the Crown had withheld evidence from her – particularly regarding the shirt Peter Smith had been wearing when he was stabbed. He'd had emergency surgery on the wound and that would have changed the shape and size of the cut. Given this, the hole made by the knife in the shirt would have offered a more accurate guide to the type of knife that had been used. Yet officials had refused to hand it over to the pathologist.

It was a remarkable statement from Dr Cassidy and it now looked like Gair was bound to win his freedom. But he would be made to wait and, in the meantime, he had another personal crisis to face.

In January 2003, with Gair still serving time in Barlinnie Prison, his mother, Norma, died. The prison arranged for him to attend the funeral escorted by two guards. As he stood there by her graveside, he no doubt remembered his promise to her – to prove his innocence of murder while she was still alive.

Finally, in June 2005, an appeal hearing was convened. The focus was on the witnesses who said they had been threatened and pressurised by the police to blame Gair for the murder. Willie McLeod turned up, as did other men who had identified Gair as being at scene of the murder, and all retracted their evidence – except they weren't allowed to.

Lords Cullen, Sutherland and Hamilton determined that, at the original trial, Willie McLeod had had plenty of time to consult a lawyer. The others were dismissed as unreliable – they'd been reliable enough to convict a man of murder but now they weren't reliable enough to have that conviction overturned. In their written judgement, the Law Lords also made reference to the witnesses being put under considerable pressure to retract their evidence. What they seemed to be referring to was the campaign to prove Gair innocent and the considerable attention given to the case by certain journalists.

The cops were cleared of underhand tactics and the journalists were found guilty. So it seemed but it left Stuart Gair no further forward.

As this book goes to print, Stuart Gair is forty-two years old and has been fighting to clear his name of murder for almost seventeen years. He is fighting still and further appeal hearings are due. At least he is now out of jail but he lives a life suspended between freedom and incarceration. Who will employ a man who may return to jail? A man who may or may not be a murderer? It is the curse of all people who refuse to give in and allow the world to believe they are a killer after all.

The whole truth may come out about the murder of Peter Smith some day soon. If Gair is found to be innocent, other serious questions are then raised. If Stuart Gair didn't kill Peter Smith, then who did? What has the killer been doing for the last seventeen years? Are there any other victims of his blade? If so, whose fault is that?

NOSE IN THE AIR

As he led her out of the restaurant, she looked as if she was going to faint any minute. He was holding her up, his arms wrapped round her. Other diners thought that she was lucky to be with such a loving, caring man. If only they knew.

They were a handsome couple – not young but attractive. And it looked as if they had money too – unusual customers for that wee restaurant. Other customers and staff in the Pancake Place on Glasgow's Union Street, right next door to the side entrance to Central Station, had already noticed them when she took ill. Her white face and jelly legs were a bit like a road accident to other motorists – they just couldn't help but look.

She was thirty-three-year-old Dorothy Niven. He was forty-eight-year-old Richard Karling. They had been lovers once but no more. It was June 1995 and, on the day following their visit to the Pancake Place, Karling would phone from Dorothy's home in Busby. He'd phone 999 and ask for an ambulance. She wasn't very well at all and he was worried. But, by the time the paramedics arrived, Dorothy Niven was dead.

Dorothy Niven was a fit woman with no major health worries and she had just died. Doctors and cops don't like that type of situation. Rightly, they don't trust it.

Interviewed by the cops, Richard told them about her becoming unwell in the Pancake Place. He apparently took her home and looked after her for a while. She'd said she was feeling a bit better so he'd left and gone back to his own place. The following afternoon, he had visited her just to make sure she was OK. She wasn't OK and was obviously very ill so he'd phoned the emergency ambulance.

Dorothy and Richard had been alone at her house. No one had any information about any fall-out or fight or any reason to suspect anything sinister. The pathologists would have to get to work.

During the post-mortem, they noticed something unusual. Dorothy's nose was quite distinctly turned up, like she had died with her face pressing into something with considerable force – like she had been smothered.

Then they did toxicology reports to test her blood and organs for any drugs or poisons. The cops were particularly keen on this because of the reports of witnesses at the Pancake Place. They said she was fine one minute, just sitting there having an orange juice, and the next she'd become 'floppy like a rag doll'.

Sure enough, the pathologist, Dr Louay al-Alousi, found temazepam in Dorothy's body. Enough of that could make her sleepy, woozy and unsteady on her legs. More importantly, it would be easy enough to slip some to her, especially in a fresh orange juice.

Glasgow junkies had a love affair with temazepam, which is also known by the trade name Restoril. It was a treatment for insomnia but, when taken in large doses or mainlined into veins, it replicated the sense of euphoria that heroin gave them – well, it came close. When they couldn't get their mitts on heroin, they'd take massive doses of that as an alternative. They called the capsules jellies and the city was crawling with them.

Aside from that, GPs prescribed the drug to people who had sleeping problems. There were a lot of insomniacs in Glasgow, it seems. And there were to be even more pretend insomniacs after the druggies discovered the hit they could get from temazepam. They paid or bullied straight people, often elderly folk, to con prescriptions from their doctors. If someone couldn't get the drug from their doctor by feigning the right symptoms, they could buy them illegally at only a few quid for a handful – more than enough to dope someone.

Too much temazepam made a person giddy, woozy, disorientated, unsteady on their feet. By the mid 1990s, it was well established as a date-rape drug.

The cops had only one suspect – Richard Karling. It wouldn't be the first time that a killer had tried to cover his actions by phoning for help for his victim. That line is more common than most murderers think. So common that the cops automatically suspect that very person in each case till they are persuaded otherwise.

Karling was charged with the murder of Dorothy Niven. The cops claimed that he had drugged her in the restaurant, taken her home and smothered her. Then he'd gone home to his own place in Ayr and left her overnight, before returning the following afternoon to run the fake call for help to 999.

Even as they charged him, they knew there was going to be a lot of public interest. There was his affair with Dorothy, which she had broken off to take another lover, only for the jealous, rejected man to be accused of killing her, in what looked like a crime of passion. But there was also the politics.

For thirteen years, Richard Karling had been married to a woman called Sheila Ross. Sheila's father was Willie Ross who had been Secretary of State for Scotland. In the days before devolution and the creation of the Scottish Parliament, Willie Ross had been political top dog in Scotland and one of the leading players in the Labour Party.

Ross had been seen as Prime Minister Harold Wilson's man in Scotland and he was a staunch unionist. It was Ross who invented the phrase 'Tartan Tories' for the SNP. He had two spells as Secretary of State and, when he retired in 1979, he was elevated to the Lords as Lord Marnock. Willie Ross had died in 1988 but memories of the major part he'd played in modern politics still remained fresh in 1995.

Though Karling and Sheila Ross were divorced, his involvement in a murder trial would still be seen as a scandal with some link to a major political figure.

Richard Karling insisted he was innocent of Dorothy Niven's murder throughout. At his trial at the High Court in Glasgow later in 1995, the main evidence against him was that he had been the last person to be seen with the victim. He had been with her when she had taken unwell and he was the person with her after she had died. In the meantime, the pathologist swore that there was enough temazepam in her system to have incapacitated her and her upturned nose indicated that she had been smothered by someone using considerable force.

The Crown called on some of Dorothy's friends, who said that her relationship with Karling ended because of his heavy drinking, tempers and jealousy. According to her pals, he hadn't wanted the relationship to end and pled with her to go back with him. Dorothy was a soft touch, they said, and, although she felt bad about Karling, she was very happy with her new boyfriend.

The way Dorothy Niven was described in court made her seem a clean-living, honourable woman no one would want to murder – apart from an insanely jealous ex-lover. Richard Karling was being placed squarely in the hot seat from every angle. The last person to be seen with Dorothy alive, he was now being described as the only person who could possibly have a motive for murder. He decided to set the record straight in court.

According to Karling, Dorothy Niven led a double life. By day, she was an administrator with the Students Loans Company but, by night, she was a call girl working in massage parlours and saunas in Glasgow. In that sleazy, twilight world, she would have met many dangerous men – men who would want to own her and, if they couldn't own her, might not hesitate to kill her.

The accused man's claims caused sensation and upset Dorothy's friends and colleagues. The problem with the argument from Karling's point of view was that it was too general. He didn't name other likely suspects. He remained the sole person in the murder inquiry to have been around at key times and with an apparent motive.

There it rested. The debate in court had been about who murdered Dorothy Niven and the jury felt there was only one man. They found Richard Karling guilty of premeditated murder and he was sentenced to life.

In prison, Richard Karling didn't hesitate to contact his lawyers and tell them he wanted to appeal. His legal team reckoned that there was little they could do about the incriminating social evidence – he had had a torrid affair with Dorothy and he had been the last person seen with her alive. So they decided to focus on other questions. Had Dorothy been murdered at all? If so, was it in the way described in court?

By 1999, four years after his conviction, Richard Karling's appeal was due to be heard in the High Court, Edinburgh. A few days before the hearing, startling information changed his lawyer's plans entirely.

The appeal hearing started and Karling's legal team made the Law Lords aware that they intended to challenge parts of the pathologist's report as it related to the temazepam. But they had to report a turn of events. They had just discovered, by accident, that another toxicology report had been provided by Guy's Hospital in London. Richard Karling's defence lawyers at the trial had never been made aware of this report.

The Guy's report appeared to have been sent to the cop in charge of the case, Detective Superintendent Ronald Edgar, prior to the 1995 trial but, for reasons unknown, it wasn't passed on to the defence. That report may well have changed the nature of arguments at the original trial in that it contradicted other reports about the temazepam levels. Lord Kirkwood, presiding, had no hesitation in agreeing that the matter should now be referred for a full appeal.

At the High Court, Edinburgh, in May 2001, Richard Karling's full appeal was heard. Unlike a trial where the Crown starts the proceedings to prove the charges against the accused, in an appeal, it is the convicted person's team who must begin, in an effort to establish his innocence.

The University of Cardiff's Professor Sir Bernard Knight was an early witness. When Herbert Kerrigan QC, Karling's lawyer, asked Sir Bernard about the original medical investigation into Dorothy Niven's death, he declared, 'It was a rotten post-mortem.' Not mincing his words, Sir Bernard went on to say that Dorothy's upturned nose was no indication that she had been smothered – the same effect could be produced if ill health had caused her to collapse face down. Further, in his opinion, the levels of temazepam judged to be in her system by the Glasgow tests and used at the trial were well within therapeutic levels. In other words, she hadn't had enough of the drug to make her, as witnesses described, 'floppy like a rag doll'.

Professor Robert Forrest, a forensic toxicology expert from the University of Sheffield, supported Sir Bernard. In his opinion, the tests shown at the trial did not indicate enough temazepam to prove that Dorothy Niven was drugged. That the jury should not have been told that she had been.

Then there was the report from Guy's Hospital – the one that had been available before the trial but that had somehow gone missing. These tests on Dorothy's blood showed no traces of temazepam at all. If that report had been made available at the trial, Karling's defence team would surely have challenged the tests. Perhaps the Glasgow tests were faulty – or so Karling's appeal lawyer suggested.

At an appeal hearing, the balance of power remains with the Crown. The onus is on the convicted person's side to prove their innocence. They have the uphill struggle – that is why so many apparent miscarriages of justice fail at appeal stage. Usually all the Crown has to do is to return to their original case and argue that due process was followed in front of a judge and jury so the conviction should stand. Not this time.

The Crown announced they were not opposed to Karling's appeal. He was an innocent man in the eyes of the law and free to go. Further, they weren't seeking to retry Richard Karling for the murder – a point they could have pursued. The statement was bold if bleak. No further action was to be taken on the mysterious death of Dorothy Niven.

The coverage of that missing report was damning to Strathclyde Police. Normally, after an appeal, they choose to say nothing. Not this time.

'Such a report was not expected by the force, given that it wasn't instructed by ourselves,' said the police spokesman. 'Any question of any evidence being withheld by Strathclyde officers is completely untrue.'

Back in 1999, Richard Karling's legal team had simply requested all the reports carried out on Dorothy Niven. In that bundle, they stumbled across the report from Guy's Hospital. If the cops hadn't requested it, who did and why did they have it?

As is ever the way, those questions will remain unanswered but there are more important questions on hand. How did Dorothy Niven die? Was she murdered? If so, how and by whom?

Questions that should concern us all. Questions that we could have had the answers to. Questions that will now remain unanswered, probably for ever.

LOST AND FOUND

'I know that park like the back of my hand,' said John Gibson,
looking tired, weary. 'Everyday, we'd go there and hike this way
and that, systematically searching every inch of the ground. And
some of it's rough terrain – muddy and dangerous. But what else
do you do when your brother goes missing?' John Gibson stopped
and began to roll a cigarette. Licking the gummed edge of the
paper, he went on, 'Trouble is we were looking the wrong place.'
He lit the fag and a plume of blue smoke floated upwards in front
of his face. 'The cops told us to look in the wrong fucking place.
Why would they do that?'

It had started back on 27 May 2004 for John Gibson and his partner Grace MacKay though they didn't know what was going on
that day. It would take days for the cops to tell them. Yet, on 27
May, John's half-brother, Robert Power, went missing. That's the
day the nightmare started.

Robert Power was a handsome man who looked much younger
than his forty-six years. With charm to match his looks, he was
never without lady friends. Women were his big weakness. Some
would say they were also his biggest risk.

Robert was never without some new lady friend – well not for
long. He had been on that day in May though. He'd had been in a
relationship with a woman called Susan Margetts but they had
called it off a few months before. Robert wasn't happy about that
and had convinced her to go out with him now and then. They'd

even gone on holiday together but the relationship was more off than on. Robert wanted it on again.

Susan Margetts would later relate that, on 27 May, she was receiving repeated phone calls from Robert pleading with her to get back together with him. She refused every time and he started threatening to do something serious to himself.

Robert had parked his car, a Mitsubishi Jeep, in the car park at Busby station and walked into nearby Busby Glen Park. From the entrance to the park, you could almost see Countryside Estate Agents, where Susan Margetts worked. The last call she received from Robert was at around 7.20 p.m. Two hours later, she called the cops, worried that he sounded suicidal.

It's usually difficult to persuade the police to act on such referrals. A lovers' tiff isn't something they'd want to get involved with but, the very next day, they were out interviewing some of Robert's former lovers and sent divers into watery areas in Busby Glen Park where he'd last been seen. Was there something in Robert Power's background that would make the cops more worried about him than most people?

Robert had been in a bit of trouble when he was a young man. He and his half-brother John Gibson grew up in a rough sector of Glasgow's south side and had fallen into thieving and the other games most of their peers got up to. They were well known in Pollok, Priesthill, Nitshill and right out to Barrhead. They knew all the players and had grown up with them yet Robert Power wasn't a street player – anything but.

'Robert was always a big coward,' John said, 'but lovable. He hated pain of any sort, wouldn't fight, rob, take pills or any risk. Worried about everything and got by on personality.' When they were young he and John had landed in jail for short sentences. 'He was petrified every second of that term. Swore he'd never go to jail again and kept his word.'

Robert Power sold suites of furniture for a living. He was successful enough to pay his bills but sometimes he ran to broke. At one of his low times, in 2003 to 2004, he'd lived with John and

Grace but that was no hardship since they were all close. Robert and John were very close – everyone knew that. Yet, as the cop divers dragged the water in Busby Glen Park, no one went near John Gibson. No one told him there was search going on for his brother.

Three days later another of John's brothers told him about Robert going missing. It was 30 May 2004 and that was the day John and Grace started hunting for Robert.

A couple of weeks of daily searches of the park went by. It's a big park and some of the ground is difficult underfoot. The couple made up flyers with pictures of Robert, handing them out in the park and asking anyone who had been there on the day he'd gone missing to contact them. They searched Shawlands, the area where Robert then lived, and went to his friends, his former girlfriends, anyone they could think of. They were getting nowhere.

Of all the family, Robert was closest to John and Grace. Legally it was complicated because of different relationships in their family of origin but they knew him best and were most likely to know where he might have gone. The cops had approached Robert's estranged son from a long-term relationship but Robert and his son hadn't spoken for nineteen years and didn't really know each other. So, it was time for Grace and John to visit the police to see if they could be of more help.

They found out that Robert had parked his Mitsubishi Jeep legally at the station, locked it up carefully and taken his keys. He had also his mobile phone with him and his house keys – just like you would. Police had also visited Robert's flat and searched it. They found nothing useful. The cops seemed very matter-of-fact and implied that Robert had gone off before. He hadn't.

Then John and Grace went to see Susan Margetts. She told them of Robert's emotional pleas and threats from the last phone conversations she had with him. 'What she was relating was Robert's style,' said John. 'He was very good at persuading women to take him back. Played every card in the pack if he had to. She must have heard all that emotional stuff from him before but she was worried enough to phone the cops within a short time.'

Susan Margetts seemed very calm by then. It just didn't strike John and Grace that this was the same women who had phoned the cops in a panic saying that Robert was suicidal.

The concerned man and woman decided that Robert couldn't have committed suicide. When he was low, it was John or Grace he'd reach out to. Yet there he was, apparently threatening to kill himself over several hours and he didn't call John once.

Convinced that he had had an accident, John and Grace with friends kept searching the park and walking a nearby railway line. They went round all the hospitals including the psychiatric hospitals in case Robert had had a nervous breakdown and was lying in one of them, not sure of who he was.

Then the cops said they had a breakthrough. They had managed to pick up a signal from Robert's mobile phone via the nearest Orange mast. This was foolproof – a scientific clue that specified where he was quite precisely, they said. Now the cops would concentrate their search on one sector of Busby Glen Park. So did John and Grace.

The cops were out there almost every day, walking that area, section by section – or so they said. During that time, Grace MacKay got a phone call from a friend that shocked her. 'I'm out at the park searching,' she said. 'I've found something – not Robert but you'd better come and have a look.'

When Grace arrived she saw her friend's point. It was a bag which contained an entire police uniform. It looked genuine and was lying slap bang in the area the cops were meant to have searched.

The theft or loss of a cop uniform is a very serious matter. People have gone to jail for taking them. A few weeks later, the police confirmed that it was a genuine uniform, number C140, and it belonged to a female cop based in Maryhill.

With Robert's well-documented reputation for womanising and sometimes not being fussy whether his partners were married or not, John and Grace's minds raced into overtime. Was there some significance to that female cop's uniform being found where the police were certain that Robert was?

As time went on, Grace and John continued their search and put adverts in papers asking for anyone who had seen Robert to come forward. Other members of the family reacted differently. One sold all Robert's furniture from his flat. Susan Margetts plagued them to take a leather chair of his that she had at her home. It was as if everyone else was resigned to the fact that he wasn't coming back and John and Grace had to admit they had a point.

'We started thinking if there was anyone around who might have wished Robert harm,' said John. 'He wasn't that type of guy but given he had disappeared off the face of the earth – we had to wonder.'

Robert's contact list was peppered with well-known Glasgow street players. Coming from his background and moving in his circles, they were among the people he knew – the folk he had grown up with. Yet his only business with them was to try to flog them suites. One time, he had sold an expensive three-piece suite to a man by the name of Gordon Ross. Ross was one of the henchmen of Thomas 'The Licensee' McGraw and he had a fierce reputation. He'd been involved in shooting a local player in Pollok mentioned at the beginning of this book – a young man called John Simpson.

Simpson, still only twenty-three, was the equaliser for Stewart 'Speccy' Boyd who ran the south side. The young man was scared of no one and with good reason. But he'd made the mistake of slashing The Licensee's brother in Barlinnie Prison one time so Ross thought he'd dole out a bit of revenge for his boss.

There was no way that even Ross wanted to tackle Simpson head on. So he laid a plan that resulted in him getting a call from a certain party when Simpson was lying on a couch fast asleep. Ross and another hit man crept into the house and blasted Simpson three times in the skull. Then they got the hell out of there, leaving the young guy for dead – except he survived. The gun Ross had used was too powerful and the bullets had gone straight through Simpson's head without hitting the vital parts of his brain. But John Simpson's troubles weren't over.

A month later, when he'd discharged himself early from hospital, he was standing in his own patch, waiting for a taxi, when a pal drove up and pulled over for a chat. As Simpson bent to say hello, a gunman who had been lying flat on the back seat sat up and blasted him several times. John Simpson died where he fell.

Robert Power didn't have anything to do with that kind of shenanigans but he did have that kind of guys' phone numbers and, when he could, he sold them suites. The trouble was that he had short-changed Gordon Ross and guys like Ross don't take too kindly to that. He's gutted men for less. But Gordon Ross didn't make Robert Power disappear for one very good reason – he himself had been knifed to death eighteen months before. But there were others.

Speccy Boyd's own gang were very fierce indeed. Not that he himself would have harmed Robert Power. Speccy knew that Robert was a likeable guy and a non-combatant but his crew were something else. For years, they had settled their scores in their own way, often resorting to killing lifelong pals because of some minor issue. Worse than that – they'd a habit of making bodies disappear in council incinerators or in the marshlands of nearby moors.

Speccy Boyd was a strong leader who held them in check but he had died in a suspicious car accident in Spain in June 2003, almost a year before Robert disappeared. Since then, his troops had lost all control.

Could Robert have fallen out with one of these local players? Cheated one of them on the price of some furniture? Got off with one of their wives? Or maybe a daughter without knowing who her daddy was? John and Grace didn't think so. Robert knew what these guys were capable of and he wasn't stupid. However, there was someone they weren't so sure about.

It's a man who can't be named for reasons that will become obvious later. He had known Robert years before, both through some business and meeting up at parties. The bloke hadn't been around for years – he'd done some time for some robbery and presumably he was just getting on with his life. Then, suddenly, he had turned up again and Robert was petrified. Not just scared but shaking, white and looking as if he'd be sick. The bloke would search him out and sometimes find him at John and Grace's house. Robert would leave with him in spite of how he felt. John and Grace asked him time and again what it was about that man but Robert wouldn't say anything, which wasn't like him either.

Since Robert had disappeared, John and Grace had caught the guy parked around the corner from their home, watching their house or driving by at different times and staring in the window. They asked around about the guy but what other people told them about him they already knew. Then, one day, a female of their acquaintance turned up saying she was worried about Robert. She asked a load of questions about the search for him. They thought it was strange because she hadn't bothered before. She took to calling and making suggestions and visited them another time. That time when she left their house, Grace went upstairs and watched her through the side of the curtains. At the corner of the street she got into the car of the man Robert had been so terrified of.

Now they were worried. They had no answer and no vital information but these people were behaving suspiciously and a man they loved had been missing for months. Then they got a call from a pal – cop divers had pulled a man's body out of water in Busby Glen Park. For hours, they dreaded the news. Then they were told it wasn't Robert. They didn't know whether to laugh or cry. They wanted so much for Robert to come strolling into their lives with a smile but the not knowing was sapping their energy, bringing them down. People going missing kills some of their loved ones from the inside. You have to be strong to live through it.

On 20 November 2004, the family received another kick in the solar plexus. John and Robert's eighteen-year-old nephew, Stuart Robert Power, was knifed and killed in the street in Ibrox. For years, there had been bad blood between him and two other young guys, Raymond McHarg and Robert McNaught. The two young men jumped Stuart as he was going back to his place on Copland Road and knifed him nine times, leaving him for dead on the street. Raymond McHarg and Stuart Power were cousins. How does a family cope with that?

Later in 2005, McHarg and McNaught would be sentenced to life with minimum sentences of fourteen and thirteen years respectively. But that was for later. Towards the end of 2004, with Robert missing for almost seven months, John and Grace were still hunting for him.

Grace was down at the park searching with a couple of friends. As they were leaving after another futile search, she spotted a robin sitting on a fence. It just seemed so peaceful, so calm. When she got home, she looked up the meaning of the name Robin and her book told her it was the female version of Robert. Then, the next day, they got a phone call – Robert had been found.

It was 2 December 2004. Robert Power was found over a mile away from the section of the park the cops had insisted he was in – a long, hard walk away from the area John, Grace and their friends had been searching daily for almost seven months. He was in an area that the Orange mast would not have detected. He was found hanging by the neck from a tree.

The cops had been called the day before, round about the time Grace was in the park. Keith Watson, a project worker for Glasgow City Council's Biodiversity Team, was carrying out some research in the area when he stumbled across the corpse. Poor man.

The place where Robert was hanging was in the grounds of Carnbooth School for kids with special needs and less than 100 yards from the school building itself. The teachers and head-mistress from the school were shocked and upset. They had passed by that tree every day in term time. How did they not see Robert?

From where Robert's body had been hanging there was a clear view of a busy road. From that road, there was a clear view of where he had been hanging. How many cars had passed by in seven months? How many passengers had they held? Why had no one spotted him?

Later, when approached by John and Grace, the school caretaker admitted to being perplexed. As part of his regular duties he cleared that area and beyond of litter. Why had he not spotted Robert?

On being asked these questions and others by John and Grace, the police first said that Robert had been hanging eighteen feet off the ground. Later they changed their minds and said it was only two or three feet. If that had been the case, surely the caretaker would have easily spotted him – as would the teachers as they went about their business.

John just couldn't get his head round his brother killing himself in that way. All his life, Robert had been petrified of heights yet there he was deciding to commit suicide by climbing a high tree. If John could ever contemplate Robert committing suicide – and he struggled with that – it might be through some booze and pills but not lynching himself from a tree.

If Robert had been threatening suicide on the phone to Susan Margetts, it would have been while he was in Busby Glen Park, a long, difficult walk away. Most experts say that, once the decision to commit suicide has been made, the majority of people are unlikely to go on that kind of expedition. Nor are they likely to delay.

'Teachers, pupils, parents, joggers, dog walkers and taxis would have passed close by daily,' said John. 'That ground is maintained nineteen times a year by the council. An area a few yards from that tree was treated for asbestos and was cordoned off to a three-metre radius. Yet still no workmen saw his body. Still the cops claim that Robert hung there unnoticed for over six months.'

Amid their grief for Robert, John and Grace were left with more questions than answers. After he was found, they continued visiting that place. It was the only link between them and him now.

Almost two months after Robert had been found, John and Grace were visiting his place. There on the ground, yards from where he had hung, they discovered his trousers, keys and wallet.

Before concluding that Robert had committed suicide, not only was a post-mortem carried out but the cops had also claimed to have searched the area thoroughly. How could they have missed such items? Why were Robert's trousers on the ground? Then they got a horror call. Robert's foot had been found by a passing member of the public. Grace and John didn't even know it had been missing.

'Wild foxes – that's what the cops blamed,' said John, 'and that's when they changed their minds about how high he'd been hanging off the ground. Suddenly he wasn't high in the air – too high for passers by to notice – but hanging near the ground so that the foxes could get at his foot.'

The foot hadn't been found near Robert's body but some distance away towards Busby Glen Park, close to the area the mobile phone mast that had picked up his signal. The cops appeared to be changing their explanation of Robert's death just to fit the facts as they emerged.

The couple struggled to get any straight answers from the police so they engaged with John's lawyer, the respected Jim Friel. He would know how to get proper information from them and he wouldn't let go until he did.

As this book goes to print, the Crown Office has been asked repeatedly for additional information on the death of Robert Power under the Freedom of Information Act. So far, John Gibson and Grace MacKay feel they have had no answers.

As this chapter is being written, the police have now denied that a police uniform was found near the scene. Maybe soon there will be a similar denial about his missing foot.

John and Grace are now challenging for more detailed information on the post-mortem. That's all they can hope for since the police advised Robert's elderly and frail mother to have the body cremated. It was.

With the help of their lawyer, John and Grace are not giving up. They have questions that need answers – answers that will benefit you and me and anyone else who wants to walks the streets of Glasgow in safety.

Did Robert Power really die hanging from that tree? Did he really die of hanging? Did he commit suicide? Or is he just another statistic in the growing list of unsolved murders? The unsolved murders of Glasgow – the Murder Capital of Europe.

INDEX

A
Abernethy, Lord 33, 68, 69
al-Alousi, Dr Louay 221
Anderson, Carl 190–192
Anderson, Kahli 165
Anderson, Kyle 165
Anderson, Russell 165
Anderson, Sharon 165
Andrew's Law 113
Ardentinny Outdoor Centre 166
Armani 2

B
Bain, Dorothy, QC 68
Baird, Stephen 197
Balmer, Jeanette 142
Bandit Lands 182, 183
Barge Pub 112
Barlanark Team 15
Barlinnie Prison 36, 48, 209, 218, 231
Barras, The 66, 136
Bassi, Gurmit 125, 127–32
Bassi, Harbej 125–27, 129, 132
Bassi, Rajwinder 125–32
Bassi, Steven 127, 129
Bates, Stephen 190–92
Baxter, John 46, 47
Beggs, William 194, 203
Bennett, Benjie 10
Bennett, Paul 12
Bible John 66, 137
Billy Boys 180
Black, Dr Marjory 190, 191
Black, Robert 82, 90

Blanco, Ricardo 26–31
Blue, Alexander 205
Bluebell Woods 154, 155, 158, 162–64
Bonini, Kevin 108, 109, 112, 113
Bonini, Mark 108–114
Bonini, Susan 112
Boyd, Stewart 'Speccy' 9–12, 231, 232
Bracadale, Lord 72, 105, 106, 196, 203
Brady, Finbar 47, 48
Brady, Ian 82
Brand, Lord 157
Broadley, Rose 70–73
Brodie, Lord 113
Brother's Bar 35
Buckingham Palace 41
Bulger, James 159
Burgoyne, Samuel 197
Burton, Amanda 212
Busby Glen Park 228–30, 233, 235, 236
Butchart, Robert 70

C
Cameron, James 47, 48
Campbell, Angus 98
Campbell, Jamie 161–164
Campbell, Kim 161
Campbell, Robert 161
Campbell, Shona 98
Campbell, TC 18, 39–42, 44, 45
Carnbooth School 234

Carpenter, Dr Anne 105, 106
Carroll, Angela 51
Cassidy, Dr Marie 212, 218
Cathcart, Samuel 131
Cathkin Braes 187–90, 192
chicken runs 139, 141
Clark, Richard 175–78
Clarke, Lord 217
Clinton, Mark 205
Cochrane, Bryan 'Dopey' 12
Colbeck, Joanna 70–73
Collins, Thomas 26–8
Connolly, Billy 2, 133
Connolly, Scott 197, 198
Cornton Vale Prison 61, 73, 80,
    103
Coronation Street 93
Coronation Throne 156
Cosgrove, Lady 122
Court of Criminal Appeal 73
Coyle, Anthony 75, 78, 79
Cullen, Lord 219
Cummings, Mark 84–90
Currie, Elizabeth 167–171
Currie, Jimmy 167–169, 171

D
Daniel Clan 22, 24
Davidson, Jack, QC 177
Dawson, Lord 89
Dear Green Place 62
Devine, Patrick 56–58
Dorrian, Lady 77
Douglas Inch Centre 105
Douglaston Golf Course 21
Doyle Family 5, 39–41, 44, 45, 205
Drug Treatment and Testing Order
    (DTTO) 108, 110
Drury, Stuart 144–153
Duffy, John 123, 124
Duguid, Ian, QC 68
dumdum bullets 23
Dykebar Psychiatric Hospital 118,
    120

E
Eastwood, Clint 209, 215
Edgar, Det. Sup. Ronald 224
Elder, James 38

Elliot, Toe 'Little General' 18
Emslie, Lord Justice General 157

F
Falkland Islands 59, 118
Fat Boab's bar 2
Ferguson, Andrew 195–203
Ferris, Paul 5
Fighting McNeilly Women 51
Findlay, Donald, QC 89, 131, 135,
    192
Fleming, Douglas 47, 48
Forrest, Professor Robert 225
French Foreign Legion 27, 28
Friel, Jim 236
Friends and Foes List 19
Friery, William 59

G
Gair, Norma 218
Gair, Stuart 208–19
Gallagher, Bryan 77
Gallagher, Jacqueline 124
Gangster No. 1 195
Garngad, The 62, 63
Garrity, Thomas 163, 166
Gibson, George 52
Gibson, Gordon 188–93
Gibson, Henrietta 52
Gibson, Jack 192
Gibson, John 227–37
Gibson, Susan 192
Gillespie, David 75, 78, 79
Glasgow Green 66, 67, 139
Glasgow Royal Infirmary 35, 63,
    208
Glasgow Two 41, 42
Glover, Bobby 5
Glenochil Prison 135, 195, 212, 214,
    216
Godfather, The 195
Goodfellas 195
Gray, Jamie 76–9
Grieve, Lord 157
Guy's Hospital 224–26

H
Hamilton, Ian, QC 156, 157
Hamilton, Lord 219

Hamilton-Campbell, Dr Isobel 118–20
Hanlon, Joe 5
Hardie, Lord 96, 184
Harper, Neil 104
Healy, John 55
Herd, James 182–84
Heron, Kara 64, 65
Hicks, Gary 96, 97
High Court, Dunfermline 32
High Court, Edinburgh 38, 47, 68, 105, 153, 163, 184, 224
High Court, Glasgow 21, 27, 49, 57, 64, 71, 77, 111, 117, 121, 128, 130, 141, 152, 155, 191, 192, 196, 211, 217, 223
Hood, Kirsty, QC 184
Holmes, Richard 63
Holy Day of Baisakhi 125, 126
Hopkinson, John 67–9
House of Commons 41
Hutcheson, Christopher 195–204
Hutcheson, Daniel 195–97, 199–204

I
Ice-Cream Wars 39, 205
IRA 20, 54, 59, 61

J
Jamieson, John 165
Jackson, Gordon, QC 104–106, 128, 131
Jenkinson, Aaron 115, 117, 119, 121
Jenkinson, Darren 115–22
Jenkinson, Frances 115–22
Jenkinson, Jacob 116, 117, 119–21
John, Elton 9
Johnstone, Lord 171
Jones, Christopher 128–32

K
Karling, Richard 220–26
Keenan, John 63
Keith, Richard 163–66
Kelly, Brian 36–8
Kerelaw Secure Unit 164–66
Kerr, Brian 110, 111
Kerrigan, Herbert, QC 225
King, James 17

Kirkwood, Lord 153, 224
Knight, Professor Sir Bernard 225
Krays 16

L
Labour Party 222
Lafferty, Margo 124
Lafferty, Thomas 'Shadda' 44
Law Hospital 42
Lecter, Hannibal 194
Leggate, Stuart 85–90
Lennox, Alan 66–9
Leverndale Psychiatric Hospital 127
Limbs in the Loch Killer 194, 203, 204
Linton, John 39, 41–5
Lockerbie Disaster 191, 192
Lofthouse, Kevin 48, 49

M
McAlinden, Edith 75–80
McAlinden, John 76–8
McAlroy, Justin 5
McAulay, Scott 196
McBarron, Anne 128
McBride, Paul, QC 111, 112, 171
McCabe, John 24
McCallum, Blair 198
McCartney, John 'The Joker' 9, 10
McLean, Catriona 173–78
McCormack, George 'Crater Face' 42
McDermott, Aileen 144, 145, 149–51
MacDonald, Dr George 120
McDonald, Ian 'Blink' 33
McDowall, Paul 36–8
McElroy, William 64, 65
McEwan, Lord 49, 119, 121
McFadyen, John Paul 26–8
McFarlane, Dr Jean 130
McGovern Family 22, 33–5
McGovern, Jamie 34
McGovern, Joe 34
McGovern, Leona 124
McGovern, Paul 34
McGovern, Tony 33–5
McGovernment, The 34
McGowan, Dorothy 172
McGowan, Gary 170–72

McGraw, Thomas 'The Licensee'
40–3, 55, 205, 231
McGregor, Ewan 217
McGregor, Dr Jim 212–16
McGregor, Karen 124
McGregor, Maureen 214, 215
McGrory, Anne-Marie 21
McGrory, Christopher 20–22, 24
McHarg, Raymond 234
McInally, Diane 124
McKay, Colin ('As Cold as Death'
only) 20–22
McKay, Colin, The Birdman of
Possilpark 36–8
MacKay, Grace 227, 229–37
McKenna, Marilyn 144–53
McKinnon, William 56, 59
McLanaghan, James 187–89, 191
Macleod, Malcolm 100
Macleod, Myra 100
Macleod, Susan 100–106
McLeod, Murdo, QC 177
McLeod, Stephen 63–5
McLeod, Willie 210–212, 214, 219
McMillan, Brian 109–12
McNaught, Robert 234
McPhee, Billy 5, 205
McPhee, Roderick 'Scythe Killer'
142
McPhie, Frank 'The Iceman' 14–24,
29
McRobert, Teresa 134, 135
MAC-10 sub-machine guns, aka
'Big Macs' 26
Mafia 27, 44, 203
Margetts, Susan 227–31, 235
Mark's Law 89
Marnock, Lord 222
Maxwell, Edward 18
Melvin, Charles 'Chas' 10, 12, 13
Mezey, Dr Gillian 106
MI5 59
MI6 59
Mills, Dougie 36, 37
Ministry of Defence 53, 59
Mitchell, Geoffrey, QC 71, 72
Mitchell, Ian 75, 76, 78, 79
Mitchell, John 'the Beggar' 197,
202

Mitchell, Stephen 26
Moors Murders 82
Morton, Andrew 109–114
Muggers' Alley 67, 68
Mulcahy, David 123
Mulhall, Derek 179
Mulhall, Stephen 179–81
Mullan, Peter 217
Munro, John 133–35
Murphy, Brian 'Spud' 63
Murphy, Sean, QC 77, 113
Murray, Alison 154–58, 162
Murray, Iain 155–58
Murray, Iain, Sr 155, 157, 158
Murray, Kenneth 157
Murray, Patrick 85, 87
Murray, Robert 36–8

N
Newell, Susan 82
New Morvern Bar 33, 34
Niven, Dorothy 220–26
No Mean City 14
Norman Conks 180
Norval, Walter 15

O
O'Donnell, Francis 55–9
O'Donnell, Manny 'The Contractor'
53–61
O'Hara, Robert 'The Birdman' 32,
33, 35–8
Operation Overlord 217
Osman, Rebaz 69

P
Pan Am Flight 103 191, 192
Pancake Place 220, 221
Park Bar 100
Penrose, Lord 122
Perth Prison 18, 19, 29
Peterhead Prison 28, 41, 194, 203
Pollok Kray Twins 91, 92, 96
Pond Hotel 57
Porter, Julie 212
Power, Robert 227–34, 236, 237
Power, Stuart Robert 233, 234
Prais, Edgar, QC 199
Prince Andrew 59

INDEX

Q
Quar, Jack 53, 54, 59–61
Queen, the 41

R
Ramsay, Lynne 115
Ratcatcher 115
Rennie, Mark 12
Richardsons 16
Richest Dustbin Man in the World,
    The 10
Roadhouse Pub 43, 44
Roberts, Marjorie 124
Rogano, The vii
Ross, Gordon 43, 231, 232
Ross, Sheila 222
Ross, Rt Hon. Willie 222
Royal Ashoka Restaurant 126
Ruchill Golf Course 63, 64
Ryan, Dean 139–43
Ryan, Mary 56–9
Ryan, Steven 139–43

S
Saughton Prison 142, 153
Scanlon, Derek 201
Scanlon, Scudder 10
Scottish Criminal Cases Review
    Commission 158
Sheiling Bar 43
Sheridan, Tommy 41, 217
Sheriff Court, Glasgow 69, 101
Shields, Thomas 182–84
Shotts Prison 42
Silence of the Lambs 194
Silent Witness 212
Simpson, John 'The Equaliser' 7–13,
    231, 232
Sinclair, Angus 124
Smith, Ann 217
Smith, Anne, QC 120
Smith, David 217
Smith, Peter 207–10, 212, 217–19
SNP 222
Southern General Hospital 110,
    152
Steele, Jim 43, 44
Steele, Joe 39–45
Stevenson, Jamie 'The Bull' 34, 35

Stewart, Amy 67–9
Stone, Gary 95
Stone, Kevin 91–6
Stone, Margaret 94
Stone of Destiny 156
Stone, Stephen 91–5
Stormonth, Marshall 137–43
Sturton, Melanie 80
Strathclyde Police 45, 89, 189, 218,
    226
Sudden Infant Death Syndrome
    (SIDS) 116
Sun (pub) 132
Sutcliffe, Peter, aka 'The Yorkshire
    Ripper' 90
Sutherland, Lord 164, 165, 219
Sweeney, James 75, 76

T
Taggart 212
Tartan Tories 212
Tennents Bar 100, 101
Thompson, Arthur, aka 'The
    Godfather' 16, 33, 55
Thompson, Fatboy 5
Thompson, Robert 159
Thorne, Paul 25–9, 31
Tinto Firs Hotel 57
Toner, Michelle 47
Toner, Martin 47–50
Toye, Gavin 18, 29
Toye, William 'The Worm' 18–20,
    24, 29,
Tron Theatre 136, 138
Turnbull, Bill, QC 27
Turner, Christina 51, 52

U
UDA 20, 54
UVF 54

V
Vendetta 5
Venables, Jon 159
Vulcan Bar 34

W
Wallace, Barry 194
Watson, Keith 234

INDEX

Waverley, The 168
Weatherall, Billy 12
Welsh Brothers 55
West, Fred 82, 102
West, Rose 102
Westguard Securities 188–200
Westminster Abbey 156
Wheatley, Lord 178
Wheatley, Pat, QC 122
Wilson, Brian 155–58
Wilson, Rt Hon. Harold 222

Wilson, William 190–92
Wood, Hector 209, 212, 214
Wylde, Tracey 124
Wylie, Jacqueline 29, 30

X
XYY Team 15

Y
Yardies 25–7, 29, 30
Young Posso Fleet 180

VENDETTA

PAUL FERRIS & REG McKAY

The Conspiracy Continues . . .

Paul Ferris ruled crime in Scotland. He had links to London firms, Manchester gangs and Liverpool faces. He'd been accused of murdering The Godfather's son, Fatboy, and found not guilty. Some cops talked of killing him. But, when he was released from prison in 2002, he told the world and the waiting press that he was walking away from his life of crime. But would they let him? As soon as his car sped away, the journalists were after him. And they weren't the only ones . . .

Vendetta tells the astonishing inside story of what happened next to Paul Ferris. And it's a story of international gangsters, hit contracts, murders, bank scams, Essex-boy torturers, corrupt politics, crack-head hit men, knife duels, Securi-wars, drugs, guns, Yardies, terrorists and more. In *Vendetta*, Paul Ferris slashes open the underbelly of Britain's streets and exposes the dark forces that police them as well as revealing the truth about what really happened to him and about the conspiracies and corruption that won't leave him alone.

For years, new enemies and old foes have tried to silence Paul Ferris. But it's Ferris who's here to tell the tale while many of them are not. And some tale it is.

£9.99 PAPERBACK (ISBN 1-84502-061-8)

*Available from all good bookshops
or, to order direct from our distributor,
call Book Source on 0870 240 2182*